Born to
Pay

BORN TO PAY

The New Politics of Aging in America

Phillip Longman

A Richard Todd Book

HOUGHTON MIFFLIN COMPANY

BOSTON · 1987

Library of Congress Cataloging-in-Publication Data

Longman, Phillip.
Born to pay.

"A Richard Todd book."
Includes bibliographical references and index.
1. Aged — Government policy — United States.
2. Aged — United States — Economic conditions.
3. Intergenerational relations — Economic aspects —
United States.   4. Social security — United States.
I. Title.
HQ1064.U5L64   1987   362.6'0973   87-3926
ISBN 0-395-38369-2

Printed in the United States of America

P 10 9 8 7 6 5 4 3 2 1

Some of the material in this book has appeared, in slightly different form, in the *Washington Monthly* and the *Atlantic*.

To Lester

Acknowledgments

This book benefited from the advice and support of far too many people to mention and of a few who would prefer not to be named. I would like to express particular gratitude to my parents, Kenneth and Mary, for their encouragement and understanding of my career as a writer, and to my brother, Andrew, who provided many early insights.

A special intellectual debt goes to my colleague at Americans for Generational Equity, Paul Hewitt, who remains my harshest and most challenging critic. I would also like to thank all the advisors and supporters of AGE, who, while not necessarily agreeing with the opinions expressed in this book, nonetheless encouraged and helped sustain me during the last several months that I spent wrestling with the manuscript.

Barbara Blake provided the original idea for the book, and was the first of many editors who helped improve my writing and thinking on its subject. Among the others were Michael Aaron and the editors of the *Washington Monthly* and the *Atlantic*, particularly Jim Fallows, Phil Keisling, Nick Lemann, Debby McGill, Tim Noah, Charles Peters, and William Whitworth. Richard Todd of Houghton Mifflin I thank for his faith, patience, and logical mind. My friend and former colleague at *New Jersey Monthly*, Randall Rothenberg, also provided much advice and encouragement.

I would also like to thank the many friends and acquaintances who helped me with the research for this book, or from whom I borrowed ideas. I am especially indebted to Gordon Green, Cynthia Taeuber, and Barbara Torrey of the U.S. Bureau of the Census; Daniel Callahan of the Hastings Institute; Pat Choate of TRW; Sen. Dave Durenberger of Minnesota; Prof. Norm

Daniels of Tufts University; Gov. Richard Lamm, now at Dartmouth College; Prof. Al MacKay of Oberlin College and his brother, Congressman Buddy MacKay of Florida; Congressman Jim Moody of Wisconsin; Prof. Rick Moody of Hunter College; Pete Peterson of the Blackstone Group; Haeworth Robertson of Mercer-Meidinger, Inc.; and Prof. Sam Preston of the University of Pennsylvania.

Finally, my deepest thanks go to my young wife, Robin, for the years she endured as I thought about aging, debt, and the fate of the baby boom generation.

Contents

Born to Pay

1

The Challenge of
an Aging Society

As I SIT DOWN to write this book, the oldest members of the baby boom generation have passed their fortieth year. Sixteen years ago many of them were marching in protest against the bombing of Cambodia and the killings at Kent State. In another sixteen years, they may well be thinking of "early retirement." Already, those at the leading edge of the baby boom generation have begun to worry over their prospects for old age. What they think and do as a result over the next few years will profoundly affect our economy and our politics.

Nearly a third of the total U.S. population, and more than 43 percent of all voting-aged Americans, belong to the baby boom generation. Comprising more than 74 million Americans born between 1946 and 1964, this generation has thus far redefined the dominant issues and concerns of American society each time its oldest members have passed to a new life stage.

In the 1950s, the flight to the suburbs, overcrowded schools, and increasing juvenile delinquency were but a few of the trends and dislocations caused by the arrival of the baby boom generation. When its older members reached adolescence in the 1960s,

the normal values and concerns of that time of life — sexual freedom, self-discovery, and idealism — preoccupied, indeed consumed, the country as a whole. In the 1970s, unemployment
rates soared and housing prices skyrocketed as the same cohort
moved into young adulthood. The materialistic concerns that
even in the best of times tend to absorb young adults as they
seek to establish careers and families came more and more to
dominate the culture of the era and to contribute to the conservative trend in politics. By the 1980s, the aging of the baby boom
generation had transformed America from a youth culture to one
engrossed with such issues as tax reform, exercise, drug testing,
and proper diet.

But this generation's most revolutionary effect on American
society is yet to come. As recently as the early 1950s, retirement
as we now know it did not exist as an institution. Nearly half the
men over age sixty-five were still in the work force.[1] Most Americans, when polled, said that they aspired to work for as long as
possible and that they viewed retirement as suited only for the
disabled.[2] But today, Americans look forward to retirement as a
pleasant time of life, as a chance to travel, pursue hobbies, and
otherwise indulge their interests. And they expect that younger
Americans will contribute substantially to the cost of this prolonged period of creative leisure, through Social Security, Medicare, and other programs. The baby boomers are paying an
unprecedented proportion of their incomes to support the current older generation in retirement, and they will expect today's
children to support them in turn. The likely result, unless many
fundamental trends are soon reversed, will be a war between
young and old.

F. Scott Fitzgerald once defined a generation "as that revolt
against fathers which seems to occur about three times a century." Since the early nineteenth century, many thinkers — including Auguste Comte, John Stuart Mill, and José Ortega y
Gasset — have attempted to develop philosophies of history that
would account for the familiar loose sense of generational rhythm

that pervades modern societies. All these theories foundered on the inherent vagueness of defining a generation in purely cultural terms. When people herald themselves members of some new "lost generation" or "Woodstock generation" or the like, they summon up invisible allies to whatever their cause, who may or may not actually agree to be counted. As Thomas Griffith has observed, in a nation of more than 240 million people, evoking a generation is but "one way that individuals make their thin little voices louder."[3]

Nonetheless, membership in the baby boom generation is not a subjective notion, but an inescapable reality. Thirty-five percent more Americans were born between 1946 and 1964 than during the previous nineteen years; 12 percent more were born than during the subsequent nineteen years.[4] Whether they fought in Vietnam, protested the war at school, or were too young to remember; whether they are yippies turned yuppies, ghetto blacks or blue-collar whites, people born during the years of the baby boom are bound together by a unique demographic circumstance that will determine their fate in the future even more so than in the past.

By having fewer children and living longer than any Americans in history, the baby boomers will become the first cohort of senior citizens unable to draw on the economic output and financial support of a much larger number of younger Americans. Historically, a graph of the age composition of the population always appeared in the form of a triangle. At its base were infants and young children, who composed the largest single age group. Even during periods of low fertility, each older cohort would shrink in relative size, reflecting the loss of more and more of its members to disease, accidents, and other hazards of aging. At the top of the chart, forming the peak of the triangle, would be the few Americans who survived these hazards long enough to become elderly. In 1900, only 4 percent of all Americans had managed to reach the age of sixty-five or older.[5]

Figures 1–1 through 1–8, which are based on Census Bureau

Age Composition of U.S. Population

Figure 1–1: 1905

Age
70 and over
60–69
50–59
40–49
30–39
20–29
10–19
0–9

Male | Female

25 20 15 10 5 0 | 0 5 10 15 20 25

Millions

Figure 1–2: 1945

Age
80 and over
70–79
60–69
50–59
40–49
30–39
20–29
10–19
0–9

Male | Female

25 20 15 10 5 0 | 0 5 10 15 20

Millions

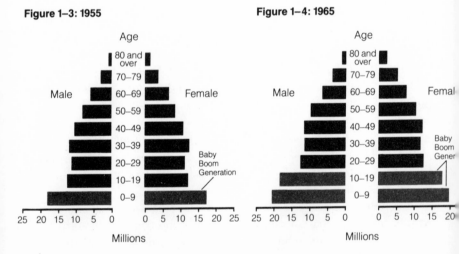

Figure 1–3: 1955

Age
80 and over
70–79
60–69
50–59
40–49
30–39
20–29
10–19
0–9

Male | Female

Baby Boom Generation

25 20 15 10 5 0 | 0 5 10 15 20 25

Millions

Figure 1–4: 1965

Age
80 and over
70–79
60–69
50–59
40–49
30–39
20–29
10–19
0–9

Male | Female

Baby Boom Gener

25 20 15 10 5 0 | 0 5 10 15 20

Millions

Source for figures 1–1 through 1–5: *Cynthia Taeuber (Bureau of the Census), "Age Structure of the U.S. Population in the 21st Century." Paper delivered at the Midwest Regional Conference of Americans for Generational Equity, Hubert Humphrey Institute for Public Policy, Minneapolis, Minnesota, January 13, 1986.*

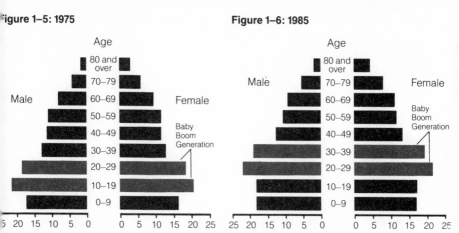

Figure 1–5: 1975

Figure 1–6: 1985

Figure 1–7: 2005 (Middle-Range Projections)

Figure 1–8: 2025 (Middle-Range Projections)

Source for figures 1–6 through 1–8: *Bureau of the Census, "Projections of the Population of the United States, by Age, Sex, and Race: 1983 to 2080," Series P-25, No. 952, U.S. Government Printing Office, 1984.*

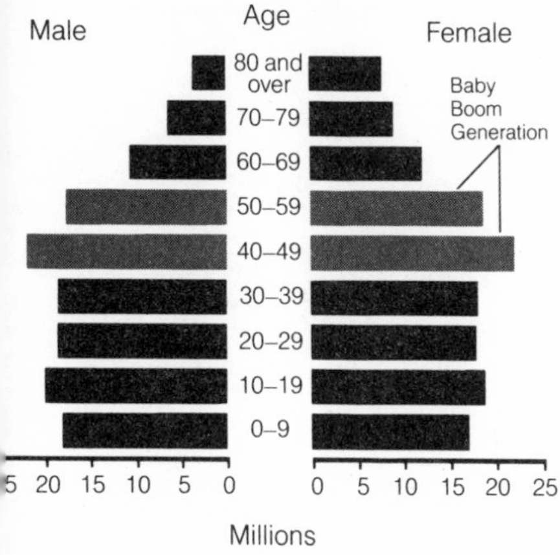

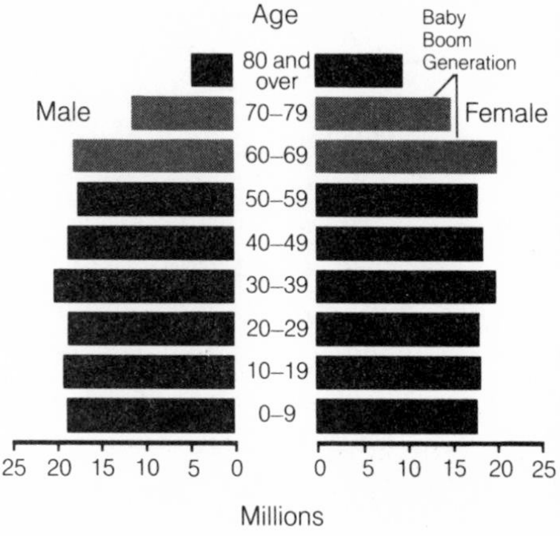

projections, show how the aging of the baby boom generation will transform the age composition from the form of a triangle into a figure more nearly resembling a square.[6] The baby boomers started out as an exceptionally large generation. Unlike members of previous cohorts, they will not shrink in number relative to younger Americans, even as many baby boomers are struck down by the ravages of age. Because of their low fertility and increasing life expectancy, the baby boomers will continue as the dominant age group well into the next century, even assuming that the country continues to absorb a very high number of younger immigrants.

We can predict few trends with any degree of certainty regarding American life in the first half of the twenty-first century. The aging of the population, however, has already built such a powerful momentum that it is hard to conceive of any likely future development that could reverse its course. Although the year 2050, for example, may seem a long way off, it is important to remember that everyone who will be over sixty-five by that time has already been born. It is reasonable to assume that mortality rates will continue to improve as medical knowledge advances. Indeed, in recent years life expectancy among the elderly has been increasing faster than for any other age group. But even if for some reason no further medical advances are achieved, the absolute growth, if not the relative growth, of the elderly population is more or less a given.

The proportion of the total population that will be elderly is only slightly less certain. As the oldest women of the baby boom generation pass beyond their prime childbearing years, the chances for a second boom are receding rapidly. To the casual observer it may seem as if the fertility rate is about to take a big jump. News magazines report a trend toward elaborate weddings. Many young women are interrupting their careers to concentrate on marriage and children. And in point of fact, the number of women giving birth each year has begun to rise. But the picture is deceptive. One reason is that the rise in the birthrate has been concentrated among women who have delayed having their first child until their thirties. Both time and, typically, economic necessity conspire against such women's ever raising as many children as their mothers did. Largely because of the trend toward deferred marriage and childbearing, the average American woman now has 1.8 children over her lifetime, whereas 2.1 are needed just to replace the population.[7]

Prevailing attitudes toward family size also argue against a significant increase in the fertility rate. In 1959, 45 percent of all Americans believed that the ideal family would include four children; today only 11 percent believe this. Over the same interval, the percentage of Americans favoring two-child families has increased from 16 to 56 percent.[8] Moreover, even if the children of the baby boomers do decide to raise large families, their relatively small numbers will ensure that the overall effect on the age composition of the population will be minimal. At least for the rest of this century, the percentage of American women who could potentially have children will continue to fall, as the baby boom generation passes beyond its prime childbearing years and is replaced by the much smaller "baby bust" generation.[9]

Thus, the baby boomers must face the prospect of becoming the largest generation of senior citizens in history, both in absolute size and relative to the number of younger citizens available to support them. By 2030, the Census Bureau projects, using cautious assumptions, more than one out of five Americans will be age sixty-five or older. Nearly one in ten will be seventy-five or older.

To some readers, it may seem that sheer force of numbers will assure the baby boomers a comfortable retirement. Today, Americans over sixty-five compose little more than 12 percent of the population. Yet they are a commanding force in American politics. Social Security, even for the wealthy, is immune to budget cuts, despite the federal budget deficits. If today's relatively small cohort of senior citizens can so effectively command public resources, why shouldn't the baby boomers look forward to an even easier time as they swell the ranks of the elderly?

So long as democratic institutions survive, the baby boomers will enjoy great political strength in old age. Politicians will bid against one another to court their vote. Entrepreneurs will organize vast pressure groups to lobby on their behalf. The baby boomers are sure to find their own curmudgeonly "spokesperson" to play the role of Claude Pepper. But while the baby boomers in old age will command far more votes and probably will enjoy far greater political influence than do today's senior citizens, they will nonetheless be forced to seek their support from a working-aged population that will be comparatively much smaller and quite likely poorer. At the same time, whatever old age subsidies they secure will have to be divided thinly because of their great numbers. The baby boomers' strength in numbers will also be their great weakness. In 1985, there were 4.9 Americans aged twenty to sixty-four available to pay benefits to each member of the population over sixty-five. By 2030, according to Census Bureau projections, this ratio will at "best" fall to 3 to 1 — assuming a dramatic increase in fertility and small improvement in life expectancy — and could well fall as low as 2.2 to 1.[10]

The Twilight of Youth

While there will be many more elderly in the next century relative to the working-aged population, there will probably also be many fewer children. This has led some observers to conclude optimistically that since the working-aged population will presumably be spending a much smaller fraction of its income for public education and other programs for the young, they will accede to paying much more for the elderly.

Several considerations argue against placing much faith in this thought. The first is that, under current spending patterns, the public cost of supporting each retiree far exceeds the amount spent on each child. Thus the savings realized by a decline in the relative number of children would probably be not nearly as large as the extra cost of providing the growing number of elderly with the same level of benefits enjoyed by today's senior citizens.

The most recent comprehensive study of the subject was published in 1977 by economists Robert Clark and J. J. Spengler. In 1975, according to their estimates, total per capita expenditures for the elderly, at all levels of government, exceeded the amount spent on children age seventeen and under — including the total spent on public education — by more than three to one. The disparity is no doubt much larger today. Social Security pensions and Medicare pensions have become much more generous, while welfare and educational programs for the young have been cut.[11]

At the federal level, according to the Office of Management and Budget, the total spent in 1983 on the population over sixty-five amounted to $217 billion, or about $7,700 per senior citizen. The amount spent per child, on the other hand, is more difficult to calculate, and the government keeps no official figures. In an article for *Scientific American*, however, Samuel H. Preston, a demographer at the University of Pennsylvania, calculated that total federal expenditures benefiting children came to $36 billion in 1984, which was about one-sixth of the total spending on the elderly. Because there are many more children than there are elderly people, the expenditure per child was about one-tenth the expenditure per older person.[12]

In our society, of course, the cost of raising children is still largely borne by individual parents. Thus the potential savings realized by a decline in the relative number of children is not fully revealed just by examining the pattern of public expenditures for the young and the old. Still, we must consider the harsh reality that most parents derive far more satisfaction and reward in spending money on their own children than in paying taxes to support the elderly in general. If parents have fewer children in the future, they will surely prefer to spend more on each child than pay higher Social Security taxes. This is especially likely since, as society grows more complex, their children will need ever more education to succeed. Single Americans also will prefer to use the money they save by not having children for purposes other than supporting the baby boomers in old age.

Finally, we must consider how working-aged Americans in the early decades of the next century will be looking to their own prospects for retirement. If fertility rates continue to decline and longevity continues to increase, today's children will face even greater difficulty in securing their own old age benefits than will the baby boomers. Before providing their parents' generation with generous old age benefits, today's children will be required by prudence to save up toward the cost of their own golden years. Thus, there is no reason to believe that a continued decline in the relative number of children will assure the baby boomers adequate support in old age, and there is good reason to believe the opposite.

Can the Baby Boomers Pay Their Own Way?

Unable to depend on population growth to finance their future Social Security and other old age benefits, the baby boomers have an inordinately great need to accumulate assets, such as savings accounts and home equity, from which they can draw income in old age. Yet it is highly unlikely that the baby boomers as a whole will ever be able to pay their own way through retirement.

The first reason is the cost of supporting today's retirees. Members of every generation, in their middle years, have sacrificed to provide support for their elders. But prior to the adoption of Social Security, Medicare, and other old age entitlement programs, such support was typically extended only to the elderly in need, not to everyone beyond a certain age. A rich father was not likely to receive payments from his children solely because he had passed age sixty-five; indeed, any transfer was more likely to be in the opposite direction, in the form of an inheritance.

Today, the Social Security system alone costs most younger Americans more than one out of every seven dollars they earn.[13] Not only do the young support the old as a whole — regardless of need — but the ranks of the old have never been larger. Today's elderly are retiring earlier and living longer than any generation in history. The average age of retirement is now sixty-two, while life expectancy for people at that age is over seventy-seven years for men and over eighty-two years for women.[14] No matter whether one applauds or deplores Social Security, no one can deny that its cost, together with other entitlement programs for today's senior citizens, diminishes the ability of younger Americans to save toward their own retirement. Since 1939, the maximum annual Social Security tax has increased by more than 10,000 percent, from $60 to $6,006; since 1960, the tax has increased by nearly 2,000 percent.[15]

The second great obstacle to saving faced by most members of the baby boom generation is their relatively low standard of living. In the 1980s, two stereotypes of the baby boomers prevail. They are depicted either as narcissistic yuppies wallowing in discretionary income, or as victims of downward mobility — unable to afford children for the price of the wife's not working, bid out of the housing market, or burdened with unprecedented mortgage payments. There is no doubt that some baby boomers are well-to-do. The generation is so large that even the small percentage of its members who are affluent attract inordinate attention from advertisers and journalists — who tend to be yuppies themselves. But the vast majority of baby boomers are better described by the second image.

In 1984, 47 percent of all Americans aged twenty-five to thirty-four who were in the work force earned less than $12,500 a year; 70 percent earned less than $20,000.[16] The typical young American family headed by a person aged twenty-five to thirty-four consisted of a husband, a wife, and a single child under age twelve. Fewer than half owned their own homes. In most families, both husband and wife worked. Before taxes, the median

income for such families, from all earners, totaled $25,157—
hardly enough to buy a BMW, or even to save much toward
retirement.[17]

The downward mobility of the baby boom generation is revealed by several other measures. The first is the unprecedented
disparity in the wages between older and younger workers.
Throughout most of American history, the premium paid for
seniority was much less than it is today. Once—largely because
they tended to be better educated—young men starting out
earned nearly the same pay as their fathers. As recently as the
mid-1950s, the median income of fully employed men in their
early twenties equaled 93 percent of the amount paid to fully
employed men aged forty-five to fifty-four. But by 1984, that
ratio had dropped to a mere 47 percent. This income disparity
is also growing among female workers. In relative terms, starting
wages for persons of both sexes have probably never been lower.[18]

The change is particularly significant when one considers the
baby boom generation's relatively advanced level of education.
Only 65 percent of Americans aged thirty-five and older have
completed high school, while nearly 86 percent of those aged
twenty-five to thirty-four are high school graduates. Some 24
percent of the younger group hold college degrees, compared
with only 15 of the population over thirty-five.[19] Yet this educational edge hasn't been enough to prevent each successive
cohort of the baby boom from slipping farther behind in its per
capita share of the nation's total income. Younger baby boomers,
who came into the work force after the economy turned downward in 1973, are doing substantially worse than older baby
boomers. A rising percentage of recent college graduates, moreover, are coming into the work force encumbered by enormous
student loans, as student aid programs have been cut. In 1986
the median debt incurred by graduates of public colleges was
$8,000; of private schools $10,000.[20]

It is still too early to tell, of course, whether the baby boomers will eventually reap the same high premium for seniority realized by today's older workers. But there are many reasons to believe that they won't. Consider, for example, the following trend line. According to a recent study commissioned by the Joint Economic Committee of the U.S. Congress, the average male worker turning age thirty in 1950 saw his income rise by 118 percent over inflation during his next ten years in the work force. Similarly, men turning age thirty in 1960 saw their real wages rise by 108 percent over the next decade. But men turning age thirty in 1970 realized almost no premium for their increased seniority. Over the next ten years, their real wages increased by a mere 16 percent.[21]

Looking to the future, the continuing decline of the U.S. manufacturing sector, the massive trade deficits, and the low wages generally paid to workers in the growing service sector of the economy all argue against the possibility that today's young workers as a whole will eventually become as upwardly mobile as were their parents in the 1950s and 1960s. In many industries, the downward mobility of the young has become institutionalized through the growth of so-called two-tier wage contracts, which exempt senior workers from sacrifice but place new hires on a permanently lower wage scale.

In 1983 and 1984, two-tier provisions were negotiated in contracts covering an estimated 450,000 workers, according to the Bureau of National Affairs, a private research group. About 8 percent of the major union contracts signed in 1984 — 17 percent of those in service industries — provided for two-tier scales. Major examples include that of American Airlines, which in 1985 paid newly hired flight attendants $11,664 a year, or 19 percent less than the starting wage paid to incumbent workers on the higher tier. The International Association of Machinists, the International Brotherhood of Teamsters, and the United Auto Workers are among the unions that have negotiated two-tier contracts in recent years in an attempt to protect their senior members from wage cuts. Some observers have even predicted the emergence of three-tier scales, as American industry continues to retrench from the excesses of the postwar period.[22]

The pressure on young families is relieved in part by the young wives who are going to work in increasing numbers. Still, even young families with two paychecks today earn little more than young families with one paycheck did in the early seventies. For young married couples, with a household head aged twenty-five to thirty-four, who *both* were in the work force, the combined median income (adjusted for inflation) in 1983 was only $3,400 higher than the amount enjoyed ten years earlier by young couples living on the husband's salary alone. Over the same period, the purchasing power of young families relying on a single paycheck declined by roughly $4,000.[23] That so many young families now depend on two paychecks to maintain even the trappings of a middle-class lifestyle is another reason not to expect any dramatic rise in the birthrate.

By another measure, net wealth, the baby boomers are also shown to be downwardly mobile. Between 1977 and 1983, for example, the average net wealth of all American households, adjusted for inflation, rose from $41,000 to $47,000. But for households headed by a person aged twenty-five to thirty-four, net wealth declined, from $18,804 to $16,651; for households headed by a person aged 35 to 44, from $44,359 to 40,710.[24]

For many baby boomers, the quest to maintain the same standard of living they knew as children requires that they go deeply and often foolishly into debt. The increase in consumer borrowing among the young is both a cause and a consequence of their general downward mobility. Between 1970 and 1983, the proportion of all families headed by a person twenty-five to thirty-four who were paying off consumer debt increased from 67 to 77 percent. Among the vast majority of young families in debt in 1983, the average amount they owed on their credit cards and installment loans was $4,781.[25] Debtors obviously have a hard time saving. In 1984, more than a third of all households headed by a person under thirty-five had no savings whatsoever on deposit with banks and other financial institutions, aside from non-interest-paying checking accounts. Only 13 percent held any assets in the form of stocks or mutual funds.[26]

Finally, the baby boomers' ability to save toward retirement has been reduced by the extraordinary inflation in real estate prices during their lifetimes. In 1949, a thirty-year-old man who purchased the median-priced house needed to commit only 14 percent of his income to meet the carrying charges. At that time, a new "Cape Cod" in Levittown went for just $7,990 — no money down, $60 dollars a month. By 1983, the combination of stagnant or falling wages, high interest costs, and mounting real estate prices meant that the average thirty-year-old man needed to commit 44 percent of his income to meet the carrying charges on the median-priced house. That same year, 65 percent of all first-time home buyers needed two paychecks to meet their monthly payments.[27]

For most of today's elderly, the vast appreciation in the value of their homes provides a great measure of security. Fully 73 percent of the elderly own their homes; the average value of their home equity in 1984 was $54,667. Elderly home owners by and large were able to save more during their working years, and they can now hold on to their financial assets longer in retirement because they have been sheltered from rising housing costs. The average value of bank deposits held by persons over sixty-five exceeded $33,000 in 1984. The average value of stock and mutual fund portfolios held by the elderly that year exceeded $42,000.[28]

The baby boomers, however, faced with extraordinarily high housing costs, will find it commensurately more difficult to save for retirement, or for any other purpose — even assuming that they manage to buy a first house. Between 1977 and 1983, the percentage of families headed by a person under thirty-five who owned their own homes declined from 41 to 34 percent.[29] Moreover, while no one knows the future direction of real estate prices, it is sobering to consider that those baby boomers who do manage to buy property will eventually see its value determined by whatever the members of the very small and so far very poor baby bust generation are able and willing to pay.

Children in an Aging Society

Polls consistently show that most baby boomers have little or no faith in receiving adequate income from Social Security and other old age programs.[30] Yet many believe that one way or another they will be able to save enough to support themselves in old age. For this to happen, the baby boomers would have to do what no other generation has done before: save up the cost of their own retirement, and, through Social Security and Medicare and other programs, pay a large share of the cost of the preceding generation's retirement as well.

Providing the baby boomers with greater tax incentives to save, such as through expanded Individual Retirement Accounts, hardly solves the problem. In 1986, IRAs cost the Treasury Department $21 billion in forgone revenue and to that extent increased the national debt and its burden on future taxpayers. Increasing savings through expansion of the private pension system entails the same dilemma. Tax subsidies for employer-sponsored pension plans increased the national debt in 1986 by more than $71 billion.[31] Moreover, as the United States moves toward a service economy, we can expect an ever smaller percentage of workers to be covered by private pension plans, which historically have been concentrated among large, unionized manufacturing industries. Between 1979 and 1983, the percentage of workers covered by such plans dropped for the first time in the postwar era, from 56 to 52 percent.[32] Although tax subsidies to support IRAs and private pensions may in the end be justified, they do not provide a panacea for the problems facing the baby boomers.

Unavoidably, then, the baby boomers' prospects for old age

depend on the success of the next generation — today's children. As Frances FitzGerald has written, "Americans in their sixties and seventies are surely the first generation of healthy, economically independent retired people in history — and, in the absence of significant economic growth, they may well be the last."[33] If you believe that today's children are bound to grow up many times richer and more productive than today's workers, then logic will permit you to believe that Social Security, Medicare, and other government programs will be able to provide adequately for the baby boomers in old age. The Social Security Administration predicts that in order for both its pension and disability funds to remain solvent over the lifetime of the baby boomers, real wages must more than double over today's levels by 2015 and increase sixfold before 2060 — and this is assuming that fertility rates increase rapidly as well, and that other demographic and economic trends are also extremely favorable.[34]

A dispassionate look at the hazards now standing in the way of the younger generation's prosperity should give pause, however, to anyone who would trust such an eventuality to fate. Consider first the alarming increase in poverty among today's children. Throughout American history, each new generation has grown up to be richer than the one that went before. And yet, as Daniel Patrick Moynihan has asserted, the United States has now become "the first society in history in which a person is more likely to be poor if young rather than old."[35] The downward mobility of the baby boomers has been compounded with a vengeance on their children. Between 1973 and 1984, the percentage of children living beneath the poverty line increased by more than two-thirds. By 1984, more than one out of five American children under age eighteen was poor.[36]

Cutbacks in federal programs for children go a long way toward explaining this alarming trend. Between 1980 and 1986, programs for children and families suffered budget cuts of over $50 billion. Due to tighter eligibility requirements, for example, Aid to Families with Dependent Children — the government's main welfare program—served only fifty-five of every one hundred poor children in 1984, compared with seventy-five of every one hundred in 1978.[37] But other deeper, more intractable problems were also at work which have affected even children nominally born into the middle class.

Of all baby boomers, those with children have generally fared the worst. During the first two postwar decades, family income among both two-parent and female-headed families with children grew by an average of more than 6 percent a year. But between 1973 and 1984, families with children saw their average, inflation-adjusted income drop by more than 8 percent, from over $32,000 a year to $29,500, despite the enormous increase in the number of working mothers.[38]

Even white families with both parents present saw their income fall—by more than 3 percent. If the increase in Social Security and other taxes were taken into account, the decline in overall family income would be even steeper. Between 1960 and the early 1980s, the average family of four saw its tax rate rise by more than 200 percent. A family of four earning poverty-level wages in 1986 paid between 10 and 12 percent of its meager earnings in federal taxes alone, up from 2 percent in 1979.[39]

The increasing poverty among children is a national scandal in its own right. But a closer examination of its causes suggests an even greater tragedy in the future. Besides higher taxes and lower wages, the rising rates of divorce and of children born out of wedlock have also contributed mightily to the increase in childhood poverty, while also eroding the bonds between the baby boomers and their children within all economic classes.

Since 1970, the divorce rate has more than doubled. More than 50 percent of all first marriages among the baby boomers are expected to end in divorce.[40] Moreover, couples today not only are divorcing more readily than in the past, but they also tend to do so earlier in their marriages.[41] Because of these trends, an estimated 43 percent of all children born in wedlock will experience parental separation before they reach age sixteen.[42]

Yet these children, it might be said, should count themselves lucky ever to have lived in an intact home. More than one out of every five children born in 1984 came into the world dependent on an unwed mother. Between 1970 and 1984, the number of black children born out of wedlock soared from 38 to 58 percent. But illegitimacy is hardly a problem confined to the black community. Its rate of increase has been even faster among whites. Over the same period, the percentage of white children born out of wedlock soared from one in sixteen to one out of every seven.[43]

Single-parent families are currently forming at twenty times the rate of two-parent families. The potentially horrendous implications for the future are revealed by the fact that children with divorced or unwed mothers are more than five times as likely to be poor as children in two-parent homes. Even those children in single-parent homes who do escape poverty may well be emotionally and economically handicapped by their experience. How many of these children find the wherewithal to finish high school or go to college? How many will have the means or be of a mind to support their aged parents, either directly, or through Social Security and other programs?

The Future Elderly and the Crisis in Education

The decline in educational accomplishment among today's children should also stand as a warning to those who would cavalierly suppose that tomorrow's workers will be well able to support the baby boomers in old age. The United States has lost its comparative advantage in basic manufacturing, probably forever. To reduce the unprecedented deficits in trade without a decline in living standards, the United States must rely on a work force with superior initiative and technological skills. As capital and information flow with increasing speed and volume across national borders, countries such as South Korea and Singapore are able to enter the industrial age virtually overnight by importing the most advanced capital equipment and industrial techniques. U.S. corporations are driven to transfer industrial production to whichever nation has the cheapest labor supply. If the United States is to succeed in the world economy of the next century without drastically cutting wages, it must excel in producing highly sophisticated products and services. Yet this will not be possible so long as American children lag so far behind the children of the nation's major trading partners in even basic intellectual skills.

In recent years, a succession of blue-ribbon panels and special task forces has documented the crisis in American education and warned of its implications for the future. The most famous of these reports, *A Nation at Risk*, released in 1983 by President Reagan's National Commission on Excellence in Education, concluded that "the educational foundations of our society are presently being eroded by a rising tide of mediocrity that threatens our very future as a Nation and a people."[44] Among the commission's specific findings: nearly one out of every eight seventeen-year-olds is functionally illiterate.

The same year, the Education Commission of the States reported a continuing decline in high-order thinking skills, such as problem solving, among American children. The commission also found that 26 percent of all math teachers were unqualified, and that elementary students generally received only four hours a week of instruction in math and one hour in science.[45]

The general incompetence of American children in these subjects was confirmed shortly thereafter in a report by the National Science Board, which concluded that "the Nation that dramatically and boldly led the world into the age of technology is failing to provide its own children with the intellectual tools needed for the 21st century."[46]

American students lag behind their counterparts in Japan and Taiwan from the earliest grade levels. In standardized mathematics and reading-comprehension tests administered to first- and fifth-graders in the three countries, American children finished last across the board. American first-graders accounted for only 15 percent of the top scorers in mathematics. All of the twenty American fifth-grade classes surveyed by the study had lower average test scores than the *worst*-performing Japanese classes at the same grade level.[47]

At higher grades, American children perform even worse in mathematics by comparison with children in advanced industrial countries. In the past, international comparisons at higher grade levels have been criticized for failing to adjust for the pronounced egalitarianism of the American public schools; in many foreign countries, all but the most adept students are diverted into vocational training before high school, whereas even mediocre American students are allowed to pursue college preparatory courses. Nevertheless a comprehensive international study of high school seniors published in 1985 found that our best math students — the 2–3 percent of American high school seniors enrolled in calculus classes — scored no better than the average for all high school seniors in other countries. By another measure, considering only the top 5 percent of scorers in each country, American students rank last in mathematics among industrial countries.[48]

The crisis in American education extends to college and postgraduate levels as well and is particularly pronounced in the disciplines most crucial to the nation's future industrial competitiveness — mathematics, engineering, and basic science. A 1986 report by the National Science Board concluded that university laboratory instruction "has deteriorated to the point where it is often uninspired, tedious and dull . . . conducted in facilities and with instruments that are obsolete and inadequate."[49]

Between 1973 and 1983, the number of undergraduate science majors fell by 15 percent. The annual number of Americans graduating with degrees in mathematics fell by half over the period. Partially offsetting these trends, enrollment in engineering and computer science has risen sharply in recent years. But a shortage of qualified professors has swelled class sizes and diminished the quality of instruction. Despite concerted efforts by universities, private industry, and federal agencies, roughly 1,500, or about 8.5 percent, of the nation's budgeted engineering faculty positions remained vacant in 1985.[50]

At the graduate level, foreign students are increasingly replacing Americans in science and engineering programs. In 1983, 42 percent of all students enrolled full-time in graduate engineering programs were foreigners; foreign students also composed 40 percent of the total enrollment in mathematics, 38 percent in computer sciences, and 29 percent in physical sciences.[51] Simon Ramo, former head of the President's Committee on Science and Technology and one of the nation's leading inventors, notes: "It used to be that most foreign-born Ph.D.s from our universities became U.S. citizens. Now more are returning to their home nations to take part in the technological boom there."[52] Meanwhile, federal aid to American graduate students in science and engineering has been cut; between 1980 and 1983, the number receiving federal support dropped by 10 percent.[53]

We know that as the baby boomers reach old age, the fraction of Americans dependent on public resources will increase. The growth of the older population alone will cause the funding of public pension and health care benefits for the elderly to become ever more difficult. But the rising incidence of poverty among today's children, along with the failure of our schools to teach so many of America's young people even how to read, much less the skills they will need to compete in the job markets of the next century, threatens to swell the ranks of dependent Americans still more. Today's poor, undereducated youth will become tomorrow's unemployed or marginally employed workers. Rather than pay taxes to support the baby boomers in old age, they will more likely collect public assistance themselves. Even if the more affluent members of the next generation decide not to subsidize the working-aged poor, we have every reason to believe that they will nonetheless be forced to commit more resources to pay for police, jails, private security guards, and other measures to protect themselves against the expanding underclass.

Wagering on Prosperity

The future will not necessarily turn out this way. But so long as current trends continue, we have no right to borrow on the assumption that it won't. In addition to the problems of childhood poverty and widespread illiteracy, the explosion of both public and private debt during the 1980s is undermining the future of today's children while also diminishing the baby boomers' prospects for old age.

In just the first half of the 1980s, the national debt doubled over the amount incurred during the previous two centuries — to more than $2 trillion. As a share of the gross national product, the national debt grew from 26.6 percent in 1980 to 38.4 percent in 1986.[54] Future taxpayers will pay for this profligacy in at least three ways.

The cost of paying interest on the debt is the most straightforward. In 1985, interest on the national debt reached $179.4 billion, or nearly 19 percent of all federal spending. This amount was only slightly less than the total spent on Social Security pensions that year, and was more than six times the total spent on all education, job training, and unemployment programs combined. Even if the United States never again runs a budget deficit, the cost of financing past deficits will continue to constrain the ability of the government to meet the needs and desires of future Americans, whether for a strong defense, tax cuts, or social programs.[55]

Throughout most of the postwar era, liberal economists tended to dismiss the idea that budget deficits encumbered future generations, with the thought that "we owed the money to ourselves." What some Americans paid in higher taxes to service the national debt, other Americans would receive in interest on

the Treasury bonds they held. Deficit spending might cause a
redistribution of income from the poor to the rich, these economists warned, since the rich were more likely to have invested
in Treasury bonds. But public borrowing would cause no transfer
between generations as a whole. "If our children or grandchildren
repay some of the national debt," the economist Abba Lerner
wrote in 1948, "the payments will be made *to* our children or
grandchildren, and to nobody else. Taking them altogether, they
will no more be impoverished by making the repayments than
they will be enriched by receiving them."

But Lerner also allowed, along with other liberal economists,
that "a nation owing money to other nations or to the citizens of
other nations *is* impoverished or burdened in the same kind of
way as a man who owes money to other men."[56] As the deficits
mounted in the 1980s, too few Americans could be found to buy
all the bonds the federal government was attempting to sell. As
a result, the Treasury Department increasingly encouraged foreigners to help underwrite our mounting national debt. The
Treasury even went so far as to promise foreign investors that
it would keep their identities secret from their home governments, thus making it easier for them to cheat on their taxes. As
a result of these and other incentives, by the end of 1985, foreign
holdings of the national debt reached $210.2 billion, which was
14 percent of the total debt held by the public. Interest payments
to foreign holders of the national debt amounted to $21.2 billion
that year. To keep this number in perspective, consider that it
equaled roughly three times the amount the United States spent
on space exploration in 1985 and 21 percent more than the entire
budget for the Department of Education.[57]

Second, the growth of the national debt has also encumbered
future Americans by discouraging private investment. In 1984
and 1985, the federal budget deficits consumed 60 percent of all
available private savings. Capital that otherwise could have gone
to build new houses and factories instead went to underwrite
the government's shortfall in revenue. The promise of supply

side economics was that by cutting taxes, especially for the rich, there would be more capital available in the private sector for investment in new enterprise. Instead, the opposite has occurred. Individuals used their tax cuts not to increase their savings but by and large to consume more luxuries, especially imported luxuries. The Reagan tax cuts bought a lot of yachts, private airplanes, and trips to the Caribbean, but very little in the way of new capital formation.[58]

Indeed, because the tax cuts were financed with deficits, they reduced the amount of capital the private sector could raise from domestic sources of credit while also driving up interest rates.[59] High interest rates, in turn, raised the price of the dollar and therefore the price of American exports, and thus contributed to the massive and compounding trade deficits the United States has thus far experienced in the 1980s. Even in high technology, the United States as of this writing is on the verge of becoming a net importer. Today's consumers enjoy cheap imports, but this situation causes further erosion of the nation's industrial base — a trend that must itself be viewed as a form of borrowing from the future.[60]

And third, because of the budget deficits, private borrowers have increasingly been forced, along with the government itself, to look abroad for sources of financing. In 1984, American companies and individuals borrowed from foreigners an amount equivalent to between 3 and 4 percent of the nation's total annual income, or roughly $125 billion.[61] Much of this debt went to finance credit card purchases, home equity loans, corporate takeovers, and other largely unproductive purposes. All will have to be repaid, with interest, and not to "ourselves."

For a nation to incur large foreign debts is often a good idea, so long as the money is used for truly productive investment. Throughout most of the nineteenth century, the United States relied tremendously on European sources of capital, for example. But we used this foreign capital primarily to build railroads, canals, factories, and other wealth-producing investments, not to underwrite current consumption. As these investments paid off, the United States had no trouble repaying its European creditors; indeed, with our more efficient industry, we were soon dominating the world with our exports and making the Europeans look to us as a source of capital. Between the end of World War I and 1982, the United States managed to build up a surplus of $152 billion in the amount of assets it held abroad over what foreigners owned in the United States. The return on that surplus became a large component of the country's rising standard of living.

But then, in just two years of massive government and private borrowing from abroad, the United States managed to liquidate seventy years' worth of asset accumulation. We went from being the world's largest creditor nation to being the world's largest debtor nation. Moreover, we were not borrowing for purposes that would make future Americans richer. Business investment remained flat, while consumer indebtedness has ballooned. And increasingly American consumers were going into debt to buy imported products.[62]

The deficits have allowed Americans of all ages to enjoy a somewhat higher standard of living over the short term. But the younger you are, the more the deficits will cost you in the future. Moreover, as is discussed in chapter 7, the deficits that the government admits to understate the true costs we are pushing into the future by failing to account for the government's enormous accruing liabilities, such as for future Social Security and Medicare benefits and for the repair and maintenance costs of our crumbling public infrastructure.

Taking all these trends together—the aging of the population; the increasing poverty and declining educational accomplishment of the young; and the massive debts we are now charging against the future earnings of the young to subsidize current consumption—it is fair to say that we have entered an era in which the circumstance of one's birthday has become a prime determinant of one's prospects for realizing the American dream.

Younger Americans — regardless of their class or ethnic origin — are caught in the spiral of what seems like permanent and compounding downward mobility, while today's senior citizens by all objective measures are, *as a whole*, the richest in history. The policy and moral implications of this unprecedented circumstance are by no means obvious. But no amount of rhetoric or ideology can disguise it as an essential truth of American society in the late twentieth century around which we must plan for the future.

Generational Conflict versus Generational Equity

Historically, conflict between generations has for the most part been waged over different ideas of moral responsibility, or over what we would today call different "lifestyles." In his ponderous history of generational conflict, entitled *The Challenge of Youth*, Friedrich Herr observed:

> A characteristic vision of liberation that goes beyond the political and economic can frequently be found in youthful rebellion. It demands liberation of the whole personality — sexual freedom, creative freedom. It envisages a "cultural revolution" to realize the full human potential. And simply because these drives are strongest in the young, and youth passes, youthful rebellion has a special, ephemeral quality.[63]

In contrast, generational conflict over issues of equity have been exceedingly rare or muted throughout human history. It is worth contemplating the reasons why. One, no doubt, is that the young can always look forward to becoming older, whereas they cannot necessarily look forward to attaining power and privileges based on criteria other than seniority. The history of the labor movement provides a good example. The working class of the past believed that it had no chance of owning the means of production and accordingly resented and frequently rebelled against those who did. But its members knew, or at least had reason to hope, that within their ranks they would each eventually attain seniority. Younger workers thus accepted union wage scales that discriminated against them in favor of older workers with the expectation that they would receive their reward in turn.

Within families, generational conflict has historically been mitigated by considerations of another kind. Before support for the elderly was institutionalized through Social Security and before the growth of banks and financial markets made saving for retirement possible, parents were constrained from abusing their authority over their children by the demands of prudence. Parents knew that eventually their support in old age would depend on their children's bonds of gratitude and affection. In purely economic terms, children were an investment, rather than, as today, a discretionary consumer item.

Also, as long as the family remained a productive unit—united in the common purpose of running a farm or a shop—the division of labor tended to be rooted in obvious biological reality; children and the old were excused from work on the basis solely of their actual frailty or inability to contribute. Finally, in most societies, children and their parents usually shared automatically in the key determinants of social standing and economic success. Within families or communities, the identity of race, ethnicity, language, and social caste between young and old tended to link them in common allegiances, in opposition to outsiders regardless of age.

In our own time, however, these underlying sources of generational harmony all are either fading away or losing force, for interconnected reasons. Consider first the role of Social Security and other old age benefits. As support in old age has come to depend less and less on the affection and prosperity of one's own children, or even on one's having children at all, individuals have correspondingly less incentive to reproduce themselves or to sacrifice on behalf of their children. One result is the falling birthrate; another is the increasing incidence of poverty and neglect among children due to the divorce and separation of their

parents, or simply to their parents' lack of direct financial interest
in their education and future welfare. Both trends undermine
the long-term financing of Social Security and other old age benefits. We thus have come to a point at which middle-aged Americans, and especially the baby boomers, can look forward neither
to receiving the same old age benefits as today's senior citizens,
nor — in many if not most instances — to receiving adequate support from their own children, even assuming that they have any.

In his book, *New Rules*, a survey of changing attitudes during
the 1970s, pollster Daniel Yankelovich concluded that "today's
parents expect to make fewer sacrifices for their children than
in the past, but also demand less from the offspring in the form
of future obligations than their parents demanded." Yankelovich
based his conclusion on several survey results. Nearly two-thirds
of all American parents reject the idea that parents should stay
together for the children's sake if the partners are unhappy with
one another. A similar majority feels that they have the right to
live well now and spend what they have earned "even if it means
leaving less to the children." But more than two-thirds of all
parents also feel that "children do not have an obligation to their
parents regardless of what their parents have done for them."[64]
The ruling ethos seems to be that parents are free to neglect
their children's interests so long as Social Security and other
benefits will relieve their offspring of ever having to support
them directly in old age.

The aging of the population is itself also a cause of the dissolving
bond among the generations. As Americans live longer, the proportion of their lives that they spend in the company of their
children decreases. White American women born in the 1880s,
for example, could expect to live about 21.3 years after their
youngest child reached age eighteen. Those born in the 1950s,
by contrast, are expected to survive approximately 34.1 years
after their last-born reaches adulthood. The average baby boomer
mother thus will spend nearly half as many years free of children
as she spends devoted to them. The change is even more dramatic

when one considers how long both husbands and wives are likely
to remain alive after their last child reaches eighteen. In the
1880s, both mates would survive this event by an average of only
1.6 years; those born in the 1950s can expect to live together
free of their children for 12.9 years.[65] Given these changes, it is
only natural to expect that adults would plan their lives with
increasing concern for themselves, rather than for the needs of
their children. Indeed, the prospect or the opportunity of attaining a prolonged, healthy, active retirement increases at least
the perceived cost of having children in the first place.

The bonds between the generations are also obviously eroded
by the increasing proportion of childless Americans. The number
of young childless couples rose by 75 percent between 1968 and
1985, compared with a rise of only 8 percent in the number of
young couples with children. In 1965, married couples with children under eighteen accounted for 42.5 percent of all households,
whereas today that number has slipped to a mere 28 percent.
Experts predict that 15 percent or more of women now in their
twenties and thirties will remain childless throughout their lifetimes, far above the historical 8–10 percent rate.[66]

By itself, the trend toward childlessness erodes political support for programs benefiting the young. But another demographic trend reinforces the bias. Increasingly, today's children
are members of minority groups. Nearly a fifth of the population
under age fifteen is black or Hispanic, compared with only 11
percent of those older than sixty-five. Taking these two trends
together, we can expect that by the second decade of the next
century, an unprecedented proportion of the elderly population
will lack any blood relationship to younger Americans, and what's
more, the generations will be increasingly estranged as well by
differences of race and ethnicity.[67]

As David Hayes Bautista has observed, by the time the baby
boomers reach retirement age, "the different generations will
have different ethnic compositions. Thus, what is an intergen-

erational income transfer will be seen also as an interethnic transfer." Writing specifically about California in the next century, Bautista warns of a scenario leading to "social collapse" in which "the baby-boom elderly see themselves surrounded by culturally different people. . . . Because age and ethnicity will correlate, things will become labeled by ethnicity. Pediatric health will be labeled as a Mexican problem. The elderly will be seen as an Anglo problem. That could be a pretty depressing situation."[68]

In the meantime, the tensions that throughout the industrial era have found expression in those two grand abstractions, "capital" and "labor," are also likely to divide the interests of young and old. As we have already seen, older Americans on average possess enormously greater net wealth than do their children. One consequence has been that the same high interest rates that generally punished working-aged Americans in the early 1980s — by causing unemployment, making home owning less affordable, and making debts more difficult to pay off — were of great benefit to the many elderly who held substantial financial savings.

But there is another more profound sense in which those who do not derive their income from paid labor will be at odds with those who do. As Kingsley Davis and Pietronella van den Oever pointed out in an essay predicting a coming class struggle type of conflict between young and old:

> If a person is not working for wages, salary or fees, regardless whether his income derives from rents, interest, insurance, retirement pay, or government transfers, he is not currently producing goods and services in exchange for those he receives. When he buys an automobile, someone else has produced the vehicle. When he buys vegetables in a grocery store, someone else has grown them. In each case the elderly buyer, if he is living from non-work income, is producing nothing in return. Doubtless, he was productive in the past, but he is not now. He surely feels that

he has worked hard in the past, has contributed to his own retirement, and is thus reaping his just reward; but if he is able to
work, his idleness entails an inevitable social cost.[69]

This is too strong. The elderly who have managed to save up
the cost of their retirement serve the interests of those who follow
by forming capital that can be used to create new jobs, finance
home mortgages, underwrite student loans, and in other ways
improve the future. Yet for performing this role, the wealthy
elderly are no more likely to receive the affection of the young
than capitalists of any age are likely to win the affection of labor.
So long as the wealthy elderly demand, in addition to return on
their capital, to be provided with across-the-board old age subsidies, the resentment of the young in general can only increase,
especially since the young will quite likely have little hope of
receiving similar subsidies from the next generation.

The Prophets of Crisis

Predictions of a coming war between the generations have by no
means been confined to the present era. Many of the trends that
are currently weakening the bonds between young and old have
quietly been at work for many decades, and a few far-sighted
observers could see their eventual implications. As early as 1951,
in a speech before the Southern Conference on Gerontology,
the economist Frank G. Dickenson warned that "the enormous
growth in the number of old people in America, and their increasing demands for pensions, may lead us to expect a new
sort of class war—between our younger and older citizens."
Dickenson prophesied that the burden of supporting the old
would grow inexorably, and that as a result "we will see workers
and employers, despite their natural respect for age, standing
shoulder to shoulder against hard-driven politicians who promise
our senior citizens impossible pensions."[70]

Today, partisans of the senior power movement frequently

attack suggestions that any real competition ever exists between the generations. In 1986, for example, the Gerontological Society of America published a study, later publicized by the House Select Committee on Aging, which argued that young and old were inevitably bound together by common interest and that any suggestions to the contrary were "intentionally divisive" and the result of an "improper frame of analysis."[71] Yet before the trends just discussed began to force the issue of generational equity, gerontologists were among the first to warn of a youthful revolt against the growing power of the elderly. Bernice Neugarten, for example, one of the country's most widely respected gerontologists, predicted in 1974 that during the rest of the decade "anger toward the old may rise . . . as a growing proportion of power positions in the judiciary, legislative, business and professional arenas are occupied by older people; as the number of retirees increases and taxes rise."[72] The next year, Robert N. Butler, who coined the term *ageism* in the mid-1960s and who for many years headed the National Institute on Aging, warned that "one unhappy aspect of the politics of aging is the pitting of one age group against another in the quest for scarce social resources. . . . The consequent resentment of younger age groups can boomerang against old people."[73]

Today's elderly probably have little to fear, despite these warnings. Indeed, throughout the remaining years of today's older people, the aging of the population will actually work in favor of more generous retirement benefits. As the youngest of the baby boomers join the work force and as the oldest gain income through seniority, their taxes are expected to swell the coffers of the Social Security trust funds for many years to come. Moreover, as life expectancy among the elderly continues to lengthen, there will be ever more middle-aged Americans seeking relief from the potentially astronomical cost of supporting their elderly parents in nursing homes or of paying for the cost of operations and catastrophic illnesses not covered by Medicare. Finally, as the percentage of households with children present continues to decline, fewer Americans will be pressing for the government to spend its money first on the needs of children. With current fertility and mortality rates, it turns out that there is no longer any stage in life when the average married couple will have more children under the age of twenty than they will have surviving parents.[74]

Instead, it is the baby boomers who need fear abandonment in old age. For it is they, along with their children, who will inherit the consequences of this spendthrift era. There are no purely technical solutions to the deficit looming everywhere in American society—in the birthrate that is below replacement level, in the declining educational performance of the nation's children relative to their counterparts abroad, in the federal budget, in the balance of trade, in the long-term financing of Social Security and Medicare. Our problem is as much cultural as it is economic. As a nation and as individuals we have committed ourselves to spending more in real resources than we will likely be able to produce over our lifetimes. Behind the abstract and bloodless debate over fiscal policy, trade, and general national decline lurk the terrifying ethical and societal issues that have created our deficit state.

Americans are by now well accustomed to the idea that virtually any act of government can serve to redistribute in the here and now wealth and opportunity among different types of citizens, among different industries, regions, and other categories of special interest. What we have not yet embraced in our politics, however, is the reality that now, as never before, government policies can also serve to redistribute wealth and opportunity from the future to the present, and therefore from younger generations to older generations over time. In most instances, the borrowing is inadvertent, the result of individuals' simply seeking to maximize their standard of living according to the rules we have collectively determined more or less in good faith. No one

generation is any less to blame for the crisis than another—
unless it be today's children.

The purpose of this book is to examine the major mechanisms
of intergenerational transfer in our society, to ask how they came
about, whether they are fair or prudent, and how they might be
reformed. The first subject to which we will turn our attention
is housing policy, which has become perhaps the greatest single
means whereby wealth is being redistributed from young to old.

2

The Mortgaging of America: Real Estate and the Future of Retirement

AT AGE THIRTY, Henry George considered himself a defeated man. With but a grade school education, he had bounced around from one odd job to another across California before coming at last to New York, where he soon enough failed as a telegraph news reporter. The year was 1864, and as George wandered the streets of that rich city, he was struck by what seemed to him a great paradox of modern political economy: that side by side with the fabulous mansions and other manifestations of vast new wealth there could exist a mass of the unemployed whose poverty exceeded that of the most wretched peasants of the Old World. In an instant, George would later write, there came to him "in daylight, in the city street—a burning thought, a call, a vision. Every nerve quivered." George resolved that he would never again rest until he had solved the conundrum of "deepening poverty amidst advancing wealth."

The result, fifteen years later, was, of course, his worldwide best seller and enduring classic, *Progress and Poverty*. The book's central thesis was so simple and seemingly unanswerable that for a long time it humiliated professional economists who had failed to discover it for themselves. George observed that in any region where the population and the economy are growing, there is an ineluctable tendency for the price of land to inflate even faster as a direct result. Yet, as George wrote, an "increase in land values does not represent increase in the common wealth, for what land owners gain by higher prices, the tenants or purchaser who must pay them lose."[1] As George might put it today, land speculation is a zero-sum game. To manufacture any product or even to provide any service requires land, labor, and capital in some combination. As more resources are committed to cover the inflating price of land, commensurately less funds are available to reward workers and those who invest in productive enterprise. To remedy this, George proposed a simple solution: a 100 percent tax on all price appreciation in land, combined with elimination of all taxes on labor and capital.

George stopped short of applying the same logic to manmade forms of real estate. In his view, a house and the lot on which it stands are of an entirely different metaphysical order, since the one is the product of labor and the other a "gift of nature." Yet had he witnessed the superinflation of home prices during the last twenty years, George would no doubt find this a distinction without much difference. In 1955, the median price paid for a new home was $13,400; by 1985 that price had risen to $88,900 — an increase of more than 60 percent after adjusting for inflation. This price increase was only to a negligible degree the result of anyone's honest labor. Indeed, had a sufficient number of workers been building houses during those decades, supply would have met demand and prices would have remained stable. Moreover, for at least the past twenty years, the ever increasing amounts of capital used to finance the sale and resale of existing houses at ever higher prices has come at the direct expense of investments needed to maintain America's industries, roads, bridges, and general standard of living. As a result, not only are today's younger Americans paying unprecedented prices for housing, but they are also earning lower real wages than they would have otherwise.

In the last chapter, we saw how by 1984, the average thirty-year-old man needed to commit 44 percent of his income to meet the carrying charges on the median-priced house. Because no lender will actually write a mortgage that consumes such a high percentage of income, home ownership rates among the young have been declining steadily. From 1981 to 1985, the percentage of home owners aged twenty-five to twenty-nine dropped from 41.7 to 37.7; the percentage of home owners aged thirty to thirty-four dropped from 59.3 to 54.7.[2] A close look at how these trends came about reveals that the same government policies that helped millions of Americans to realize the dream of home ownership in the 1950s and 1960s have inadvertently served to make real estate vastly more expensive for today's younger Americans, while also providing tremendous capital gains for many of today's older Americans.

With the possible exception of agriculture, there is no other sector of the economy in which government is so directly and thoroughly involved in manipulating prices than in real estate. For nearly thirty years, the results were all to the good. From the Depression on, the federal government has provided mortgage credit and tax benefits aimed at making houses affordable for as many Americans as possible. As recently as 1946, the majority of Americans were renters. Then, within the space of one generation, more than two-thirds of us became home owners. At the local level, towns have regulated land use, enforced building codes, constructed sewers to ensure pleasant neighborhoods and to promote public safety and health. Meanwhile, although detractors like Lewis Mumford have made it intellectually fashionable to denounce suburban sprawl, suburbia's shaded sidewalks and detached single-family homes are just what the majority of Americans still and probably always will desire.

But over time, government policies have come to serve more those who already own homes than those who would like to buy one. Increasingly, local regulations do not serve objective public interests but are used instead to prop up real estate prices and to exclude "undesirables," such as young families with children. At the same time, as more of the nation's wealth has been consumed by real estate speculation, and as home owners have increasingly come to rely on the inflating value of their homes as a substitute for saving, there has been correspondingly less financial capital available for investments needed to maintain the country's industrial competitiveness and to provide decent-paying jobs for today's younger Americans.

The Mortgaging of America

Mortgages are largely an invention of the twentieth century. Before World War I, they carried a stigma; the best families were expected to buy their houses outright. During the twenties, however, mortgages became widespread enough to finance a housing boom. The terms of these mortgages seem quaint by today's standards. Even savings and loans, which had been formed specifically to hold the savings of working people and to provide them with home mortgages, would not lend money for longer than three to five years, after which time the loan would be refinanced. Bankers refused to write long-term mortgages because they had to provide their depositors with ready access to their savings. As the cardinal rule of banking puts it, "If you borrow short, you cannot afford to lend long."

With the onset of the Depression, wages and prices declined, making it more difficult for people who owed money on their houses to keep up with their monthly payments. In 1926, roughly 68,000 home mortgages were foreclosed; by 1932, the number was up to 250,000; by the next year, fully half of all mortgages in the United States were in technical default.

Foreclosures accelerated a decline in housing prices. A typical house worth $5,000 in 1926 was worth about $3,000 in 1932. During the same period savings banks were beset by lines of depositors demanding their money back. The result: hundreds of savings and loans failed, threatening the entire U.S. banking system with collapse.

On July 22, 1932, President Herbert Hoover responded to the emergency by creating the Federal Home Loan Bank Board (FHLBB). Initially funded by a $125 million line of credit with the Treasury, the board was empowered to lend funds to the savings banks, using their mortgages as security. The idea was that the agency would then turn around and sell bonds, backed by these mortgages, in order to raise more capital to lend to the savings banks. This would enable the savings banks to write still more mortgages, and on better terms, while also maintaining enough cash on hand to satisfy their depositors.

Almost needless to say, the scheme flopped. No one would buy the bonds, which were not federally guaranteed. Moreover, the FHLBB would lend money only to home buyers who qualified to borrow from private lenders. But the Bank Board set an important precedent. For the first time, the federal government was using its powers to divert more credit to potential home buyers as a way of protecting both the banks and the home owners from the consequences of falling real estate prices.

Soon after the election of Franklin Delano Roosevelt, the government raised the stakes enormously. If investors found it too risky to put more of their money into home mortgages, then the obvious solution was for the government to *guarantee* these mortgages against any loss. Among the myriad new agencies that sprang up during Roosevelt's first hundred days was the Home Owner's Loan Corporation — an institution that would revolutionize home financing. Empowered to sell up to $2 billion in bonds backed by the full faith and credit of the United States, the HOLC for the first time made it possible for at least some lucky home owners to take out mortgages running as long as fifteen years, rather than the usual two or three years.

Yet this infusion of new and cheaper credit into the real estate markets was still not enough to arrest the downward trend of home prices. Between 1929 and 1934, according to the Census Bureau, the average price of owner-occupied houses slipped by more than 20 percent.[3] Nor was this infusion of credit enough to end the massive unemployment in the construction trades. In 1934, Congress passed the centerpiece of Roosevelt's housing legislation, the National Housing Act, which established the Federal Housing Administration (FHA). Lewis H. Brown, a prominent housing expert who helped the administration craft the legislation, enthusiastically described its purpose in an article for the *New York Times*.

> "Everybody who has studied real estate and building knows," Lewis asserted, "that the short term mortgage, that on which the lender may demand his money at the end of three or four years, was the panic element in the collapse of real estate values." The solution, Lewis concluded, was obvious: entice lenders into offering longer-term mortgage money, with monthly payments going not only to pay interest, but also to retire the principal. "Under this bill," Lewis explained, real estate mortgages will not only be insured by the government, but the lending bank . . . will be getting its money back each month. There will be no better security in the world than these amortized real estate mortgages."[4]

Thus was born that happy instrument of the last generation of home owners: the long-term, self-amortizing, low interest rate mortgage. With the passage of the National Housing Act, the government committed itself to insuring mortgages running for as long as twenty years, at 6 percent interest and with as little as 20 percent down. The program, which was administered by the FHA, did not catch on immediately. Some bankers doubted that Congress could insure anything beyond its own term. Others resented all the paperwork, insurance fees, and appraisals the

FHA required. As late as 1939, FHA-insured mortgages constituted only 10 percent of the total.

But gradually loan officers overcame their habitual sense of caution. Before insuring any mortgage, the FHA investigated the property and approved the neighborhood. This extra measure of security made FHA mortgages easily tradable. Banks found that they could sell FHA mortgages even to investors in distant parts of the country who knew nothing about the property on which the notes were written. If for any reason a home owner fell behind on a mortgage guaranteed by the FHA, the agency would take over the debt, thereby insulating the mortgage holder from almost all risk. In effect, the government had made it much safer for an investor to put his money into FHA mortgages written by any small local bank or savings and loan than to underwrite even the largest, most secure corporations. As a result, for the first time in American history, it became cheaper—in terms of monthly payments—to buy a home on credit than to rent.[5]

Quonset Huts to Levittown

With the end of World War II, veterans returned home to face an acute housing shortage. Through the Depression and the war, residential construction had been minimal; the yearly average of new homes built had been fewer than 100,000. Now demand for houses surged. Newspapers chronicled the result. In Omaha, a newspaper advertisement read: "Big Ice Box, 7 × 17 feet, could be fixed up to live in"; in New York, two newlyweds became squatters in a department store window. As late as 1947, 6 million families were sharing quarters with friends or relatives, while half a million were living in temporary structures such as quonset huts.

But the housing shortage had a built-in solution. Since consumers had found so few items to buy during the war, banks were overflowing with savings. These savings allowed the federal government to provide, through the FHA and a new Veterans

Administration loan guarantee program, the opportunity to purchase a first house with little or no money down and at interest rates below 4 percent.

The initial result of these cheap mortgages was a surge in house prices, which many feared would soon lead to a bust. In an article entitled "Don't Get Stuck with a House," John P. Dean, an expert in city planning, warned the readers of *Harper's* magazine in 1945:

> As though the ordinary risks of home purchase were not formidable enough, the home market for the next few years will be charged with special dangers, most of them obscured by our abundant faith in "home-ownership" and in the promise of the "Postwar World." . . . Post-war home prices will reflect not only the general increase in price levels caused by freer circulation of money but also will represent an inflated write-up resulting from too few homes for too many people.[6]

By 1947, Federal Reserve Board Chairman Marriner S. Eccles was warning Congress that "excessively easy mortgage credit for housing . . . has greatly increased the effective demand for both old and new housing far beyond the supply and this has greatly inflated prices." Eccles railed against the government's growing commitment to providing easy mortgage terms to veterans and other Americans, concluding, "Manifestly, this is not in the best interest of the general economy."[7]

The fear was widespread. Writing the next year in *Harper's*, Eric Larrabee observed, "Nearly everyone is agreed that today's housing values are inflated, and that the collapse will have to come someday."[8] Yet what Larrabee and other critics of the mortgage financing boom overlooked was that the enormous infusions of cheap credit into real estate, while initially serving to drive up the price of existing houses, would soon inspire an unprecedented building boom, and so prices would rise only modestly for many years to come. The number of houses built rose from 114,000 in 1944 to 937,000 in 1946, to a peak of 1,692,000 in 1950. Overall, a yearly average of 1.4 million houses were built between 1945 and 1965.[9] Moreover, these homes were, by the standards of the time, both relatively easy to afford and generally of high quality.

Probably the best known of these houses were those built in Island Trees, Long Island, subsequently renamed Levittown. In his book *Crabgrass Frontier*, Kenneth Jackson describes how William J. Levitt's ingenious mass production technique put up houses quickly and efficiently:

> After bulldozing the land and removing the trees, trucks carefully dropped off building materials at precise 60-foot intervals. Each house was built on a concrete slab (no cellar); the floors were of asphalt and the walls of composition rock-board. . . . Freight cars loaded with lumber went directly into a cutting yard where one man cut parts for ten houses in one day. The construction process itself was divided into 27 distinct steps—beginning with laying the foundation and ending with a clean sweep of the new home. Crews were trained to do one job—one day the white-paint men, then the red-paint men, then the tile layers. Every possible part, especially the most difficult ones, were [*sic*] preassembled in central shops.[10]

Between 1945 and 1965 mortgage debt outstanding on homes containing between one and four families increased by more than elevenfold, from $18.6 billion to $212.9 billion. As a percentage of the nation's gross national product, residential mortgage indebtedness increased over this period from 9 to over 30 percent.[11] Yet by diverting such vast amounts of capital into the real estate markets the nation bought something real and sorely needed: new houses. And since supply rose to meet demand, these new houses were provided at affordable prices. Through the 1950s and early 1960s, home prices increased by an average of around 5 percent a year. Yet even this statistic exaggerates the true rate of inflation. The median-priced house was increasing in price largely because it was also increasing in size and luxury. In 1969, the President's Committee on Urban Housing, for example, found that "most" of the rise in home prices between 1953 and 1965 was the result of a 40 percent increase in the floor space of new, median-priced houses, combined with the introduction of "air conditioning, better thermal and sound insulation, more and better appliances, more tasteful design and landscaping, and many other features."[12] Home buyers were thus not cheated when they paid higher prices for houses, because having paid the extra money, they increased their real standard of living—they got more house.

Walling the Suburbs

Although federal housing policy proved a success during the two decades after World War II, after the mid-1960s it began to falter. The volume of mortgage debt continued to climb; between 1965 and 1984, it increased by another sixfold, from $213 billion to more than $1.3 trillion. As a fraction of GNP, it rose from just under 31 percent to 37 percent.[13] But a smaller proportion of this money was spent on creating new houses, which were sorely needed as the baby boom generation came of age. Instead, the money tended to be spent on buying and selling existing houses at ever higher prices.

The ratio of total mortgage lending to the value of new home construction provides a rough measure of the degree to which capital flowing into real estate is being used either to increase the supply of new houses or to inflate the price of existing houses. During the 1950s, the amount of mortgage money lent each year averaged about *one-third less* than the total value of new residential construction. Yet in the years to come, with each new dollar of credit committed to mortgages, a declining share went toward financing new home sales and a higher share toward financing the resale of existing homes at ever higher prices. During the 1960s, the amount of mortgage lending rose to within 10 percent of the value of all new construction. During the first half of the 1970s, mortgage lending for the first time surpassed the value of all new construction. Between 1975 and 1978, the amount of residential mortgage lending rose to be *nearly half again as large* as the value of all new homes built.

Writing in 1981, Anthony Downes, a housing expert at the Brookings Institution, noted that the phenomenon could be explained in part by lower down payment requirements for new homes. But most of the increase in mortgage lending over the value of new construction, Downes wrote, "resulted from greater use of mortgage funds for sales of existing units and for refinancing without sales." "Insofar as these employments of funds merely inflated the value of existing inventory," Downes concluded, "they did not add to socially useful wealth or productivity."[14]

Much of the capital flowing into real estate during the seventies actually wound up being used for other purposes. By 1979, according to a study by the U.S. League of Savings Associations, typical home owners selling one house and buying another received $30,877 in equity from the house sold. This gain was so large that on average, even after paying an inflated price for the second home, the typical owner realized a profit on the transaction of $10,498, which he could use for any purpose he liked.[15] By diverting more and more credit into real estate, the government may have thought it was aiding young people in buying a first house, but much of the capital was actually going instead to underwrite trips to the Caribbean and other forms of pure consumption by those old enough to own a home already. Meanwhile, even as house prices continued to soar, new houses were no longer increasing in size and luxury. Between 1980 and 1983, the median floor space of new houses actually declined slightly, while at the same time a declining percentage of new houses contained such amenities as basements and garages. And still, the median price of new houses advanced 16 percent.[16]

Paying more and getting less is the true definition of inflation. The large question is, why did policies that were so successful during the early postwar period begin to fail just as the baby boom generation came of age?

In part, the sheer size of the generation was responsible for inflating home prices. The baby boomers, moreover, because they tended to remain single longer than members of previous generations had and because of their high divorce rates, created even more demand for housing than they would have if they had assumed the lifestyle of their parents. The total number of households, which had grown from 53 million in 1960 to 63 million in 1970, then jumped to 77 million in 1979. The rate of increase was three times faster than that of the population as a whole.[17]

But demography is not destiny. For a variety of purely political reasons, capital that might have been used to build new affordable houses for the baby boomers went instead toward enriching current home owners. Among the most important of these reasons were the many barriers to new house construction thrown up during the late sixties and seventies by the early residents of suburbia. During this period, communities across the country enacted ever more restrictive zoning ordinances, elaborate and time-consuming building permit processes, land use restrictions, and a host of other measures often overtly designed to limit growth and push up local property values.

Building codes and zoning restrictions can serve valuable public purposes. At the most practical level, they can ensure that new houses will be built safely; to a certain degree they are also helpful in maintaining the character of a neighborhood or town. Historical preservation, for example, can be a laudable means of preventing the casual destruction of buildings that pass on from one generation to the next a sense of cultural heritage. On a less exalted level, prohibitions that proliferated early in this century against building outhouses improved public health enormously, to say nothing of the quality of life.

But when towns require, as many now do, that all new homes contain more floor space than any that were built in the 1940s and 1950s, that they have copper rather than plastic pipes, and that they be placed far back on a minimum of half-acre lots, with four-foot sidewalks, paved driveways, and "tasteful" landscaping, then it shouldn't surprise anyone that prices become prohibitive. These local policies limit the supply of new houses. Meanwhile, the federal government's massive diversion of credit into the mortgage markets compounds the resulting inflation by preserving effective demand even in the face of higher prices. Taken together, local and federal housing policies thus help create a cycle wherein fewer homes are built, home prices soar, buyers go more deeply into debt, and sellers reap large gains. The cycle might continue indefinitely, except that as more and more capital is committed to financing the sale and resale of existing houses, less is available for the productive investment needed to maintain the earning power of the young, as well as to construct new houses.

By the late 1960s, more than 78 percent of all municipalities with populations greater than ten thousand had some form of land use regulation. More than half had zoning ordinances, and nearly 45 percent had enacted subdivision regulation. Roughly a quarter of the towns in the United States required that new homes be built on lots of at least half an acre.[18] Two blue-ribbon panels of the time—the President's Commission on Housing and the National Commission on Urban Problems—reported that such regulations were frequently being used to limit residential development to large, expensive single-family houses, and that the effect of this was to restrict the supply and inflate the cost of all housing. Most young people no longer had the option of buying a new, no-frills, unfinished "starter house" of the size and kind that Levitt made famous, for in most towns across the United States building such houses had already been declared illegal.

Yet in the years to come, the web of federal, state, and, most significantly, local regulation would become much more complex and exclusionary. In 1982, President Reagan's Commission on

Housing found that "unnecessary regulation of land use and buildings has increased so much over the past two decades that Americans have begun to feel the undesirable consequences: fewer housing choices, limited production, high costs and lower productivity in residential construction." The commission concluded that such regulations had pushed up the cost of houses in some communities by as much as 25 percent of the final sales price.[19]

Consider building codes, which in most communities today go far beyond what is required to ensure public safety and indeed effectively outlaw low-cost housing. Modern labor-saving techniques such as preassembled roof trusses and prewired panel boards are often forbidden. These restrictions reflect in part the political power of construction unions, whose members feel threatened by the prospect of such labor-saving techniques as prefabrication costing them their jobs. But the phenomenon also results from pressures generated by home owners intent on enhancing the "quality" of the neighborhood and, by extension, their property values.

Another method commonly used to raise property values is limiting the supply of land. Examples of such regulations include site development plans that require extrawide streets and large lots, farmland preservation acts, and environmental protection measures. Again, as with all building regulations, land use restrictions can be used to meet legitimate public interests or abused merely to inflate property values. The line is often difficult to draw. If, for example, some farmers on the fringes of a city are on the verge of bankruptcy, should they be allowed to save themselves financially by subdividing their land for development, even if that leads to raising the property taxes for those farmers who remain? The question is difficult to answer without knowing precisely the extent to which land use restrictions actually raise the cost of housing. But it is not surprising to find that during the 1970s, when all forms of growth control were proliferating across the country, the price of land for new homes rose faster than the price of labor, material, or any other cost component except financing. By 1980, nearly a quarter of the cost of the average new home would go just for the cost of the lot.

Another means by which home owners restrict growth and raise property values is by having newcomers assume the full cost of new schools, roads, utilities, and other infrastructure that might be made necessary by an increase in the local population. During the fifties, such expenditures were traditionally borne by the community as a whole or else simply postponed. But in 1978, the U.S. Department of Housing and Urban Development's Task Force on Housing Costs found that "local governments are steadily transferring from the community at large to the developer, and thence to the new housing consumer, a greater share of the public capital costs of growth."[20]

" 'Controlled growth,' " Martin Mayer observed in his book *The Builders*, "turns out to mean loading all of the costs of growth on the newcomers, and giving all the benefits to the existing residents — especially those who had the best cabins on the ship before the political leaders lifted the gangplank."[21] In San Diego, Mayer reports, the city council approved a prize-winning development in the north end of the city only after the developers agreed to build *all* public facilities — schools, water plants, sewage plants, police stations, firehouses, libraries, and parks — with their own — that is, the new residents' — money. Even so, Mayor Pete Wilson opposed the plan, claiming that the new residents would still need other city services costing $2.5 million a year.

Other towns are more subtle in the ways in which they force new residents to assume all the burdens of growth. Tactics range from such backdoor measures as high permit and development fees to the levying of special taxes on newcomers who are not yet able to vote. The local politics of growth, like the national politics of Social Security or deficit spending, are heavily skewed against all late arrivers. Writes Bernard Frieden, a professor of urban studies at MIT:

Suburban governments that enact and implement growth controls are responsive mainly to already established residents who elect local officials. Potential home-buyers usually live elsewhere and have no representation in the regulatory proceedings. They are not organized as a political force, and indeed there is no way of knowing who they are until they turn up to look at model homes. Because the politics of growth control exclude families that want to move into the community, it is not surprising that compromises are struck at their expense.[22]

The Inflation Bubble

Local barriers to new construction were not the only reason real estate prices began to soar in the 1970s. Also important were three additional factors acting in combination: (1) the creation of new government agencies that pumped mortgage money into the housing market faster than new houses were actually being built, (2) tax subsidies that failed to discriminate in favor of new house construction, and (3) the incentives created by inflation itself. In 1968, the Council of Economic Advisors, in its annual report to the president, predicted that 20 million new housing units would be required during the 1970s "to meet the needs of the postwar baby boom." Yet the housing industry was building only about 1.5 million houses per year. A logical response might have been for the federal government to take measures to coax more capital specifically into new house construction. Instead the government directed dollars into new and existing houses alike.

The Federal National Mortgage Association, commonly known as "Fannie Mae," started life as a minor New Deal program. Under the terms of the Housing Act of 1968, however, it evolved into a "quasi-government agency" with enormous powers to attract capital into mortgage lending. Fannie Mae's mission is to purchase mortgages, thereby allowing the banks and other lenders to write more mortgages. To raise the necessary capital, Fannie Mae sells bonds, as well as special securities—backed

by pools of mortgages — to private investors. With a call on the
Treasury to buy $2.25 billion of its offerings on demand in the
event that the market dries up, Fannie Mae has little trouble
luring capital away from other sectors of the economy. Investors
assume that the federal government would never allow Fannie
Mae to collapse.

The Housing Act of 1968 also brought Fannie Mae a little
sister, "Ginnie Mae," formally known as the Government National Mortgage Association (GNMA). Shortly afterwards, they
were joined by a little brother, "Freddie Mac," the Federal
Home Loan Mortgage Corporation. Ginnie Mae works in much
the same way as Fannie Mae, but its issues are formally guaranteed by the full faith and credit of the U.S. Constitution.
Freddie Mac also raises money by selling bonds in the open
marketplace but uses the capital solely to purchase mortgages
from savings and loan institutions. Between 1968 and 1980, these
three so-called federally sponsored credit agencies, along with
other agencies designed to provide low-cost mortgages to farmers, sold $361 billion in bonds and pumped all of that money
into home finance. To realize the significance of this figure, consider that it amounted to more than 72 percent of the total increase in home mortgage indebtedness over the period.[23] Because
this great diversion of credit came at a time when local policies
were increasingly preventing the construction of new houses, the
government thus became, wittingly or unwittingly, the principal
underwriter of the great housing inflation of the era.

At the same time, the tax advantages of owning a house were
growing more compelling. Ever since Woodrow Wilson signed
the income tax into law in 1913, "interest on indebtedness"
had been exempt. When tax rates rose during the 1940s, the
mortgage-interest deduction became a significant factor in
spurring people to buy houses. Similarly, as the inflation of
the 1970s automatically pushed Americans into higher tax
brackets, more and more of them sought to shelter their earnings in real estate. Between 1965 and 1980, for example, "bracket

creep" increased the marginal tax rate for a median-income family from 17 to 24 percent.[24]

By far the largest tax subsidy for home owners — again, one that became much more valuable during the seventies and especially for the rich — is the exclusion of what tax specialists like to call a home owner's "imputed rent" from taxable income. Unlike other investments, such as stocks, bonds, or even savings accounts, buying a home of one's own guarantees one a very real and highly valuable form of return that is entirely free from taxation: the pleasure of living in it. A renter, by contrast, not only must pay for his shelter with aftertax dollars, but must pay the money to someone else. Moreover, any return from his savings, with few exceptions, is fully subject to taxation.[25]

Effective tax rates on businesses also skyrocketed during the seventies, largely because the government failed to adjust the rules for depreciating new plant and equipment in accord with inflation. As businesses paid higher taxes, their stocks and bonds became correspondingly less attractive to investors, while speculating in real estate became correspondingly more attractive. At the same time, Americans were encouraged to invest in real estate by the tax rule that exempts home sellers from paying taxes on any of their real estate gains, provided they use their equity to buy a new home within two years. What's more, for Americans who just happen to be over age fifty-five, any profit on their homes is entirely free from taxation, up to a high limit.

Taken together, these features of the tax code made it ever more costly *not* to invest in real estate while at the same time doing nothing to increase the supply of housing. By the late 1970s the only shelter many Americans were seeking was shelter from high taxes. Young families in need of a home found themselves bidding against an ever greater number of speculators and other buyers seeking tax advantages.

Moreover, once the inflation spiral got underway, millions of Americans who otherwise would have elected not to buy homes felt compelled instead to get into real estate in the biggest pos-

sible way just because its value was inflating. Home ownership
has always had its virtues, and yet, except during the seventies,
it has never been for everyone. Senior citizens, for example,
have often found it more convenient to move into an apartment
after their children have left than to try to keep up a large, empty
house. Many upper- and middle-class urban families once pre-
ferred apartment living to the hassle and financial risk of owning
property. Single people generally have little need of a house.
But during the 1970s, the only alternative to owning a home of
one's own was to pay rent and try saving money, while inflation
and rising taxes ate one alive. And because the federal government saw to it that the supply of cheap mortgages would continue
to expand, while local governments made sure that fewer new
houses would be constructed, home owners found that there was
virtually no limit to what they could get for their property. During the late 1970s, net increases in home owner equity were
three to four times larger than total personal savings out of income.[26]

Largely as a result of government-sponsored real estate speculation, by the end of the 1970s, the thrift ethos in the United
States was nearly extinct. The American middle class took its
counsel from scores of best-selling authors, popular lecturers,
and other savants who had discovered how to get rich quick in
real estate using other people's money. Even those home owners
who were too afraid to leverage or pyramid their inflating home
equity into untold fortune still looked more and more to their
"investment" in real estate as a substitute for savings. And who
could blame them? Their rising property values did reduce their
need to save. Moreover, so long as the federal banking regulations forced banks and thrift institutions to hold interest rates on
savings accounts well below the general rate of inflation and since
interest income remained fully taxable, only a fool would expect
to retire comfortably on a passbook account.

By 1982, a survey of recent home buyers revealed that 40
percent had bought their houses primarily for "investment pur-

poses" and 25 percent primarily for "tax reasons." Only 4 percent gave as their reason: "Want to own my own house, don't want to pay somebody rent."[27]

The Morning After

Yet the real estate boom could not continue indefinitely as long as Americans collectively continued to borrow more than they saved. By the end of the 1970s, the ledgers of the nation's savings and loan institutions—the principal providers of mortgage credit—revealed a clear if limited accounting of the great intergenerational transfer of wealth brought about by the real estate markets. After years of writing long-term mortgages at what turned out to be less than the underlying rate of inflation, S & Ls found themselves holding mortgage portfolios of ever diminishing real value. By mid-1981, the thrift industry as a whole had lost more than $111 billion on the mortgages it had previously written to home owners.[28] In effect, one generation of borrowers had managed to consume rather than return much of the capital the banks needed to go on lending to the next.

Consider the case of an older home owner who took out a 4 percent mortgage in 1950. Thirty years later, the amount he had repaid his local savings bank was but a small fraction of the amount needed to finance the resale of his house to a young couple or to anyone else. Where was the money to come from to cover this shortfall? For a while, the government could save appearances by diverting ever more credit from other sectors of the economy into home mortgages. But eventually, the chain letter scheme would be revealed, and reform, principally at the expense of all latecomers, would become inevitable.

Two key pieces of legislation sought to resolve the crisis. The first came in March of 1979, when banking regulators, for the first time since the Great Depression, permitted all of the nation's thrift institutions to write variable rate mortgages. This meant that thrift institutions would no longer be forced to assume all the risk of future inflation or high interest rates but rather could shift most of that burden to the mortgage borrower. Holders of variable rates would have no way to "inflate out from under" the burden of their debt. By 1983, more than two-thirds of all home buyers took out variable rate mortgages.

The next major reform came in March 1980 when Congress passed the Depository Institution Deregulation and Monetary Control Act. With this measure, the government committed itself to a full-scale assault on banking regulations that, for the course of two generations, had served increasingly to pamper and protect mortgage borrowers from the rigors of the open credit markets. The act called for the total elimination, by 1986, of all interest rate ceilings on savings accounts and struck down regulations that, for more than sixty years, had forced thrift institutions to invest their deposits primarily in residential real estate lending. No longer would savers be forced to subsidize borrowers; savers would earn whatever the market decided was the real price of money, through such new vehicles as money market accounts. By the end of 1980, more than a third of all savings in S & Ls had shifted from passbook accounts, which paid 5¼ percent, to money market certificates paying an average of around 15 percent. As a result of the increasing cost of raising funds, both commercial banks and S & Ls were forced to raise interest rates on all loans accordingly.

Meanwhile, home mortgage borrowers would no longer be guaranteed a place first in line at the nation's credit window. With the thrifts free to invest their assets more or less as they pleased, people wanting to borrow for a house would be forced to compete for funds with IBM, AT & T, Exxon, the U.S. Treasury, and others. Most thrifts continued to invest primarily in real estate, as it turned out, but they increasingly favored going into highly speculative partnerships with developers of commercial property rather than underwriting home owners. Just between 1979 and 1983 the share of all S & L lending flowing to nonresidential real estate, such as office buildings and shopping malls, increased from 3.6 to 12.9 percent.[29] By the mid-1980s, most major cities across the country faced a serious glut in the amount of available office space while also enduring acute housing shortages.

This time the problem was once again largely due to tax policy. In 1981, Congress radically reduced the amount of time it took to write off a new investment. Previously, the period of depreciation for business property had been twenty-five to thirty years. Now, under the new accelerated cost recovery system (ACRS), that period was reduced to fifteen years. Since, as Henry George observed, land values are one of the few things in life that are virtually guaranteed to appreciate over time, and considering that few buildings crumble after fifteen or even thirty years, granting generous tax depreciations on commercial real estate proved to be one of the least sensible tax cuts of the Reagan era. Combined with an investment tax credit of up to 10 percent, which applied to such things as hotel furniture, and assorted other tax breaks, ACRS forced the government to pay out more deductions to real estate investors than they paid in taxes. This fact once moved Senate Majority Leader Robert J. Dole to remark before an audience of real estate lobbyists, "Maybe we ought to exempt real estate from the tax code altogether. No taxes, and no deductions either. The revenue estimators tell me that would raise $15 billion by 1987." Retelling the story later, Dole reported, "Three real estate guys fainted in the back of the room."[30] Fortunately the 1986 tax reform bill should reduce the worst abuses by commercial real estate investors, although the bill does nothing to end the tax subsidies flowing to Americans who invest in residential real estate.

Affordable Housing for First-Time Buyers

Today, the problem of housing affordability is almost exclusively confined to first-time buyers. Americans who became home owners before the 1980s have actually seen their housing costs decline as inflation reduced the cost of their fixed rate mortgages. Many have leveraged their inflating equity in order to trade up to more luxurious houses, and it is for such people that the housing industry is now primarily building. While the pace of housing construction has been strong during recent years, a major study published in 1986 found that "residential construction activity is being stimulated primarily by current owners moving up to higher quality houses." The same report concluded that "unless young adults achieve substantial income growth or unless the cost of homeownership declines to more traditional levels, many more young families than in the past will find themselves unable to purchase a home."[31]

As we have seen, much of the problem can be blamed on the way the government, directly and indirectly, has inflated the price of houses. But there is another side to the government's role in the mortgaging of America: the problem of where the money hasn't been spent. Between 1965 and 1981, the value of the country's stock of residential real estate increased by an annual, inflation-adjusted average of 6.7 percent. During the same period, the real value of corporate bonds and equities actually decreased by an annual average of 0.9 percent.[32] As two noted critics of government subsidies to home owners observed in 1981, "One of the visions that haunts efforts at projecting housing realities into the future is one of a splendid tract development surrounding an abandoned factory."[33]

It isn't quite fair to say that the United States has simply built too much housing in recent decades; indeed, most people would find it obvious that we have not built quite enough to shelter the baby boomers and their children in the style of the previous generation. But it is clear that as a nation we have been diverting far too much financial capital to bidding up the price of existing houses and not enough into maintaining our roads and bridges and other infrastructure, or into improving the competitiveness of our manufacturing base or the earning potential of our labor force.

Throughout the postwar period the rate of savings and investment in the United States has actually been rising slightly as a percentage of GNP. But meanwhile, the supply of available workers has been growing tremendously, especially since the early seventies with the arrival in the work force of the baby boomers. There is no principle in economics that says a large new generation must be a downwardly mobile generation. But there is a sturdy law that says any increase in the labor supply must be matched by a commensurate increase in the rate of productive investment or else the inevitable result will be declining growth in productivity and falling real wages.

The ratio of capital to labor, not just the size of the labor force alone, is the principle determinant of where wages for new workers will settle. The liberal economist Lester Thurow notes that in 1982 the average American worked with $58,000 worth of plant and equipment. Just to maintain that year's productivity and wage rates, new workers thus needed to be equipped with at least that amount of new capital equipment. But over the years, the necessary investments haven't been made. Thurow concludes: "Implicitly the parents of the baby boom generation were promising not just to bathe, feed and educate their babies, but to save $58,000 to equip each of their babies to enter the labor force twenty years later as the average American worker. And for every wife who entered the labor force the family was implicitly promising to save another $58,000. These implicit promises weren't kept."[34]

That is a harsh way of looking at the problem, but it contains an essential truth. Not only is the American savings rate the lowest of all industrialized countries, but the nation squanders an enormous proportion of what capital it does form on unproductive investments. And there is no greater example of how the nation's scarce capital has been abused than that of the flow of funds' going to finance the sale and resale of existing real estate at ever higher prices. A particularly telling statistic reveals that the typical Japanese family saves 21 percent of its disposable income and spends 5 percent on housing. Americans squirrel away less than 6 percent and spend 15 percent on housing.[35]

How are we to reconcile our still pressing need to invest in new housing while at the same time form the capital we need to put our industries back on their feet? The best solution would be for Americans to save more; the larger the pool of savings, the less harsh the tradeoff between investment in housing and investment in factories and education.

Meanwhile, whatever we invest as a nation in real estate ought to go primarily for new construction, rather than for underwriting existing housing. Any tax credit or mortgage subsidy that does not, for whatever reason, lead to the creation of new homes does nothing to make housing more affordable. Instead, such subsidies serve to drive up the price of existing houses by raising demand without increasing supply. Furthermore, because such subsidies cost the government forgone revenue, they aggravate the problem of the budget deficits and cost all Americans — and particularly the young — more money in the long run. In 1986, the mortgage interest deduction on owner-occupied houses alone contributed more than $27 billion to the budget deficits, the deferral of capital gains on home sales contributed more than $2.5 billion, and the exclusion of capital gains on home sales for persons aged fifty-five and older contributed another $1.2 billion.[36]

Another step toward more affordable housing would be to require the federally sponsored credit agencies like Fannie Mae and Ginnie Mae to place more and perhaps all of their investment portfolios into new rather than existing residential units. Similarly, voters should demand that local governments refrain from passing exclusionary zoning laws and building regulations that merely serve to reduce the productivity of the building trades and drive up house prices. Tax subsidies for real estate serve to enrich present owners at the expense of all who follow unless they are targeted to encourage new construction.

Increasing public investment in highways and mass transit

systems is also a prerequisite to holding down housing costs. It will be a long time before home buyers again enjoy the great advantages provided by technology in the 1950s, when the combination of the eight-cylinder engine, synthetic rubber tires, and the limited-access highway rapidly expanded the supply of land that was within commuting distance of any place where one was likely to find a job. But the nation ought at least to maintain adequately the transportation system it has in place. Today, despite the trend of businesses' moving to the suburbs, falling investment in roads, bridges, and mass transit is actually lengthening commuting times and in effect shrinking the supply of land. In 1982, Houston city planners estimated that snarled traffic annually costs motorists in that city over $800 per capita in lost time and wasted fuel alone.[37] Nationally, the problem will get much worse unless we invest much more in improving our transportation network. Of the nation's 557,000 bridges, over 126,000 are structurally deficient. The Federal Highway Administration reports that 9 percent of all primary roads and 14 percent of all secondary roads are in poor condition; half of the nation's roads are classified as being in no better than fair condition.[38] Deferring maintenance on our public infrastructure not only pushes costs on to future taxpayers, it also raises the property values of home owners in the cities and inner suburbs, while making home ownership generally less affordable for the young.

Before these needed reforms can find a constituency, however, cultural values must change. American home owners have come to view rising property values as an entitlement. It is not enough simply to enjoy our houses as a place in which to live. We have come to expect more money back from our houses than we ever paid in, with the next generation paying the difference. In this, our attitudes toward real estate resemble our attitudes toward the next great and equally unsupportable entitlement addressed in this book: Social Security.

3

Social Security and the
Baby Boom Generation

DESPITE ITS RECURRING FINANCIAL CRISES and its ever
mounting cost, Social Security remains today far and away the
most popular social program ever invented in the United States.
It is not difficult to understand why. On the third day of every
month, the system mails out checks to 36 million Americans, or
more than one out of every seven citizens. Most of the recipients
are retirees, of course, but their survivors and disabled persons
of all ages also collect. Furthermore, even for the majority of
Americans who are not currently eligible to receive direct benefits, the system still provides real value. Anyone with an aged
parent living independently on Social Security, rather than in
the spare room, is likely to be an enthusiastic supporter of the
system. And most of us expect ourselves one day to turn sixty-
two — now the most common age of retirement on Social Security.

Now more than half a century old, Social Security has thus far
offered a fabulous deal to its contributors. Unlike most private
pensions, Social Security delivers even to those who choose or
are forced to change their jobs frequently. Unlike annuities,

Social Security benefits are protected against inflation. Unlike an Individual Retirement Account, Social Security provides survivor and disability insurance.

Moreover, for all recipients to date, Social Security has delivered a fantastic rate of return on the taxes they have paid into the system. In 1986, according to the Congressional Research Service, a married worker retiring at age sixty-five who paid the maximum amount of Social Security taxes required under law, would recover his or her contributions to the pension trust fund in just twenty-one months. Low wage earners recover their contributions in as little as twelve months.[1]

Yet few Americans are aware of how such rich returns have been made possible. To know the answer is to realize that today's younger Americans are in acute danger of being stranded by Social Security just as it becomes their own turn to retire. For the underlying trends that have allowed the system to work so well for their parents and grandparents are, quite simply, no longer in effect.

Social Security is, as Sen. Bill Bradley of New Jersey has said, "the best expression of community that we have in this country today."[2] The system embodies the noblest of all American values: that of mutual aid to protect against life's hazards and of respect for the needy. But the fact remains that, under current law and by the design of Congress, younger Americans are not even promised a fair return on their investment in Social Security. What is more, even the government's promise of severely reduced benefits derives from specific, highly unlikely assumptions about the future on which no individual American would wager a day's wages, let alone a lifetime's payment of Social Security taxes.

A Ponzi Scheme That Worked — for Today's Senior Citizens

One day in 1919, Charles Ponzi, Italian immigrant and failed Boston fruit peddler, hit upon an idea that would soon make him the most famous financier in the United States. He announced to the world that through an obscure investment strategy involving International Postal Union reply coupons, he could take anyone's money and return a 50 percent profit in just ninety days. Soon, widows, orphans, and even staid financiers were rushing to press their cash into his eager palm. Ponzi hired sixteen clerks to rake in the money, and still the lines outside his office grew longer. After his desk drawers overflowed, he was forced to keep his multiplying bushels of cash in wastebaskets. In a few months, he collected $15 million, all the time paying off investors promptly. Indeed, he delivered the promised return in just forty-five days rather than ninety, and still more cheering investors rushed to his door.

But then, inevitably, the bubble burst. At one time, Ponzi may have honestly believed that he could make a fortune for everyone with postal coupons. But when that failed, he decided instead simply to pay off his early clients with the money he collected from latecomers. In the end, he was scouring the world for ever more contributors, just like anyone caught on the end of a chain letter. When finally arrested, he had assets of about $4 million and liabilities of about $7 million, although no one knew for sure since he kept no books. Loathed by tens of thousands who had lost their life savings to his scheme, he died in Brazil in 1949 with an estate of $75.[3]

Critics of Social Security, even before its adoption in 1935, have frequently likened its method of financing to Ponzi's scheme. In some essential characteristics, the comparison is fair. Like a Ponzi scheme, Social Security does not in any true sense invest the money it receives from current contributors. Rather, it uses their tax dollars to pay off previous contributors whose benefits have come due. In the parlance of the system's actuaries, this is known as "pay-as-you-go" financing, although the phrase is somewhat misleading. Since the late 1950s, the system as a whole has collected just about the same amount every year as it has paid out. But in the meantime, of course, by paying their Social Security taxes, workers have been building up legal as well as moral claims to future benefits. No large reserves exist to cover the cost of these claims. Today, the assets of the Social Security system are generally sufficient to cover only a few months' worth of benefits. At the same time, the system's total liabilities — that is, the cost of paying benefits already promised to workers — exceed $11 trillion.[4] In this sense, Social Security has thus far been anything but a pay-as-you-go system.

Social Security is also like a Ponzi scheme in that, over time, it can offer fair rates of return to its contributors only if there are always more of them. From month to month, Ponzi needed to compound the number of his paying customers for the simple reason that he had no other source of cash for paying off his previous investors. So too, essentially, with Social Security, which has promised all previous and current recipients far more in benefits than they ever paid in taxes and which has already used their taxes to meet previous obligations. Unless the population of younger workers paying into the system remains constantly on the rise, the only alternative to reneging on future benefits is to collect more revenue from younger Americans and those not yet born.

This does not necessarily mean, of course, that in the absence of rapid population growth, tax rates must always go higher in order for Social Security to continue offering generous benefits. When wages rise, from one generation to the next, the system's revenues increase automatically without tax rates necessarily needing to go up. If both wages and the number of workers contributing to the system are growing rapidly over a prolonged period, as they were during most of the postwar era, then Social Security benefits can be made very generous indeed without threatening the system or unduly encumbering the young.

As Paul A. Samuelson, arguably the most influential economist of the postwar era, explained in a column for *Newsweek* in 1967:

The beauty about social insurance is that it is *actuarially* unsound. Everyone who reaches retirement age is given benefit privileges that far exceed anything he has paid. . . . How is this possible? It stems from the fact that the national product is growing at compound interest and can be expected to do so for as far ahead as the eye cannot see. Always there are more youths than old folk in a growing population. More important, with real incomes growing at some 3 percent per year, the taxable base upon which benefits rest in any period are [*sic*] much greater than the taxes paid historically by the generation now retired. . . . Social Security is squarely based on what has been called the eighth wonder of the world — compound interest. A growing nation is the greatest Ponzi game ever contrived. And that is a fact, not a paradox.[5]

We should be kind to Samuelson. When he wrote these words, the United States was just coming to the end of the greatest, most prolonged period of mass affluence ever recorded in the history of mankind. After more than twenty years of rapid economic growth and rising wages, it was easy to believe that the prosperity would go on forever — that each generation of Americans would inevitably be much more affluent than the one that came before. And while the birthrate had been falling for a decade, it was still not clear that the baby boom was finished; the call for zero population growth (ZPG) was just then gaining urgency as Americans witnessed the crowding and social dislocations caused by a tidal wave of youth.

But twenty years later, our preoccupations need be of a wholly different sort. We have learned that economic growth is not automatic, that our standard of living doesn't necessarily rise from generation to generation just because this is the American dream. And we can see, both at home and throughout the industrialized world, that birthrates are falling below the level needed to maintain a steady population. The ideal of ZPG has yielded to the reality of APG — Aging Population Growth. We can no longer count on there always being more children than elderly.

Ponzi Meets Tonti

"Frankly face the facts, and see the results," Ralph Waldo Emerson once wrote. "Tobacco, coffee, alcohol, hashish, prussic acid, strychnine, are weak dilutions: the surest poison is time." There is another demographic factor, less often discussed, that is also working against the long-term solvency of Social Security. After age thirty, the life tables tell us, the chances that one will die within the next twelve months double every eight years. Yet while those odds eventually catch up with everyone, they have nonetheless already improved so much in this century as to revolutionize the financing of all old age benefits. Among persons born in 1900, for example, only 41 percent managed to survive until age sixty-five. But more than three-quarters of all Americans born in the last decade can expect to reach sixty-five, even assuming no further improvement in mortality rates.

The implications for Social Security are clear. Within any generation, the living can no longer draw on large subsidies from the dead. In financing Social Security we will no longer be able to rely on so many taxpayers' dying before or shortly after they reach retirement age. The same principle holds true for all private pensions and health care plans. As life expectancy improves, particularly for those already over sixty-five, the economy's "ghost dividend," as it were, dwindles every year.

In 1653, the Neapolitan banker Lorenzo Tonti invented a financing scheme that well illustrates this feature of the economics of mortality. Tontine schemes were once all the rage in Europe and were even used to help finance the French national debt, as well as houses, hotels, and bathhouses. The idea was for a pool of investors each to receive an annuity for life, which increased in amount as their numbers were diminished by death. The last survivor enjoyed the whole income from the initial investment and usually became very rich indeed.

These days, aside from the obvious incentive for murder, one reason such schemes are no longer popular is that mortality rates have improved so dramatically; one simply has to wait too long for one's coinvestors to die off. But in a larger sense, the economy as a whole still profits from the same dark reality embodied by a Tonti scheme. The rate of capital formation, for example, is improved by those who save for retirement but never quite make it. And so is the ratio of capital to labor, which ultimately determines productivity and wages. But as more and more people survive well past retirement age, these dividends are reduced, and to an ever greater extent we all must actually pay our own way through life.

Where Do Your Social Security Taxes Go?

Before proceeding to a fuller discussion of what is wrong with Social Security and how the problem might be remedied, we need to become acquainted with a few more features of the system's current method of financing. Truth always lurks in the details. After more than fifty years of demagoguery and willful misrepresentation by some advocates of the program, few Americans have any idea, according to the polls, of how the system works or of who actually pays for the 432 million checks it writes out every year.

Social Security is funded primarily through a tax on paid labor, the payroll tax. An employee's portion of the tax is deducted automatically from his or her payroll check under the column mysteriously marked "FICA," which stands for Federal Insurance Contributions Act.

The payroll tax for employees as of this writing is 7.15 percent of their gross wages, with wages above $42,000 per year not subject to taxation. Employers are also required to forward another 7.15 percent of each worker's gross wages to Social Security, up to the same limit, for a combined maximum Social Security tax of $6,006. Under current law, by 1990, the combined employer-employee payroll tax will rise to 15.3 percent, with wages above $51,600 not subject to taxation. This will bring a maximum tax bill of $7,894 per year — or $236,820 over a thirty-year career, assuming that tax rates and ceilings don't go higher. Starting in 1990, self-employed workers will also pay 15.3 percent of their gross income, up to the same limit.

Each month, the revenues collected through the payroll tax are forwarded from the Internal Revenue Service to the Social Security Administration (SSA), where they are appropriated, under a formula set by Congress, to each of the system's three major trust funds. About 70 percent of the revenue is entered into what the government calls the Old Age and Survivors Insurance (OASI) trust fund and goes primarily to cover the month-to-month cost of providing pensions for today's senior citizens. Another fifth of the revenue goes to the Hospital Insurance (HI) trust fund and is used to finance current hospital care benefits for the elderly under the Medicare program. The remaining 10 percent of your payroll tax dollars goes to the Disability Insurance (DI) trust fund. DI pays benefits to handicapped workers of all ages provided they have previously paid taxes into the system for at least five years, or, if under age thirty-one, for at least a year and a half.

The flow of funds through these three accounts obviously depends in the long run on the broad course of American society. The key determinants of the system's solvency include future rates of mortality (how long people live on average) and morbidity (how prone to sickness and disability they become); immigration and emigration; the fertility rate; the rates of inflation in prices and wages; the unemployment rate; trends in work force participation, and retirement decisions. All in one way or another affect the ratio of contributors to recipients and of taxes to benefits.

Recognizing how indeterminate any projection of the system's long-term financing must be, the SSA always publishes in its annual report four separate projections for the future of the system, ranging from what it labels "optimistic" to "pessimistic." While these projections, along with their underlying assumptions, are available to anyone who asks for them, they seldom receive much scrutiny from the press or from members of Congress.

It is the so-called II-B, or intermediate-range forecast, that is supposed to be the government's "best-guess" estimate of what the future holds in store for the system. According to the 1986 forecast, we can expect the following:

- The HI, or main Medicare trust fund, will slip into deficit in 1991, and its reserves will be completely depleted by 1996
- The disability fund, according to the system's actuaries, will be "exhausted" by 2026
- The pension trust fund, what the majority of Americans count on most from Social Security, is projected to be running in the red by 2020, just as the bulk of the baby boomers reach retirement age, and to be completely bankrupt by 2054, which is well within the lifetime of today's children[6]

How likely is it that this forecast will come true? The first thing to note is that the actuaries implicitly assume that any reserves the pension fund builds up in the future won't be used to replenish the near-term deficits they project for the Medicare trust fund. During the period when the Medicare trust fund is expected to collapse, the pension fund is projected to be building up a substantial surplus, for reasons we will come to shortly. If past experience is any guide, it is quite likely that Congress will adopt the quick fix on interfund borrowing. The pension fund's reserves will go to bail out the Medicare trust fund, with no means of repayment in sight. If this occurs, the pension fund and probably the disability fund will go broke much earlier.

But this forecast is also based on many other, highly questionable assumptions about the future. The model assumes, for example, that wages will rise above inflation by at least 25 percent before the end of the century, that real wages will double by

2032, and triple by 2059. This might happen, yet real wages have been flat over the last fifteen years.[7]

The forecast also assumes that the United States will experience no more recessions. Every year, it posits, the economy will grow by 2–3 percent. This is not an unreasonable rate of growth to expect over time, yet we know from the past that between good years come bad. A recession at any time in the future would probably throw the Medicare trust fund into instant insolvency.

Among the other assumptions underlying this forecast: the actuaries presume that after 1993 unemployment will never again exceed 6 percent; that the fertility rate will rise by nearly 10 percent by the year 2010; and that life expectancy at age sixty-five will increase by no more than three years and four months for men and by four years and four months for women by the year 2060.

Even given these relatively optimistic assumptions, the actuaries conclude that in order for the system as a whole to survive, payroll taxes will have to rise dramatically. To cover the cost of providing even reduced benefits for the baby boomers, the system would need to collect 23 percent of the next generation's wages, according to the actuaries' best estimate.

A more likely scenario for Social Security, or at least one for which we ought to be planning, is provided by the actuaries' so-called pessimistic model. But even this forecast calls for the economy to perform better in the future than it actually has during the recent past. Under the SSA's official worst-case scenario, after 1990, inflation never again rises above 5 percent and real wages increase by an average of 1.14 percent each year. Yet from 1973 to 1983 inflation averaged 8.2 percent and real wages actually declined by an average of 0.9 percent a year. The model also assumes one mild recession in 1990, followed by uninterrupted economic growth. The unemployment rate never again exceeds 7.7 percent.

If the economy behaves according to this scenario, the SSA predicts that the Medicare trust fund will be exhausted by 1993, the disability trust fund by 2006, and the pension fund by 2025. The only alternative, according to this model, would be for payroll taxes to rise to 42 percent of taxable income. Again, this model assumes that the pension fund's assets are not used to make up the shortfall in the other two funds. Moreover, and this is the most egregious and little-known feature of all official forecasts for Social Security, the actuaries assume that today's younger Americans will receive significantly lower returns from the system than do today's senior citizens.[8]

What's Promised to the Baby Boomers and Their Children

It is current law, not stargazing, that leads the actuaries at the SSA to make this assumption. In 1983, Congress passed new amendments to the Social Security Act designed to save the pension and disability trust funds from a then imminent financial crisis, which had been brought on by the deepest, most prolonged recession since the beginning of Social Security. Following months of acrimonious debate and secret negotiations among White House staffers and congressional leaders, all conducted under the cover of a special commission that included advocates for the elderly as well as business and union interests, the amendments were sold to the public as an "artful compromise" between raising taxes and lowering benefits. From the perspective of the players involved, the package was indeed an ingenious compromise, and there was much self-congratulation and promotion all around. Indeed, the mainstream press even went so far as to herald passage of the 1983 amendments as proof that the American process of government could still be made to overcome deadlock and special interest politics.[9] Yet had younger Americans, who had no formal representation in the proceedings, been aware of the details of the resulting agreement, they would not have considered it a compromise at all, since its principal effect was to raise *their* taxes and cut *their* benefits.

The amendments contained these essential features:

1. A series of stiff payroll tax increases between 1984 and 1990. Increased payroll taxes amounted to roughly 40 percent of all the projected savings under the 1983 amendments.
2. A gradual increase in the retirement age for younger Americans. The age of eligibility for full benefits is now scheduled to rise from sixty-five to sixty-six between 2000 and 2009 and to sixty-seven between the years 2017 and 2027.
3. A requirement that all new federal employees join the Social Security system. The measure provides a temporary influx of payroll taxes but does nothing to improve the system's long-term prospects: eventually civil servants hired after 1983 will be owed their Social Security pensions, and future taxpayers will be forced to pay the cost.
4. A six-month delay in cost-of-living adjustments (COLAs), which may or may not reduce benefits in the future.
5. A provision that any COLAs be based on increases in wages or prices, whichever is lower, in the event that the pension and disability trust funds near insolvency. Under current projections, this benefit cut will go into effect only when the baby boomers reach retirement age.
6. A requirement that retirees with independent annual income above $25,000 and retired couples with independent income above $32,000 pay federal income taxes on half their Social Security pensions. All revenues thereby raised go to the OASI and DI trust funds.

It is this last feature that most reduces the benefits promised to baby boomers and their children. Today, the measure affects only the wealthiest 10 percent of all Social Security recipients. But by the design of Congress, all but the poorest baby boomers will have to pay income taxes on their pensions. This is because, under the terms of the amendments, the threshold at which pensions become taxable does not rise with inflation. Given just the modest inflation rates assumed by the SSA's intermediate-range projection, an income of $25,000 will buy less in 2030 than $4,000 buys today. So by the time the baby boomers qualify for Social Security pensions, the program will be effectively means-tested, if it survives at all. Under current law, only the poorest baby boomers are even promised a fair return on their contributions to the system.

Of course in the coming decades, as an ever higher percentage of the elderly find themselves paying income taxes on their benefits, they may succeed in convincing Congress to raise the current threshold. But if they do, Social Security will go bankrupt just that much sooner. According to congressional documents, between 25 and 30 percent of all the projected savings under the 1983 amendments are supposed to derive from just this one feature of the bill. Under both the SSA's intermediate- and pessimistic-range projections, by 2035, nearly 13 percent of all taxes flowing into the pension fund are expected to come from the baby boomers themselves, as they continue contributing to the system through old age by paying taxes on their benefits.[10]

As a result of these and other features of the 1983 "compromise" on Social Security, many if not most younger Americans will probably pay more into the system than they will collect. In a study published in 1983 in the *Cato Journal*, Anthony Pellechio and Gordon Goodfellow of the Department of Health and Human Services calculated the financial consequences of the 1983 amendments, given the SSA's II-B assumptions and constant 1983 dollars. Here are some of their specific findings for Americans now under age twenty-five: All members of this generation who remain single over their lifetimes, except for women who earn no more than $10,000 a year, will be net losers. A single man who earns $35,700 or more will lose some $80,000 on his "investment" in Social Security. All two-paycheck families with incomes higher than $20,000 (the typical baby boom family) will likewise pay more in taxes than they will receive in benefits.[11]

These findings have been widely confirmed by other experts.

Prof. Michael Boskin of Stanford concludes from his studies that under current law, the younger one's age, the lower the rate of return one should expect from Social Security. Boskin calculates, for example, that among median-income married couples in which only the husband works, those who retired in 1970 will receive an average 8.5 percent rate of return on their contributions, whereas those who retire in 2025 can expect only 2.2 percent. Boskin also notes that "Social Security will not be doing very much for future cohorts of poor people." For families earning an annual inflation-adjusted average of $10,000, he concludes, "the present value of benefits and taxes roughly cancel."[12]

Even the Social Security Administration concedes the reality of the trend. In a 1984 memo developed at the request of Sen. Dave Durenberger of Minnesota, the SSA's Office of the Actuary projected the ratio of expected pension and disability benefits to expected contributions for different age groups as a whole. As in the memo, the numbers in table 1 are expressed in present values using a 2 percent discount rate (that is, they are adjusted to reflect the return taxpayers might have realized, after inflation, had they been free to invest their tax dollars in the private economy).[13] The contributions of both workers and their employers are combined in column B in accord with the view, confirmed by almost all economists, that both taxes are borne ultimately by workers alone.

Table 1 clearly shows that for younger Americans as a whole, Social Security will be collecting more in taxes for its pension and disability programs than it will ever pay out in benefits. In terms of purchasing power, the population aged twenty-one in 1984 is expected, under current law, to get back only ninety-eight cents on the dollar for its contributions to the OASI and DI trust funds. And this is assuming of course that the system as a whole remains solvent over their lifetimes, and that taxes will not be raised still more to cover the enormous projected deficits in the Medicare trust fund, as well as in the other two funds.

Reducing Social Security benefits—at least for the well-to-do—may be a practical necessity. But by postponing the sacrifice, the full burden of reform is put on the unsuspecting young.

Social Security and the National Debt

Unfortunately for today's younger Americans, Social Security's finances may get better before they get worse, thus stalling the movement for equitable reform and compounding problems in the future. For the remainder of this century, and up until the baby boom generation reaches retirement age, the Social Security pension and disability trust funds are projected, under the SSA's highly optimistic midrange assumptions, to build up substantial reserves. There are three reasons why these projected surpluses might actually occur. The first is that the rate of growth in the population over sixty-five will begin to taper off in the early 1990s owing to the paucity of children born during the 1920s and 1930s. The second reason is that the baby boomers will by then be at the life stage when earnings are usually highest. Finally, because of the provisions of the 1983 amendments, all workers will be paying into the system at unprecedented high

Table 1. Present Value of OASI & DI Benefits and
Contributions for Cohorts of All Workers at
Selected Ages (in Billions of Dollars)

A. Age of Cohort in 1984	B. Present Value of Employee-Employer Contributions	C. Present Value of OASI & DI Benefits	D. Ratio of OASI & DI Benefits to Contributions
65	62.0	156.8	2.52
60	80.8	152.6	1.88
45	116.4	127.6	1.09
21	178.0	175.6	.98

Source: Office of the Actuary, Social Security Administration

rates. If all goes according to plan, by 2020 the OASI and DI trust funds will have collected $9.3 trillion more in revenue than they paid out in benefits over the preceding thirty-five years, leaving it with assets expected to equal an incredible 26.7 percent of the gross national product.[14]

Despite the awesome size of this figure, it still will not be sufficient, again under the SSA's midrange assumption, to cover anywhere near the projected cost of providing even reduced benefits to the baby boom generation. By 2020 the trust funds are projected to start running substantial and compounding deficits. The accumulation of these projected deficits will completely exhaust the reserves of the OASI and DI trust funds somewhere between 2045 and 2055. By 2060, according to the SSA's best guess, the OASI and DI trust funds will have combined net liabilities of more than $35.6 trillion, or more than 10.4 percent of the expected GNP of the time.

Still, the question remains, if indeed we do manage to build up large reserves in the OASI and DI trusts between now and 2020, will this in any way benefit the baby boomers and their children? Since passage of the 1983 amendments, workers have been paying more taxes into the system than have actually been needed to meet its monthly expenses. Younger Americans have been asked to believe that by paying these extra taxes over the remainder of their careers, they will in effect "prefund" some of the immense cost of the baby boom generation's retirement, thereby decreasing the burden on the baby boomers' children. It is a noble thought. Unfortunately, it is wrong-headed, at best.

The most likely result of even beginning to build up a substantial surplus in any of the Social Security trust funds will be increased benefits for today's senior citizens at the expense of all who follow. Never in the history of Social Security has Congress been able to resist the temptation of giving away any build-up in the system's reserves. Furthermore, because of the way the Social Security trust funds are invested, it is highly unlikely that a surplus of any magnitude would actually benefit future taxpayers. Indeed, it is all but inevitable that building up a surplus in Social Security will not only cause a reduced lifetime standard of living for the baby boomers, but will also increase the burden they will present to their children in old age.

The most important fact to bear in mind in thinking about this issue is that, under current law, any surplus appearing in any of the Social Security trust funds must be spent in the year in which it is accrued. Social Security is not allowed to invest its reserves in real, wealth-producing assets. Rather, it is required to lend any surplus it accrues to the U.S. Treasury. The Treasury in turn uses these funds either to help underwrite the government's current deficits or to refinance the national debt. Having thus spent the money it borrowed from Social Security, the Treasury — and by extension future taxpayers — must find a way to repay the system as its notes come due. If you suspect that this is not a prudent way to invest what is supposed to be the baby boom generation's nest egg for retirement under Social Security, your doubts are well founded.

If in every year from now until the time the baby boomers reach retirement age the federal government as a whole were to run a balanced budget, then building up large surpluses in the Social Security trust funds just might, with one additional provision, be of some benefit to future taxpayers. Under this highly unlikely scenario, the surpluses would be used not to underwrite current deficits or to refinance previous ones but actually to pay down the national debt. This in turn would reduce the cost to future Americans of servicing the national debt and, in the meantime, would make more capital available for private investment. If such private investments were to pay off, future Americans would be better able to support the baby boomers in old age.

But even in this case, the problem remains that any funds Social Security lends out to the Treasury are supposed to be returned, with interest. And it is future taxpayers who will be liable for these IOUs, come what may. Moreover, Social Security is counting on its loans to the Treasury being repaid; if it does not receive back its principal plus interest, the trust funds will go broke just that much earlier.

The following is what the SSA's current plan envisages. Under the SSA's midrange forecast, the Treasury, and by extension future taxpayers, will remit the OASI and DI trust funds $25 trillion in principal and interest, payable over twenty years beginning in 2019. Over most of the period, the annual cost of retiring this debt will range around 1 percent of GNP, as is shown in table 2. This is no small amount of change. By way of contrast,

Table 2. Official Estimates of Payments of Principal and Interest That Will Be Owed by the U.S. Treasury to the Social Security Pension and Disability OASI and DI Trust Fund under Midrange II-B Economic and Demographic Assumptions

	In Billions of Dollars		
Year	Net Transfer from Treasury to OASI & DI Trust Fund	Anticipated Gross National Product	Transfer as a Percent of GNP
2020	81	34,904	.23
2025	351	46,053	.76
2030	640	61,021	1.05
2035	890	81,198	1.10
2040	1,087	108,017	1.01
2049	1,678	191,283	.88
2055	Fund exhausted	N/A	N/A

Source: Martha A. McSteen, Acting Commissioner of the Social Security Administration, Memo to Sen. Dave Durenberger dated September 4, 1985. GNP numbers for selected years are from Harry C. Ballantyne, "Long-Range Estimates of the Social Security Trust Fund Operations In Dollars," Actuarial Note No. 125, April 1985.

the *total annual cost* of Social Security, including Medicare, today hovers around 6 percent of GNP.

Because all funds lent by the Social Security trust funds to the Treasury must be repaid with interest by future taxpayers, it is hard to see how such transactions can benefit future generations. Even if the funds are used to retire the privately held national debt, a new public debt is thereby automatically created in the form of Treasury notes held by Social Security, for which future taxpayers will become liable. The only certain effect of building up surpluses in Social Security is to reduce the amount the federal government would have to borrow from private investors to finance a budget deficit of any given size. As the government becomes able to raise more and more credit by simply borrowing from the Social Security trust funds and from those who are forced to pay into them, its response might well be just to run larger deficits. Private investors at least have the option of refusing to lend to the government if it seems too profligate in its finances, whereas those who pay Social Security taxes have no choice but to play the role of the government's "friendly banker."

As even the original architects of Social Security realized, the bottom line in these matters is that there is only one way that any generation of recipients can effectively "save up" the cost of its own retirement under the system. It must succeed, by one strategy or another, in raising the productivity of the next generation. The economist Eveline M. Burns, for example, who was one of the primary theoreticians of the social insurance movement, addressed the question of surpluses in her 1949 book, *The American Social Security System*. Her conclusions were unambiguous.

> The economic burden on any society of maintaining a large number of non-producers at some future date can be reduced in only one way: the present generation must take action to increase the productivity of future generations over what it would otherwise be. . . . The income the retired aged will enjoy in 1989 or 2000 will reduce correspondingly the current income available to the

rest of the population living at that time. If the present generation wishes those living in 2000 to be no worse off than themselves, in spite of having to support a much larger proportion of non-producers, they must so add to or improve the material and human capital of that society that productivity will increase by the extent of the additional burden.[15]

In other words, building up a surplus in Social Security will do no good for future Americans unless the funds are invested in ways that lead ultimately to those future Americans' becoming more efficient workers. How this end can be accomplished by investing the funds in either current or previous government deficits is far from clear.

Some of what the government might borrow for, of course, could return rich dividends in the future. Deficit spending for education, for example, might be viewed as a gift to the future, provided it actually succeeded in improving the technical skills of the next generation. Borrowing for public works can make all Americans richer in the future, as long as the money does not go for boondoggles and pork barrel projects. But most of what the federal government spends goes solely to meet the needs of the here and now. Building up large Social Security surpluses might make sense in a socialist country, where the government would use the capital to invest directly in real wealth-producing assets, such as factories, mines, and shipyards. Still, judging by the experience of such countries in recent decades, I think most Americans will agree that we are better off not letting the government invest our Social Security tax money in whatever industries might happen to win Congress's favor.

Most likely, no substantial surpluses will ever accrue in the pension trust fund. As we have already seen, the projections calling for such a surplus are based on highly optimistic assumptions. But already some politicians, including Ronald Reagan, have begun to use the projected surpluses as an argument for keeping Social Security exempt from budget cuts. Far from contributing to the deficits, these politicians have claimed, Social

Security with its surpluses is actually helping to reduce government borrowing. In point of fact, Social Security spending contributes to the deficits just like all other forms of government spending. The taxes Social Security collects in excess of what it spends temporarily diminish the government's need to borrow from the private sector. But in the long run these taxes are supposed to be returned to those who paid them — in the form of future benefits — and are thus debts that future taxpayers will be asked to pay.

The Moral Hazard of Social Security

In her 1941 classic, *Nation and Family*, the Swedish Social Democrat, Alva Myrdal, sought to impress the English-speaking world, and especially the United States, with rousing arguments for joining Sweden along the road to "cradle-to-grave" socialism. Yet Myrdal, unlike most advocates of social insurance then and now, was fully aware of the problem of generational equity inherent in her program. The greatest danger attending the creation of any welfare state, she warned — specifically addressing herself at times to the United States' nascent Social Security system — was that the needs of those in the cradle might easily wind up being sacrificed to the interests of those approaching the grave.

"In all countries . . . the cost of supporting both the unproductive young and the old is increasing," Myrdal observed. "Whether the increase in costs for the young, owing to improved health and school standards, is higher than the increase in cost for the old, with larger pensions and finer funerals, is difficult to say." But of one trend Myrdal was certain: "While investment in human capital is unprofitable with regard to the old, the actual outlook is that the aged nevertheless are going to inherit the earth."[16]

Myrdal's prediction, which also figured prominently in the writings of her husband, Gunnar, derived from what she perceived to be a fundamental moral hazard created by all social insurance programs for the elderly. On the one hand, the long-term solvency of such programs depends on an ever increasing supply of younger workers with ever higher wages. Yet in any society, as provision for the elderly becomes more a collective responsibility and less a burden to be borne by individual families, working-aged citizens are correspondingly relieved of any direct economic incentive to reproduce themselves. Further, with their security in old age no longer contingent upon the generosity and gratitude of their own offspring, the members of the working-aged population become just that much less inclined to invest their energies in being good parents, or in supporting educational or social programs for the young in general.

This skew of incentives, Myrdal warned, would tempt individuals, and by extension generations as a whole, to attempt taking a free ride through life and would lead to the ultimate demise of any welfare state that did not furnish countervailing measures. Speaking of her own generation in Sweden, which came of age in the 1920s and 1930s, Myrdal predicted that it "will go down in history as the most ravenous of all. It has increased its spending income per consumption unit by not bearing enough children to replace itself, and at the same time, by self-insurance and by social legislation, it has usurped legal rights to a labor-free income in old age."

Such "consumption at both ends," Myrdal argued, was fundamentally at odds with the underlying requirements of the welfare state. Dependent for their long-term financing on rapid population and economic growth, social insurance programs for the elderly actually served to erode both trends. Being a committed socialist, Myrdal found a solution to this dilemma in advocating that the state offset its subsidies to the elderly with equally generous "family allowances" and other subsidies designed to spread the cost of raising children from individual parents to the society as a whole.

In Sweden, of course, her warning was at least partially heeded.

But despite massive expenditures for family welfare programs, including the creation of universal children's allowances, the country never succeeded in spending its way out of the vicious circle Myrdal prophesied. Over the last twenty years, the real value of family benefits has steadily declined, due to both inflation and competing claims on the budget, especially the demands of the ever growing number of elderly. Today in Sweden, more than 20 percent of the population is over sixty-five; interest on the national debt exceeds the cost of any single social program; and the government has annual deficits amounting to more than a third of its entire budget.

This evidence does not provide conclusive proof that any social security system must ultimately fail. But it should serve to warn us against viewing the financial difficulties of our own system as purely technical issues that are distinct from broader questions of statecraft. If Social Security is to serve a moral purpose in American society, then it must not itself create incentives that undermine its ability to endure through the generations. Nor should its long-term financing be made to rely on broad economic and social trends that we have no good reason to believe will come to pass. (Note: the optimistic forecast for Social Security requires a *reversal* of current trends.) If the Social Security system continues to require rapid population growth to remain solvent in the next century, then we must embrace the need to raise the birthrate by whatever means, encourage immigration, and live with all the consequences. If the system continues to require that our children become much more productive than we are, then we must sacrifice for that end, investing heavily in the rigorous education of the young and in new industry and infrastructure. Finally, if we are unable or unwilling to gain the conditions upon which we have predicated Social Security's long-term financing, then we must either accommodate the system to different conditions or willingly let it go.

There is a great irony in the terms *pessimism* and *optimism* as they are used by the actuaries at the Social Security Administration. To paraphrase the words of former commerce secretary Pete Peterson, the great Jeremiah of the Social Security debate, more babies, immigrants, and shorter lives are not everyone's idea of an optimistic forecast for the next century, even if such prospects brighten the annual report of the Social Security system's trustees. Liberals especially should be appalled by the assumptions upon which the system's financing is now premised. The only future that would give the present system even a remote chance of succeeding is a future most of us would find abominable: a world of fantastic population growth leading to severe strains on the environment, a future with no real progress in life expectancy despite all our investments in medicine, clean air and water, exercise, and proper diet—a world, in short, that is crowded, dirty, and dangerous.

But the essential criticism of Social Security is purely moral. How is it right for us to bet the future of the system against such long odds when the cost of our being wrong would be disastrous, both to the baby boomers in old age and to their children? Everyone is entitled to hope that the future will in all ways turn out to be convenient to the financing of Social Security. But we have no right to expose our future selves and future generations to the enormous risk that such hopes will prove to be unfounded.

Any reform of Social Security must be equitable to members of all generations—to today's elderly no less than to the elderly of the next century. But before we can even begin to address that challenge, we must confront another with which it is inseparably entangled. Not even the most stalwart defenders of Social Security see any prospect for the Medicare trust fund's escaping insolvency, in the absence of stiff tax increases between now and the end of the century. In the next chapter, we will address the acute problem of health care in an aging society.

4

Death and Taxes: Confronting America's Health Care Crisis

A CYNIC, Oscar Wilde once quipped, is "a man who knows the price of everything, and the value of nothing." Health care is a domain in which it is often considered unseemly to talk about money. All of us want to believe that there must be some goods in life for which we simply cannot or at least should not fix a price, and the preservation of human health is one such. Yet only a true cynic would discount the costs that our current health care system is pushing into the future. Indeed, the most wretched cynics of our own time are those who simply assume that one way or another the next generation can be made to pay for the staggering health care needs of the aging baby boomers.

While the problems of Social Security discussed in the last chapter may have seemed depressing and difficult, they pale in comparison to the health care crisis facing younger Americans, of which the near-term collapse of Medicare is only a small part. The issues addressed in this chapter are so tough and appalling that one's mind yearns for distraction. Solutions can be found. But only by admitting the dimension of the problem do we stand any chance of finding them.

For lack of money or the insurance it will buy, thousands of Americans die every year of theoretically curable diseases and injuries. An estimated 36 million Americans, primarily the young and the working poor, lack any medical insurance. Lack of affordable health insurance is a major incentive for going on welfare. But meanwhile, resources committed to the health care sector of the economy become unavailable for other valuable purposes, such as building new houses, schools, or factories. Between 1960 and 1986, the percentage of the nation's gross national product consumed by health care has more than doubled, from 5 to nearly 11 percent. Only an affluent society can afford universal access to the wonders of modern medicine. At some level, however, expenditures for health care, particularly if they go largely for patients who have little prospect of returning to productive labor, come at the expense of future economic growth and by extension of adequate future health care for all generations. Roughly a third of all Medicare dollars and 10 percent of the total amount spent for health care go to patients who die within a year.[1]

Inevitably, there are limits to what any society can prudently and justly pay for health care, and rules must be set for who lives, who dies, and who pays. As Joseph Califano, President Jimmy Carter's former secretary of Health, Education, and Welfare, has written, "The omnivorous appetite of health care for our financial resources adds an urgency that demands action, under threat that our society will be torn apart by a debate over death control that will make the debate over abortion seem like genteel tea-party chatter. Unlike fetuses, the old can speak for themselves."[2]

These are not pleasant truths. But in this era of high deficits, rapidly advancing medical technology, and population aging, they are truths that cannot be covered over with sentiment and happy talk about the future.

The Cost of Living

The first and primary cause of the crisis is once again the aging of the population. Older people, on average, inevitably require much more health care than do the young. About one-third of all health care spending in the United States is consumed by the 12 percent of the population over age sixty-five.[3] And so, as the elderly's share of the population increases, so too will the demand for health care.

Yet it is not simply the increasing number of elderly Americans but a subtrend known as "the aging of the aged" that presents the most severe challenge to our traditional ways of financing and allocating health care. The good news is that more and more Americans can look forward to reaching very advanced ages. The bad news is that many will end their lives after long periods of debilitating illness, the cost of which they will not be able to afford on their own.

The most rapidly growing age group is the population aged eighty and over. Today there are only about 5.9 million Americans alive who have reached age eighty. But by 2030, the number will jump to 17 million — and may go as high as 26 million by 2050 — according to the U.S. Census Bureau's "best-guess" or "middle-series" projections.[4] At these advanced ages, people tend to require vastly more expensive medical care than even those in their sixties and seventies. For example, whereas only about 2 percent of all senior citizens enter nursing homes during their midsixties and early seventies, 23 percent of all those above eighty-five eventually require such care. Recent evidence indicates that the incidence of one of the major chronic diseases of aging, Alzheimer's disease, may be as high as 15 percent among the population over eighty, with the percentage afflicted rising by 3 percent per year in each age group over forty.[5] Because of the rapid growth in the number of the very old and their high morbidity (or proclivity to disabling illness) independent researchers estimate that a new 220-bed nursing home will have to be opened every day between now and the year 2000 just to keep even with demand—and this is long before the arrival of the baby boomers.[6]

Long-term nursing home care is extremely labor intensive and will therefore always be extremely expensive. Today, at a minimum, it costs $12,000–$15,000 a year to stay in a nursing home—a cost that Medicare doesn't cover. The House Select Committee on Aging estimated in 1985 that nearly two-thirds of all senior citizens living alone would impoverish themselves after only thirteen weeks in a nursing home.[7]

As the demand for nursing home care increases and as the relative supply of available workers decreases with the aging of the population, costs can only go higher. Today Americans are spending $35.2 billion a year for nursing home care, which is nearly five times the total amount spent for medical research and nearly seven billion more than is spent for drugs and medical supplies.[8] Yet if government ever provides a universal entitlement to nursing home care, this will increase effective demand, driving up costs still more. The same is true if private insurance for nursing home care ever becomes widely available.

Yet there is really no way for society to avoid these costs, aside from euthanasia. Even when such care is provided by children or relatives, the economic burden on society is still very real. People who otherwise would be free to take on jobs or perform useful volunteer work, or simply to stimulate the economy by spending their own money, must instead stay at home around the clock and often under conditions of stress that threaten their own health.

In addition to the ever mounting cost of and need for nursing home care, each year brings expensive new medical technologies—such as, most recently, artificial hearts and PET scanners, or positive emission tomographers—that drive up health care costs for the elderly and for everyone else. Operations such as heart and other organ transplants that once were considered experimental become routine procedures, ones to which even the prison population becomes legally entitled. The Congressional Office of Technology Assessment estimates that technology-related price components accounted for 24 percent of the 93 percent increase in per capita hospital costs between 1977 and 1982.[9] More recent estimates show that increases in the intensity of care given to patients, which is largely driven by advances in technology as well as by the aging of the population, accounted for one-fourth of the rise in health care costs between 1985 and 1986.[10]

Since the beginning of modern medicine, each succeeding generation has invested massively in researching and developing new medical technology. But such investments are never matched with reserves designed to pay for the cost of applying whatever new medical knowledge comes as a result. For this reason alone, the financing of health care becomes ever more problematic, with each new generation inheriting valuable new medical techniques but no dedicated capital to pay for their use.

When a promising new treatment for acute kidney failure was discovered in the mid-1960s, for example, funds had to be diverted from other areas not only to pay for the manufacture and distribution of extremely expensive dialysis machines, but also to cover the future health care and retirement costs of tens of thousands of patients who otherwise would have died. While it is true that some of those saved will go on to repay society for the cost of their treatment, the older they are the more difficult this becomes.

The Economics of Mortality

Students of history have often suggested that the money nations spend for military defense often becomes itself a cause of war. While this is a tricky proposition, in the realm of medicine, the same underlying principle often applies. The more we spend for heroic operations and intensive care, for instance, the more we need to spend, because such interventions allow patients to live long enough to contract other diseases or to require nursing home care. And indeed, since rates of morbidity rise with age, the longer such patients live the more frequently they will need new treatment. Also, the more we spend for health insurance, whether privately or as taxpayers, the more we need to spend, because patients covered by health care insurance are less cost conscious and because they are able to afford more expensive treatments.

Moreover, spending for health care often necessitates increased spending in other budget categories, primarily for public and private pensions. In the last chapter, we briefly discussed how the economy's "ghost dividend" was declining, as more and more Americans survive long enough to collect old age benefits for which they had been paying during their working years. The optimal ghost dividend is reaped when people die right before or near the age of retirement, when their accumulation of assets is usually at a maximum and when there is no offsetting cost to society in the form of lost labor and taxes. With this principle in mind, one can easily see the great fiscal strain created when health care spending results in declining mortality among those already beyond retirement age. For one inevitable effect of this is to increase the liabilities of both public and private old age insurance plans, without any compensating increase in taxes or contributions, as occurs when mortality among younger persons declines. The old have already paid their dues, as it were, whereas the young are still liable for their contributions. In macroeconomic terms, declining mortality among the elderly means that society as a whole consumes more than it otherwise would, or the young consume less, while total production remains the same.

While these sorts of relations are extremely difficult to quantify, some sense of them can be gained from the following statistics. It has been estimated that in 1978 the government would have had to pay an extra $5.9 billion in retirement and other benefits if all deaths by homicide and automobile accidents had somehow been eliminated. But because such deaths occur primarily among the young, the government would have gained nearly three times that amount in extra taxes in one year alone, for a net gain of over $10 billion.

On the other hand, if all deaths from heart disease and cancer had been eliminated that year—afflictions concentrated among the elderly—the government's finances would have been in much worse shape. The Treasury would have taken an extra $43 billion in taxes from those who survived. But because the overwhelming majority of these survivors would be elderly, the government would have been forced to pay out an extra $73 billion in retirement and other benefits. [11]

A second consequence of increased life expectancy among the elderly, especially when the trend continues over long periods of time, is that it probably causes each generation to convey fewer assets to the next. During their middle years, most people anticipate how long they will live by looking to the experience of the current elderly, particularly of their own parents. Common sense dictates, although the economists can't prove it, that such people make their decisions on how much to save for their own retirement based on such observations. Yet by the time they reach the age at which they planned to retire, their life expectancy will inevitably have lengthened over that of the previous generation of elderly. In the first instance, this situation creates a clamor and a need for more old age subsidies. But also, the longer people survive through retirement, the more they usually use up their savings, leaving smaller or no inheritances for the next generation.

This dissaving can have major effects on the economy as a whole. In Japan, where the population is aging at about the same rate as that in the United States, the government's 1985 economic white paper warned that the trend would cut the nation's saving rate in half by the turn of the next century and would prohibit the country from any longer exporting capital. Given the amount of capital that the United States is borrowing from Japan to finance its recurring budget deficits even while the baby boomers are still in their prime, this prediction ought to alarm policymakers in this country much more than it does those in Japan. But unlike its counterpart in Japan, our government is reluctant to contemplate much less plan for the long term.

How Long Will We Live?

Over the last two decades mortality rates for all age groups have improved. And yet it is among the elderly, especially the very old, that mortality rates have improved most dramatically when compared with historical trends.[12] Just between 1970 and 1977, the decline in mortality rates among the elderly ranged from 4 percent for men over eighty-five to 16 percent for women aged sixty-five to seventy-four.[13]

Economists Barbara Torrey and Douglas Norwood have developed a thought experiment that hints at the fiscal implications of such a trend. They ask us to imagine a society in which a million children are born each year and have been born each year for the past sixty-six years. Everyone in this society starts work at age twenty, retires at sixty-five, and then spends one year in retirement before promptly dying. In such a society, there will be forty-five workers contributing to the retirement system for each retiree.[14]

But now suppose that the age of death increases by 3 years, to age sixty-nine. In three years, the number of retirees will quadruple, while the number of workers remains the same. This means that if old age benefits are to remain even, taxes rates must also quadruple. And all this happens because the age of death has risen by a mere 4.5 percent. If the increase in life span were accompanied by an increase in morbidity, as it usually is in the real world, tax rates for increased health care would need to go still higher.

The increase in the life expectancy of the elderly has been so dramatic in the last two decades that researchers are at a loss to explain it fully. One of the largest contributing factors, for example, was a steep decline in the incidence of heart disease. Beginning in California in the early 1960s and then gradually spreading throughout the country for the next twenty years, rates of death by heart attack and other heart failures mysteriously began to decline. The national rate, having soared throughout most of the century, peaked in the mid-1960s and then declined by 25 percent over the next fifteen years. While many hypotheses have been put forward to explain this decline, such as increased exercise, changing diets, and reduced smoking, none applies very well to the actual population of the elderly at the time and none is consistent with the full range of data available. The trend, so far as medical researchers can explain it, seems simply to be an act of providence.[15]

How much more will mortality rates among the elderly improve? There is no consensus view. A key question, however, is in what sense people ever really die of old age. As more and more of what were once thought to be the natural ravages of age, such as senility, arthritis, and bone weakness, are revealed instead to be the result of specific diseases or dietary and environmental factors, there appears to be no theoretical reason why the passage of time alone must lead to death. This is not to imply that man may even potentially be immortal. But if indeed no natural or innate limits to the human life span exist, then there is no reason to believe that the current rapid improvements in life expectancy among the elderly won't continue indefinitely.

The strongest challenger of this view is James F. Fries of Stanford University, who received widespread attention in the early 1980s for a paper he published in the *New England Journal of Medicine*.[16] Fries's argument began with the observation that while the average life expectancy for the population as a whole has increased dramatically in the last two centuries, this situation has not been caused by any significant increase in the maximum age at which people die. As far as can be documented, the longest any human has ever lived is 114 years. The laws of probability argue that at least some people would have lived to much greater ages if all that such an achievement required was the avoidance of specific diseases or environmental hazards. Thus, Fries theorized, there must be some biological factor, such as a limit to the number of times human cells can divide themselves, that eventually and inevitably undoes every human being.

Using purely statistical arguments, Fries went on to state that, for any given population, the maximum possible life expectancy at birth is probably around age eighty-five. According to his data, this is the age at which current trend lines of improved life expectancy for different age groups eventually converge; by 2045, he predicted, more rapid improvements in life expectancy for the young than for the old would lead to a situation in which both a newborn infant and a sixty-five-year-old would have an equal chance of reaching age eighty-five but very little chance of living past it. Thus, he concluded, for any society age eighty-five must be the approximate outer limit for life expectancy at birth; with better health care and exercise and diet, people might put off the natural onslaughts of age for a long time, but this could only lead to a "compression of morbidity" as they bump up against the biological limits of the human life span. Like the "one-hoss shay" in Oliver Wendell Holmes's famous poem, the elderly of the future will fall apart all at once, according to Fries, and repair will be impossible.

As it has turned out, however, Fries's statistical arguments, while mathematically elegant, relied on assumptions that are already being contradicted by events. The most recent data show, for instance, that while life expectancy at birth improved 4.3 percent during the 1970s, life expectancy at age sixty-five increased by more than double that rate.[17] What's more, it is among the oldest of the old that mortality rates are now improving the fastest. Indeed, those who reach the age of eighty-five, according to some studies, seem to gain a reprieve of sorts; their chances of dying no longer increase from year to year at the same high rate as they do for younger persons.

For example, in what may be life's ultimate Catch-22, living to an advanced age may even reduce one's statistical risk of contracting most forms of cancer. Contrary to what many Americans believe, the chances of being struck by cancer, while rising rapidly in midlife, actually decline after one passes age sixty-five. Of those persons dying between the ages of sixty-five and sixty-nine, 28 percent are taken by cancer, but that drops to 12 percent for persons dying above the age of eighty-five.[18] At the same time, however, the very old are turning out to be extremely frail and vulnerable to other slow, debilitating assaults, particularly Alzheimer's disease.

Whether the high morbidity of the very old means that there are innate limits to the human life span is unclear. We now know that the body's basal metabolic rate changes hardly at all after age thirty. Although most organs undergo functional declines with aging, none is sufficiently compromised, even at extreme ages, for death to result in the absence of disease.

Many scientists now believe that diet alone may explain much of the aging process. According to different estimates, anywhere from 15 to 50 percent of Americans over age sixty-five consume insufficient amounts of calories, calcium, iron, the B complex vitamins, and vitamin C. Many of the elderly are too poor to afford a proper diet; others suffer loss of appetite due to the effects of medication. Undernourishment may cause much of the weakening in immunological defenses commonly attributed simply to aging, holding out the prospect that Americans may vastly improve their life expectancy just by eating better.[19]

More theoretically, it has repeatedly been shown, contrary to Fries's supposition, that cells taken from animals and raised in test tubes will continue to divide long past the normal life span of those animals. And even if our genes do contain some sort of death message that eventually signals the cells to stop reproducing, many researchers believe that emerging biogenetic technology will allow a way for such messages to be blocked. Entropy, or the general tendency (posited by physicists) of all things to fall apart eventually, may well be the only theoretical principle standing in the way of man's immortality.

"Tables of longevity may be everywhere considered the touch-stones of government," the Frenchman J. P. Brissot de Warville remarked in 1788, "the scale on which may be measured their excellencies and their defects, the perfection or degradation of the human species."[20] That so many Americans are now surviving to advanced ages should not be viewed pessimistically, but as a testament to the grand success of American culture. But from that very success has come a deep moral obligation to prepare for its financial consequences. In 1974, the Social Security Administration projected under its "best-guess" scenario that life expectancy at birth would reach no higher than 69 years for men and 76.9 years for women by the year 2000. As it turned out, life expectancy for both men and women improved by more than that by 1983. This is but one more instance of the government's simply assuming away its obligations to younger Americans.

The Prospect for Medicare

What most Americans refer to as Medicare is actually two programs. The Supplementary Medical Insurance program (SMI) pays for doctors' fees, laboratory fees, and other outpatient services for the elderly. The Hospital Insurance program, or HI as the government calls it, helps pay for the hospital costs of the elderly and also provides some very limited protection for those needing convalescent care. Despite recent draconian measures that have been taken to hold down the costs, the financial outlook for both programs is dismal. Indeed, to put the matter precisely, these are not programs for the elderly but programs for the current older generation. As currently financed, they cannot be sustained — not even for the parents of the baby boomers.

What makes the picture even more bleak is that when measured against the medical needs of today's elderly, these programs are not particularly generous, and for some forms of care they are woefully inadequate. Today, SMI and HI together pick up 48 percent of the health care costs for the elderly. But because of medical inflation and the availability of new technology, the elderly are actually paying more out of their own pockets for health care than they did in 1965 when these programs were first put in place.

Looked at from a purely fiscal point of view, however, SMI and HI are exceedingly generous — to the point that it is inconceivable that younger Americans will ever enjoy the same level of subsidy. While not begrudging today's elderly their medical benefits, we must be frank about who is paying for them and with what prospects for reimbursement. So long as only incremental reforms are being considered in Washington, it is simply unjust for the government not to put younger Americans on notice that they can expect little or no return for the tax dollars they are contributing to Medicare. That Medicare cannot fully meet the needs of today's elderly only underscores the dimension of the challenge facing the baby boomers and their children.

Consider first the financing of SMI. The program is entirely voluntary. But it offers such an attractive return on investment for today's senior citizens that virtually everyone over sixty-five elects to participate. As of January 1, 1985, the cost of joining SMI was set at $15.50 per month. For this SMI pays 80 percent of any doctor bill, after the patients pays a $75 deductible, up to what SMI deems a "reasonable" limit for any given service. While it is true that many doctors charge more than this limit — at the extreme expense of the elderly poor — SMI still offers an extraordinary value. The elderly currently enrolled in SMI are receiving benefits worth *four times* on average the value of their contributions. With premiums sufficient to pay for only about a quarter of the actual cost of the program, the shortfall is being covered with funds raised by federal borrowing and by the taxpayers in general. And these shortfalls are increasing. By 1990, more than 83 percent of the cost of SMI will be covered by general revenues. By 2005, the cumulative subsidies required to sustain the program are officially estimated to exceed $1.5 trillion—a sum equal to three-quarters of the current national debt. And this is well before members of the baby boom generation become eligible to participate.[21]

But the problems of SMI pale beside those of the Hospital Insurance program. As was discussed in the last chapter, the HI program—what most people mean by Medicare—is funded primarily through payroll taxes levied on younger workers. In 1986, the combined employer-employee payroll tax designated for the HI program was 2.9 percent of a worker's earnings, up to a maximum of $1,218. But these contributions go to cover the costs only of current beneficiaries. In the best of circumstances, the HI trust fund has reserves sufficient to pay for just six months of benefits and generally much less. By paying into the system, younger workers build up a legal entitlement to future hospital care coverage without any funds' actually being set aside to meet the cost of this promise.

For today's elderly, this pay-as-you-go system has provided an extraordinarily good deal. As Carolyn K. Davis, the former administrator of the Health Care Financing Administration, which oversees Medicare, testified before Congress in 1985, today's beneficiaries are receiving benefits far beyond the contributions they paid into the system. "For individuals who became eligible for Medicare in 1983," Davis told the House Select Committee on Aging, "the average contribution made during their years of employment, even with accrued interest, is $2,690. However, we estimate they will receive $34,000 in benefits if they are female and $28,000 if they are male. That's anywhere from 10 to 12.5 times their contributions."[22]

A separate study by the Congressional Budget Office showed that married couples retiring in 1982, even if both had contributed to the system over their entire working careers, would still receive back from Medicare seven times what they had contributed.[23] This statistic captures the essence of the system's fiscal crisis. Since Medicare has only been in place since 1965, most of today's elderly paid into the system for but a portion of their working years. For this reason, one would expect their rate of return to be high, just as it was for the early recipients of Social Security pensions. But now we see that, given the tax rates that have prevailed since the beginning of the program, today's elderly could not have paid their own way even if the system had been fully mature, as it will be for the baby boomers. Either benefits will have to be cut, or taxes raised, or both. For the baby boomers and their children, there will be no free ride.

Further underscoring the dismal prospects for Medicare is the fact that the government has already taken drastic measures to hold down its cost — measures that may already be reducing the quality of care received by the elderly. The single most revolutionary attempt at reform came as part of the 1983 Amendments to the Social Security Act. Under pressure from an exasperated Congress, Medicare adopted a new prospective payment system for hospitals, to be phased in over three years. The new system sets specific price schedules for 470 so-called diagnostic-related groups (DRGs), ranging from heart attacks to broken hips. Medicare notifies hospitals in advance of what it is prepared to pay for each of these DRGs, based on the hospital's previous cost for treating such illnesses, the age of the patient, whether other complications exist, and other factors. When fully phased in, DRGs are expected to be based on a single national payment structure, accounting for differences only between urban and rural hospitals. If the hospital can cure a Medicare patient for less than the amount Medicare has specified for his ailment, then it can keep the difference; if it costs the hospital more to treat the patient than the specified limit, the hospital must take a loss.

Even though Medicare spending has continued to increase inexorably since 1983, the adoption of the prospective payment system has undoubtedly helped to hold costs below what they otherwise would have been. Under the old "fee-for-service" system, the government would reimburse hospitals for virtually any expense they incurred in treating Medicare patients, and so hospitals had no particular reason to strive for efficiency. But they also had no incentive to provide anything but the highest quality of care for Medicare patients.

Among the 5,405 hospitals operating under DRGs in 1984, the average length of stay for Medicare patients dropped from 9.5 to 7.4 days. Defenders of DRGs point to such statistics as proof that hospitals were previously providing unnecessary care for Medicare patients. But meanwhile there have been widespread charges that hospitals have released Medicare patients while they were still in danger of relapse. Moreover, unless DRG price schedules are set at a sufficiently high level, hospitals have a strong incentive and perhaps even an economic imperative to shift costs on to non-Medicare patients, and so once again younger Americans wind up footing the bill.

There are still no definitive studies to show whether DRGs are leading either to a two-tier health care system or to significant cost shifting. But of one thing everyone is sure. Neither the savings thus far realized under the prospective payment system nor the dramatic run-up in recent years in the amount of deductibles and copayments charged to Medicare patients have been anywhere near enough to save Medicare from imminent insolvency.

Figure 4–1 is taken from the 1986 annual report of the Federal Hospital Insurance Trust Fund. It shows that under all but the most optimistic scenario, alternative I, the trust fund will be bankrupt before the turn of the century. And that optimistic scenario is taken seriously by no one. The four alternative scenarios presented in the chart are based on the same economic and demographic assumptions used for projecting the future of Social Security's disability and pension trust funds. And as we saw in the last chapter, even the most "pessimistic" of these scenarios actually calls for a level of economic performance that exceeds the U.S. experience of the last fifteen years. Further, when it comes to one of the most crucial variables affecting future Medicare expenditure — the question of how long people can expect to live past the age of sixty-five — the actuaries refuse to accept even the possibility that the rate of improvement already realized in the 1970s will continue in the decades to come.

Figure 4–1. Short-Term HI Trust Fund Ratios

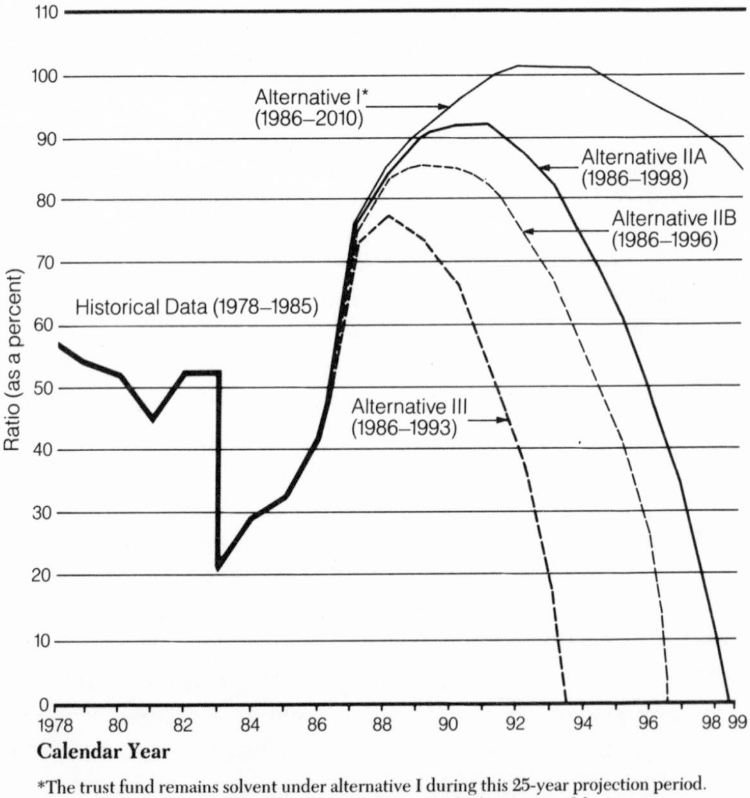

*The trust fund remains solvent under alternative I during this 25-year projection period.
Note: The trust ratio is defined as the ratio of assets at the beginning of the year to disbursements during the year.

Source: *1986 Annual Report of the Board of Trustees of the Federal Hospital Insurance Trust Fund.*

More Promises from the Past

The crisis in Medicare is replicated throughout the American health care system. The nation's largest health care provider, for example, is the Veterans Administration. The VA is keenly aware of the long-term consequences of promises made in the past. As of mid-1979, the agency was still making monthly benefit payments to 103 widows and 142 needy children of Civil War veterans, both Union and Confederate.[24]

But these days the VA is confronted with a financial crisis for which there is no precedent. The first mission of the VA's health care program is treating veterans with service-related disabilities, regardless of their age. But the VA also offers free hospital and nursing home care to all veterans who happen to make it over age sixty-five, whether their health care needs are service related or not.

The cost of this entitlement, while already large, will soon become astronomical, due not only to the general aging of the population, but also to the legacy of World War II and Korea. Largely because of the huge number of Americans who served in uniform during these two wars, by 1990 six out of every ten men over age sixty-five will be veterans. In 1976 there were 128,000 veterans over age eighty-five; by 1985 their number had increased to 231,000, and by the turn of the century it is predicted to reach 303,000.

Because of the growing number of old soldiers, the demand for VA nursing home care will more than double by the turn of the century, and other health care costs will rise proportionately as the veteran population ages. In 1973, the VA's total medical outlays were just $2.7 billion; ten years later they reached $8.3 billion, and will exceed $15.4 billion as early as 1990 in the absence of deep benefit cuts.[25]

Medicaid, which is designed to provide health care to the poor of all ages, is also seeing more and more of its available resources consumed by the burgeoning number of elderly on its rolls. More than 40 percent of all Medicaid spending now goes to persons sixty-five and over, most of them indigent nursing home residents.

Because of the extraordinarily high cost of nursing home care, even middle-class Americans must face the prospect that they will eventually come to rely on the Medicaid program. Indeed, a cottage industry of consultants has sprung up to advise the elderly on how they can hide or convey their assets so as to meet this welfare program's strict means test.

Although standards vary from state to state, in most states Medicaid patients, while allowed to keep their homes and household possessions, cannot show more than $1,700 in financial assets, or $2,550 if married. In addition, their income generally must be below three-quarters of the poverty line. As more and more Americans reach advanced ages and require long-term nursing and other health care, the numbers qualifying for Medicaid even under these extremely harsh requirements can only grow.

Nor is the private sector preparing to meet its health care promises to the baby boomers and their children. In 1984, the unfunded postemployment health care liability of the *Fortune* 500 companies alone approached $2 trillion. Yet the total assets of those companies was only $1.4 trillion.[26] In other words, to meet the cost of health care benefits already promised to their workers when they retire, these companies would have to sell off everything they own, and still they would come up 30 percent short. Just as with all the Social Security trust funds, private employee health care benefits are funded on a pay-as-you-go basis, essentially using the principles of both a Ponzi and a Tontine scheme.[27] But just as the Ponzi principle is being undone by the decline in fertility, the Tonti principle is undermined by the decline in mortality.

In 1984, the Chrysler Corporation paid $530 in health care benefits for every car it sold. Of this amount, approximately 40 percent went to people who were not even working for

Chrysler—retired workers and their dependents.[28] When the company first agreed to pay such benefits, back in 1966, it seemed a comparatively cheap and also humane way to buy labor peace—paying the price would largely be the problem of the next generation of labor and management. But no one imagined that the price would be so high. As has happened throughout the U.S. manufacturing sector, the ratio of workers to retirees has since declined dramatically, owing both to layoffs and to the increasing life expectancy of the elderly.

At Armco, Inc., the diversified Middletown, Ohio, steel company, the ratio of active employees to retirees shrank from 5 to 1 in 1975 to 1.8 to 1 last year. During the same interval, Armco's annual retiree health care cost soared from $5 million to $40 million. The recent collapse of the LTV corporation, which cut off health care benefits to more than eighty-thousand retirees, further dramatizes the challenge that awaits all businesses in the years to come. It is a challenge that is not confined merely to "sunset" or currently declining industries. RCA, which is currently paying only 1–2 percent of its payroll for health care benefits, estimates that within twenty years its health care bill will rise to 20 percent of payroll, due to demographic trends and the declining size of the work force.[29]

The increasing cost of health care is severely reducing the ability of the United States to compete in foreign markets—a burden that can only compound as the population continues to age. Already, U.S. automakers as a whole are spending more for health care than for steel.[30] Since 1975, employer payments for health insurance, in all sectors of the economy, has been the fastest-growing component of total labor costs.[31]

The health care crisis in the United States thus cannot be compartmentalized into the problems of specific programs—it exists in all programs, both public and private, and the underlying causes are everywhere the same. Nor can the crisis in health care be considered an issue distinct from the crisis in the Social Security pension and disability funds, nor from the massive unfunded liabilities to be found in all our social accounts, since all these issues are essentially tied to the question of what the members of the different generations owe to one another and to their future selves.

The Economy of Ethics

Health care in this country, as in every country, is, always has been, and always will be rationed. This is the first and inescapable point of departure for any serious discussion of health care reform. Under our current system, access to health care and the quality of care received is rationed according to many criteria, but the two most important are personal wealth and seniority.

A brief revisit to our major health care programs shows how this is so. Medicaid provides a fatally limited standard of care to the very poor. The program's meager budget ensures that many who could be saved are not, for lack of access to the same doctors and treatments available to richer and to most older Americans. Medicare, on the other hand, provides comparatively generous protection to anyone who manages to survive life's traumas until age sixty-five. But the program still requires deductibles and copayments that effectively ration care away from the elderly poor, particularly if they are not poor enough to qualify for Medicaid. Meanwhile, roughly 10 percent of the population under age sixty-five, predominantly the working poor and their children, have virtually no access at all to adequate health care because they can't satisfy the means-test for Medicaid and at the same time lack private medical insurance. Even if such an ad hoc and unjust system of allocating health care resources could be maintained in the future, sooner or later, Americans could stand its inequities no more and would demand reform.

So we must push back to first principles. Granted, the need for greater efficiency in the provision of health care is paramount so long as what we spend in the aggregate for health care is competing with other vital social needs. And there is indeed a great deal of unnecessary surgery and other forms of waste, fraud, and abuse throughout the health care sector that ought to be our first target of reform. A look at the rate at which different medical procedures are performed in different parts of the country, for example, reveals that if there is any general agreement among the members of the medical profession on what constitutes appropriate treatment, individual doctors and surgeons are flouting it routinely. A recent national survey by the *New England Journal of Medicine* found that of 123 medical procedures studied, 67 showed at least a threefold difference between regions with the highest and lowest rates of use.[32]

Further underscoring the inefficiency of the American health care system is the fact that we in the United States spend more per capita on health care than do people in any other country in the world, and still we rank fifteenth in life expectancy at birth for males and eighth for females. Even such poor countries as Cyprus and Spain have achieved higher male life expectancy at birth than has the United States.[33]

But to say that the crisis in health care can be solved just by regulating out waste, fraud, and abuse in the current system is simply disingenuous. The current system is unjust in the first place because it denies so many Americans access even to inefficient treatment. Furthermore, as we have seen, the aging of the population, combined with advances in medical technology, will severely challenge our ability to provide even for those categories of the citizenry who are currently favored with adequate access to high-quality health care. Before we can come anywhere near solving the long-term crisis, we will be forced to reexamine the basic social values underlying our system of health care. Specifically, we will have to ask ourselves why, so long as we must ration health care by some criteria, we should so largely favor the rich and the elderly, and especially those who are both.

Seniority

When Medicare was first enacted, the principal argument used in its defense rested on two premises. The first was that the elderly were much more likely than members of other groups to be in need of medical treatment; the second was that few elderly could afford the cost.

In a very rough sense, both premises remain true today. It is true, of course, that the population over sixty-five is, *on average*, dramatically better off than it was twenty years ago. As rapidly as the economic status of the elderly has improved, though, the cost of health care has soared still higher.

This still leaves open the question, however, of why the mere circumstance of one's reaching one's sixty-fifth birthday should ever have become a condition for entitlement to Medicare in the first place. Obviously there are many on both sides of that age who are needy and many who are not. And it is by no means self-evident that subsidizing only those in need would be more expensive, especially in the long term, than subsidizing all the elderly.

Indeed, as we shall see later in this chapter, many countries provide full medical benefits to all their citizens for but a fraction of what the United States spends per capita on health care, and they still have comparable life expectancy rates. If this practical truth can be accepted for the moment, we are left with the purely philosophical question: What has turning age sixty-five got to do with one's right to adequate health care?

In this realm, the question is particularly pointed. Distributing pensions on the basis of seniority, by contrast, does not per se increase a younger person's chances of dying before becoming old enough to collect back his or her contributions. But rationing health care in favor of senior citizens does do this. It is not as if one can say to a young person dying for want of an operation that he or she can't afford, "Just be patient and you too will get your turn to enjoy the benefits of Medicare, and in the meantime all we ask is for you to continue paying your taxes." This was no less true when Medicare was enacted than it is today.

This raises another line of questioning. Then, and even more so now, many of the elderly were financially secure and did not require public funds to pay for their health care. In effect, providing such funds amounts to an inheritance protection program. What Medicare provides for the affluent elderly, they are free to pass on to their heirs and often do. This is of obvious benefit to those in the favor of a rich parent or grandparent. But why should the poor or any of the rest of us be taxed just so that such people can enjoy a larger bequest?

There is simply no end to the contradictions involved in distributing medical subsidies on the basis of seniority. If entitlement to Medicare is justified on some basis other than need, why does such an entitlement not also apply to younger Americans, regardless of *their* means? Either access to publicly funded health care is a right of citizenship or it is not. If it is, on what basis is such an entitlement denied to younger Americans? If it is not a right of citizenship, why is it extended to everyone — rich and poor alike — lucky enough to have reached age sixty-five?

The same questions apply, with only somewhat less force, to the broad range of our social programs. As Elizabeth Ann Kutza has pointed out, age has always played some role in determining a citizen's rights and privileges.[34] At age sixteen, in many states, an individual is deemed "old enough" to drive a car or to leave school. At age eighteen one is allowed to vote, and may be allowed to drink in a public place or to marry without one's parents' permission. Age twenty-one has generally been accepted as the legal age of transition from minority to majority status. But over the past half-century, passing from one's sixty-fourth to one's sixty-fifth year has become without question the most significant milestone of American life, carrying with it an enti-

tlement to benefits and social services that are denied even at
the cost of life to younger citizens. Are there any arguments that
can justify this pattern of age discrimination?

Some advocates of senior power have argued that the elderly,
along with veterans in general, are due special compensation by
virtue of their previous contributions to society.[35] Yet as the
philosopher Daniel Callahan has noted, "It is by no means evident why mere survival, the living of a life through adulthood,
in and of itself merits the bountiful social blessing of fully
subsidized health care. Just as not all the aged are financially
needy, not all of them will have led lives worthy of automatic
honor."[36]

More critically, Callahan adds, this line of reasoning could just
as well be used by younger Americans, who could demand compensation for their ongoing or future contributions to society. No
one generation can show the superiority of its claim to virtue, if
for no other reason than because no one ever knows what challenges and possible triumphs yet await the young. There is no
particular reason to believe, for example, that today's elderly will
be the last generation to live through a major depression or to
fight a major war.

Nor is it easy to find any other justification for age-based entitlements. It may be said that today's elderly as a whole supported their own parents through old age and that this is the
basis for their claim to across-the-board old age subsidies from
today's young. Pointing to history, however, does not get senior
power advocates where they want to be. Before the advent of
Social Security pensions and Medicare, the young were indeed
often called upon to provide full support for their elderly parents.
But not all of today's senior citizens made such a sacrifice. More
fundamentally, let us recall that for those who did, their support
was contingent upon the actual, individual need of their parents,
not upon their parents' age alone. A rich father did not expect
payments from his children merely because he passed his sixty-
fifth birthday, and it is fair to say that none ever received such

tribute. If our current entitlements of age are to be justified by appeal to the patterns of intergenerational financial assistance that once prevailed within families, then it is clear that these programs must all be means tested.

Further undermining the concept of reciprocity, particularly as applied to health care, is the brute fact that the burden of supporting the old, although now divided among the working-aged population as a whole, has been growing exponentially over the last generation and will most likely continue to do so in the future. Today's older Americans are retiring earlier and living longer, with more generous pensions and health care benefits, than any previous generation in history. This by itself is a wonderful achievement. But its costs to younger Americans certainly cannot be justified on the basis of what today's elderly once provided for their own parents.

The baby boomers will be bound by the same general principle. Although members of this generation may be much more generous than previous generations in providing for the elderly, this will not win them a right to still more generous treatment from their own children. This will remain true no matter how much the baby boom generation might need increased subsidies to meet the high cost of health care in old age or to keep individual pensions at a decent minimum.

Finally, even if our society did have a long tradition of providing entitlements on the basis of seniority alone, this still would not necessarily justify the practice so long as it unfairly encumbered or violated the rights of all latecomers. An analogy can be seen in the sometimes fatal and usually dangerous practice of hazing that goes on in fraternity houses each fall. The fact that most sophomores will survive being buried alive and the like does not justify such practices, even if the survivors are allowed the pleasure of taking out their humiliation on next year's recruits. Such hazing is simply wrong in the first place. So too is any practice or policy that asks its victims to be content with the chance to oppress the next generation, in turn.

How do these principles apply to Medicare and to our other entitlements of age? They show fundamentally that even if these programs could be sustained over the lifetime of today's younger Americans, that fact by itself would not justify the practice of using seniority as a basis for conferring benefits, particularly health care benefits. That all these programs for the elderly are headed toward insolvency only emphasizes an issue of justice that would exist anyway: that of why the poor should be taxed during their working years in order to benefit the rich when they pass age sixty-five. In the realm of health care, conferring benefits on the basis of seniority and without regard to need is especially egregious, since it reduces the chances of younger Americans' becoming either elderly or rich themselves.

Our society is marked by many competing ideas of justice. But no theory has ever been devised to justify allocating life-giving resources on the basis of seniority alone. Such practices violate the strict utilitarian test of doing the greatest good for the greatest number over time, since the elderly are the least likely of all groups to be able to repay society for the cost of their benefits. Moreover, such practices violate the essentially liberal view of justice as a fair social contract among different segments of society. For none of us, I submit, would contract for the terms of our current health care system if given the opportunity before we were born.

Health Care without Politics

Suppose that, in considering the fairest principles for reforming American health care, we could forget for a moment our own special interests as young people or old people, as rich people or poor, and the like. In his monumental work, *A Theory of Justice*, the philosopher John Rawls proposed that what we really mean by justice is revealed by the social arrangements we would opt for were we somehow prevented by a "veil of ignorance" from knowing of our special interest in the outcome.[37] This is the idea of justice as fairness and as such seems to capture our everyday notions of what makes an institution just or not. While Rawls did not specifically take up the question of health care in his book, we are free to borrow his method of argument. What if we were forced to decide, before we came to earth and discovered our time in history and station in life, how much of society's wealth should go for health care and by what rules that sum should be divided? Such a thought experiment, while difficult to perform, provides insight into this extremely complex and vital moral question.

The first issue we would need to consider is whether society should at all times allocate an unlimited amount of resources to health care. Clearly there would be a great temptation to vote in favor of such an option. For it would be hard for anyone to think of any higher purpose to which we could commit society's resources. Still, if we were shrewd, we would be forced into the realization that in the long term, as technology advanced, the cost of providing unlimited care would eventually preempt investments needed to maintain economic growth, which in turn would constrain the ability of later generations to educate the young, to provide for shelter, or even to gain access to the health care itself. Being prudent and not knowing into which generation we would be born, we would thus be wary of allowing spending for health care to outpace the growth of the economy. For to do so would be to run the risk, at the very least, of our being born into an impoverished generation, one that could not afford to operate whatever high-tech hospitals and other health facilities it might inherit from the past.

We would thus be forced to decide, as in the real world every society collectively decides in some ad hoc fashion, on criteria for limiting health care spending in the aggregate and, by extension, on how different forms of health care should be rationed among different types of citizens. One method of achieving these ends might of course be simply to let the market decide the amount and distribution of health care resources. Here again, the choice would be extremely difficult. As Lester Thurow has observed, when it comes to health care, most of us are simultaneously capitalists and egalitarians. We want the right to spend our money as we see fit, especially for health care that may save our lives. At the same time, we don't want to see ourselves or anyone else die just because of an inability to afford medical care. [38]

Yet, when placed originally in a position of not knowing whether we would wind up rich or poor, this conflict of values would seem much easier to resolve. The reason, I believe, would be simple risk aversion.

When it comes to deciding on the distribution of such luxury goods as emeralds, mansions, and sports cars, by way of contrast, we might well decide for independent reasons to let market forces prevail, rather than insist that all such things be shared by the public at large. We might convince ourselves, for example, that by doing so, everyone would be provided with a greater incentive to work hard and to start new enterprises, and that this would enrich society as a whole. But more important, we would realize that the prospect of finding ourselves without access to emeralds, mansions, and the like would be no great hazard, for it is more than possible to get along in life without such things. In short, because such luxuries are not essential to the pursuit of happiness, we would at least be tempted to take the risk of our not having them at all in exchange for the possibility of exclusive ownership.

But when it comes to health care, the calculation of risk would come out much differently. Maintaining one's health is a precondition to every other pursuit of life, including the pursuit of money. If having money were to become a precondition for access to health care, many if not most of the poor would be irrevocably condemned. And none of us would have any idea whether he or she would become poor. Thus, from behind the veil of ignorance, prudence alone would dictate that we declare at least some minimal access to health care as a basic right of citizenship.

Just what we would mean by "minimal access" is hard to say. Obviously, the actual cost of being denied access to any health care increases tremendously as medical knowledge expands from generation to generation. In the eighteenth century, when blood-letting was a common medical procedure, one was often lucky *not* to have access to the "best" doctors in the community, whether one knew it or not. Still, let us assume for the moment that we could eventually settle on some rule for determining the minimum amount of health care to which each of us would want to be entitled in any given era. This would leave open the question of how we might want that amount of health care distributed to us over our lifetimes. Here again, we brush up against the issue of seniority.

Faced with limits on what we could prudently spend in the aggregate for health care, we might, for example, decide to commit the largest share of our available resources to providing health care for the young, who stand to gain the most time from medical treatment but who need it comparatively infrequently. Or we might decide to ration health care in favor of the elderly, who, though they have but a relatively short time to live in any case, more frequently depend on access to health care for survival, and on very expensive treatments at that.

The issue here is not whether the young are more or less deserving than the old. The issue, again, is prudence. In this context, we would all be assured of being young, at least for a while. And we would all face some more or less likely prospect of becoming old, depending in part on how we chose to allocate health care resources over our own lifetimes. In effect, as the philosopher Norman Daniels has observed, this question comes down to a choice between giving ourselves, on the one hand, an enhanced chance of having a normal life span, and on the other, a reduced chance of having a normal life span but with the compensation for those who do of living a few extra years.[39]

This may seem a Hobbesian choice, but it is nonetheless one that our society collectively faces every day. In the early 1980s, many states tightened their Medicaid eligibility requirements for children and young women. As a result, infant mortality rates have soared in many communities. Obviously, those infants who are dying have no chance at becoming senior citizens. But the great irony is that, under our current laws, if they had somehow managed to survive to age sixty-five, society would have spared virtually no expense in prolonging their lives a few more years. Would any of us, before we were born, opt for such an allocation of resources?

Apart from all other considerations, our decision on this issue would have to take into account the following dynamic. The more resources that were committed to extending life just a few years beyond the normal life span, the more all younger persons would need to decrease their overall level of consumption in order to support those of the previous generation who had managed to live to advanced ages. When life expectancy improves among the young, this increases the number of workers and at least potentially creates new wealth. But the same cannot be said when life expectancy increases among the very old. Thus, if forced to decide on these issues before we were born, we might well conclude that it hardly makes sense to expend vast resources on extending the normal life span. For by doing so, not only would we be reducing our chances of reaching that age in the first place, we would be guaranteeing that we would all be poorer than otherwise in the meantime.

I don't mean to sound as if my judgments on these questions are self-evidently right, or that everyone would calculate their self-interest in the same way if forced behind a "veil of ignorance." Still, it seems that, if most people were forced into such a position, they would probably reach a clear idea of how they would want medical treatment allocated over their lifetimes. Faced with an inevitably limited budget for health care, we would probably decide to reserve access to high-cost, life-extending technologies for our younger years, reasoning that by doing so we would improve our chances of actually becoming elderly. And with the savings realized by this rule, we would probably decide to provide generous social services for those of us who did indeed survive to old age, reasoning that this would vastly improve the quality of life for older people and that such an improvement would be well worth the price of a slightly shorter life expectancy for those already beyond the normal life span.

Back to the Real World

As it turns out, the situation just described is very nearly the pattern of care actually provided by Great Britain's National Health Service. The total amount spent on health care per capita in Britain is but one-third the amount in the United States. And yet life expectancy at birth is actually slightly higher there for men than in the United States and only marginally lower for women. How is this achievement possible? In part, it results from lower compensation for doctors, almost all of whom work as salaried employees of the government rather than as medical entrepreneurs. But the lower cost of the British system also results from a very real form of age-based rationing. In effect, British citizens have traded access to heroic, costly treatments in their later years for an enhanced chance of becoming elderly in the first place.

Although it is nowhere written into law that health care should be rationed by age, by tradition and under the constraint of budget pressures British doctors tend to reserve such treatments as kidney dialysis and coronary heart surgery for patients with the best chances of recovery. And by and large, such people tend not to be old. Among the population over sixty-five, the percent receiving dialysis treatment in Britain is but one-tenth the rate for other Western European countries.[40] Largely because of such rationing, by age sixty-five, British citizens have a significantly lower life expectancy than their counterparts in the United States. But British senior citizens are entitled to generous social services, such as in-home nursing care—services that are often vitally important to maintaining the elderly's quality of life but that are largely denied to American senior citizens.

Is the British system moral? Before dismissing it out of hand, we ought to compare it with our own. The British effectively ration health care by age. But so do we. Only our system favors the chronically ill elderly, whereas theirs favors both the elderly before they become chronically ill and the young in general. Meanwhile, the British do not let people of any age die just because they are neither poor enough to qualify for public support, nor wealthy enough to pay for their own medical needs. And because the British system is much more cost-effective than ours, it allows more resources to be devoted to other social purposes outside the realm of health care. Socialized medicine may go against the American grain. But in the face of rapid population aging, it remains an open question whether we can afford not to imitate the British example, particularly if we fail over the next decade to undertake the massive investments required to restore economic growth and to improve the productivity of the next generation.

Save the Children

As the population ages, the social cost of denying children and the young in general an entitlement to adequate health care will increase inexorably. Because of falling birthrates, workers will be in ever shorter supply in the next century; at least we have no good reason to believe otherwise. The labor shortage will be particularly acute if the United States continues to experience slow growth in productivity. This gives us all a practical as well as a moral imperative to see to it that members of today's very small younger generation have the best possible prospects for survival into adulthood. For even if we are selfishly thinking only of our own prospects as senior citizens, we must realize that the problem of financing Medicare and other old age benefits for the baby boomers can only be exacerbated in the long run if current rates of infant and child mortality are not improved and if we do not at the same time invest adequately in the education and future productivity of today's children.

Although this may seem a cold and calculating argument, so far sentimental appeals seem to have had little effect. The greatest danger of the senior power mindset is that it denies, or fails to perceive, that investment in the interests of children is ultimately the only means of benefiting the elderly. When those investments are not made, or do not pay off, it is precisely the elderly of the next generation who must pay the heaviest price. Thus we must face the issue squarely. None of us wants to be denied access to medical care in old age. And it is true that under a unified or national health care system like that in Britain the elderly are forced to compete directly with younger patients for access to high-cost, life-extending technology; the tighter the budgets for health care are set, the more the old and the terminally ill will be denied aggressive treatment. But the specter of death control will hang still more ominously over members of the baby boom generation and over all the future elderly as long as we do not somehow reduce the mortality and morbidity of younger Americans. And this is because every child we allow to die or remain disabled for lack of medical treatment is a child who will not even potentially contribute to the cost of our old age benefits, who will not be available to doctor us, or nurse us, or in any other way provide for our needs in old age.

Thus we are left wrestling with the same old snake, only now with tighter twist: the more capital we commit to extending our own lives to advanced ages, the less we can commit to the health care of the young, as well as to other productive purposes, such as investments in education and in rebuilding the economy. And the fewer resources we commit to those purposes, the smaller and poorer the next generation will become. And so it comes about that as we commit more resources to extending our own life expectancy in old age, we decrease the likelihood that the next generation will be able or willing to pay the bill. Let no one say, then, that the only humane thing to do is to vote the elderly—and by extension our future selves—everything they might want.

Lessons of a Failed Revolution

Shortly before the enactment of Medicare, President Lyndon Johnson declared to Congress and to the American people, "We can—and we must—strive now to assure the availability and accessibility to the best health care for all Americans, regardless of age or geography or economic status."[41] In those heady days, and for decades before, the fight for Medicare was always seen as but one battle along the road toward a national health insurance program for all Americans. As it turned out, liberals of that era won the battle but lost the war largely as a result.

The cost of Medicare exploded beyond all expectations. Originally projected by Congress to cost no more than $8 billion by 1990, Medicare was paying out more than three times that amount by 1979 and nearly ten times that amount by 1985. More than for any other reason the movement for national health insurance was destroyed by the example of Medicare. Its descent toward insolvency has convinced many Americans and nearly all policymakers that the country simply cannot afford adequate health care for the young. But the lessons being drawn from Medicare are largely incorrect. There are many reasons the cost of Medicare skyrocketed. But among the most important is the fact the program was limited primarily to the elderly.

Unlike the British program with its unified budget for the National Health Service, the U.S. system forced neither doctors and hospitals nor members of the public at large to confront hard choices about the cost-effectiveness of new life-extending technology or to think hard about the competing interests of the elderly and the rest of the patient population. Instead, these questions of triage were simply denied, because Medicare placed the health care of the elderly on an open-ended budget kept separate from the rest of the population. The needs of the elderly were thus never seen as competing with those of other patients.

The British system forces doctors to say no to patients who are beyond the point of effective treatment, for both moral and fiscal reasons. The doctors know, and the patients and their families know too, that such treatment would come at the direct expense of patients with better prospects of recovery who are often just down the hall and are in any case covered under the same fixed budget.[42]

In the United States, by contrast, the care of patients in any given hospital or doctor's office is being paid for with hundreds of different accounts: Medicare, Medicaid, private insurance, as well as individual pocketbooks. Rationing care among patients thus seems inappropriate. For under our system, there is no reason to believe that by withholding care from a terminally ill patient, the life of a child might be saved. Instead, the money saved by such withholding of treatment would be just as likely to wind up going to help the government buy more missiles, or to finance treatment for other terminally ill patients, or perhaps even to finance a tax cut so the rich can buy more yachts. There is no law or any political tradition in the United States that would prevent any given doctor or patient from coming to this conclusion.

The other reason Medicare failed is that it pumped billions of dollars into the health care system without providing the government with the means to control the resulting inflation. The idea at the time was that by investing massively in increasing the number of doctors and hospital beds, supply could be made to match the extra demand for health care created by the sudden availability of Medicare subsidies. But the strategy did not work. Indeed, there is good reason to believe that the increased number of health care providers by itself contributed to the inflation in health care cost, because of the peculiarities of medical economics under our system. As Joseph Califano writes:

> In business — manufacturing and selling cars, television sets, umbrellas, shoes, hats or balls — the more suppliers, the lower the cost, because competition drives the prices down. In the economic upside-down cake of medicine, however, more doctors do not necessarily mean lower prices. Indeed, in a provider-controlled system, the more doctors, the more medical services; the more surgeons, the more surgery; the more psychiatrists, the more fifty-minute patient hours on couches; the more specialists, the more referrals to specialists.[43]

Again, because doctors under our system do not operate under the constraints of a fixed, unified budget, they have a powerful incentive to maximize medical treatment. Added to the profit motive is the threat of malpractice suits, which compels doctors to order batteries of tests and other procedures that they might not otherwise think were necessary.

There are, moreover, other reasons to doubt that market forces alone can ensure maximum efficiency within the health care sector. As Robert Kuttner has written, "It would be hard to think of a less appropriate sphere for market economics than health care. In the medical system, decisions are primarily made by providers, not consumers; and the patient is seldom likely to change doctors or hospitals in order to save costs, when his life may be at stake."[44] As patients, we are simply not in a position to bargain for the best care at the lowest price, because we are ill or injured and because we are highly dependent on the good will of whatever doctors and nurses are ministering to us at the moment. Even employers and private insurance companies, while they have much more clout than patients, can only go so far in pressing for more efficient use of their health care dollars because all third-party payers are ultimately in competition with each other.

Neither is government regulation of prices the answer. "A

major problem with the regulatory approach," writes Sen. Dave Durenberger, former chairman of the Senate's Health Care Subcommittee, "is that it overlooks the fact that hospitals do not have cost-sensitive consumers. In fact, hospitals stay in business by filling their beds. And, they do that by attracting physicians with lures of better facilities, better equipment, and better services, whether or not they are needed by the community in general or the patient in particular."[45] Limiting the amount that doctors and hospitals can charge patients might bring short-term relief from medical inflation, but it would do nothing to solve the long-term crisis created by the aging of the population and by continuing advances in medical technology.

Only government ownership of the health care sector is sufficient to force maximum efficiency, as the example of Britain illustrates. But let us be frank about what *efficiency* means in this context, as most advocates of nationalized health care are not. To some extent it means that doctors no longer perform unnecessary surgery or order unneeded tests, because to do so entails more work for them without compensation and because it leaves them with a diminished budget for treating future patients. But efficiency in this context also means that, however informally, medical treatment is rationed on a "cost-effective" basis. Under the constraint of a fixed budget, resources will naturally go first to patients with the best prospects for recovery, who are usually young, and not to prolonging the lives of the dying, who are usually old.

This is the order of triage that is already practiced in nearly all emergency rooms in the United States and elsewhere, not by policy, but as a reflection of the hospital staff's ethical instincts. It is the order of triage that emerges under battlefield conditions, and wherever ordinary people are confronted with the moral dilemma of choosing whom to help first in a disaster. And it is the order of triage that would likely emerge within an American national health service, as its staff members rose to the challenge of maximizing the health and well-being of all Americans within the constraints of a fixed and unified budget.

Pushed to the Wall

Under current rates of mortality, roughly a quarter of all children born in the 1980s will die before reaching age sixty-five. Can we afford to do more for the young without doing less for the elderly as a whole? So long as current demographic and economic trends continue, the only honest answer, I believe, is no. The United States must contain its health care costs, as well as all forms of consumption, if it is to meet the challenge of educating the next generation, of rebuilding its dilapidated infrastructure and obsolete factories, and of repaying its massive debts from the past. At the same time, however, it would be unconscionable to deny medical technology to anyone as long as we could not be sure that the savings would be contributed toward a higher moral purpose, such as restoring the life of a child. These considerations bring me to a conclusion that most other Americans will probably feel uneasy about as well: Unless we can somehow stop the aging of the population while at the same time engineering much faster growth in the productivity of the work force, we will be forced for both moral and financial reasons to move toward a nationalized health care system.

It will not do simply to extend health *insurance* to all Americans. Taken by itself, such a move would fuel massive inflation in health care costs. Patients who otherwise would have been unable to afford access to health care or who otherwise would have been paying out of their own meager funds would then be relieved of having to worry about the cost-effectiveness of any treatment they might desire. Meanwhile, doctors would have the same incentive they have today to maximize the amount spent on each of their patients; the more operations, tests, and drugs they administered, the greater their profit.

The experience of countries such as Canada shows that health care costs can be reduced through massive regulation without fully nationalizing the health care system. There is also no doubt that greater use of health maintenance organizations and other prospective payment systems, which set fees in advance of treatment, can go a long way toward making health care less expensive than it otherwise would be by giving health care providers strong incentives to economize. But as William B. Schwartz, a professor of medicine at Tufts University, has stated, "Even if all useless care were gradually eliminated, we could anticipate only a temporary respite from rising costs unless the forces sustaining the real rate of change . . . were simultaneously eliminated."[46] Given the pressures created by an aging population, advancing technology, and a stagnant economy, we may have no choice but to follow the British example all the way and accept both the benefits and the drawbacks of fully socialized medicine.

Practical Possibilities for Reform

Should we seek to avoid the necessity of fully socialized medicine at all costs? Before deciding, consider that, in addition to relieving fiscal pressures, a nationalized health care system might bring other advantages that must be weighed. For example, such a system might allow us to do more for the elderly before they become chronically ill. Already, as the "living will" and "right to die" movements attest, many of today's elderly are fearful not so much of losing their right to heroic medicine as of being forced to exercise this right under conditions of extreme pain and at enormous emotional and financial expense to themselves and their children. At the same time, there is also a growing movement among the elderly that is crying out for home nursing care and other vital nonmedical services for which Medicare currently will not pay. As the need and demand for such "quality of life" services, including access to nursing home care, become more pressing, the chances for a redrafting of the contract between the generations along the lines set by the British may come to seem more and more attractive.

And for the future elderly, particularly members of the baby boom generation, the larger point still stands. The fewer members of the next generation who die in childhood or during their working years, the greater the numbers of taxpayers potentially available to help support the baby boomers in retirement. By the same token, the fewer resources committed to marginally extending the life-expectancy of the elderly baby boomers, the more will be available to assure their quality of life before they become chronically ill. A nationalized hospital system would also stamp out the insidious practice, now becoming ever more common, of hospitals' using scarce resources for advertising in a desperate attempt to attract paying customers away from one another.

The final and most obvious advantage of a national health care service would be, of course, that it would provide for the poor and be of even greater benefit to the nearly poor, who are currently disqualified even from Medicaid's meager benefits. But here again we must be frank about the hidden implications. There are compelling moral reasons for extending adequate health care to the poor, in any case. But if that goal is not matched by an even stronger commitment to raising standards of education and job training, the consequence will be an expanding underclass in the next century that will further undermine all our national ambitions. As Marc S. Tucker, executive director of the Carnegie Forum on Education and the Economy, has written, so long as we fail to raise educational standards, "the growing population of old people in our society can confidently look forward to closing years filled with poverty and social unrest, because a very large fraction of the work force, which is itself a declining proportion of the population as a whole, will be unable to support themselves, to say nothing of others."[47] To improve the life expectancy of such a class, without improving its life prospects, might still be moral but would bring its own special perils.

Financing a National Health Care Service

Although massive amounts of revenue would be needed to finance a national health care service, it should not be forgotten that its creation would most likely save money for the American people as a whole. We would pay more in taxes but much less for health care in general. This is because, as the British example proves, the practice of medicine would become more "efficient" — in the double sense explained earlier — than under our current ad hoc semiprivate system.

How could a national health care service be funded? There would be no need to rely on a single tax. But the choice of any source of revenue ought at least to be consistent with and at best to promote the cause of public health. Thus, for example, one logical source of revenue would be a sales tax on unhealthy or hazardous consumer items, such as cigarettes, alcohol, and firearms, as well as, possibly, on high-fat and high-protein foods, such as beef. I love to drink, I love to smoke, and I love to eat red meat, and still this suggestion seems to me consistent not only with the public interest but with my own as well. While there are limits to how much such items can be taxed without creating a large black market for them, their taxation at some level provides an appropriate and just means of financing any form of public health benefit, whether or not we move to nationalized health care.

Reliance on a payroll tax should be avoided for three reasons. First, such taxes are highly regressive — that is, they present the greatest burden to the working poor. Second, payroll taxes directly increase the cost of labor and as such reduce American competitiveness in foreign markets and cause unemployment. Finally, as we have already seen in the case of Social Security pensions and Medicare, reliance on payroll taxes creates an unwarranted ethic of entitlement among the population by encouraging people to believe that their individual contributions are going to prepay their individual benefits, rather than to meet the needs of their fellow citizens in the here and now.

Taxing savings should also be avoided. This is because of the overarching importance of increased capital formation in an aging society. Individuals need more savings for retirement; industry needs more capital for investment in raising the productivity of the shrinking labor force. In the absence of such investments, the health care system itself, whether publicly or privately organized, becomes increasingly difficult to finance. The fairest and most utilitarian way to finance a national health care service, or even our current system, would thus be to tax consumption —with unhealthy forms of consumption taxed at the highest rate and necessities not taxed at all in order to relieve the burden on the poor.

The Slippery Slope

I am not at all happy with the general conclusions of this chapter. The greatest reason is that I fear being discriminated against when I am old and sick. One may well agree intellectually and in advance to forgo expensive, painful treatments that only prolong one's death. Yet who is to say when a patient has actually reached that point or how he or she will feel about it at the time? As the aging of the population puts more pressure on the financing of health care, we face the real danger that everyone above a certain age will be declared, for medical purposes, to be effectively in the process of dying or to have no prospect for "quality of life." In a society that already denies fetuses any legal or human rights up until the third trimester, it is easy to imagine similar arguments being used against those passing some arbitrary age toward the other end of life. And from this point, it is easy to imagine patients' being denied treatment not because they are deemed terminally ill, but because they are deemed to be of little value to society, just like the terminally ill.

The slippery slope is real, and because of it we should strive for ways of rationing health care that do not involve us in making life and death decisions about individual patients on the basis of their membership in some abstract group, such as, for example, the population over age eighty. One way this might be done would be for the government to direct funds for health care research toward preventive medicine and away from technologies that are likely only to prolong the agony of the dying. But it is far from clear that the course of medical invention can actually be controlled in this fashion. Moreover, even if all medical research ended today, we would still be possessed with technologies too expensive to offer everyone. The need for triage will not disappear.

But it can be reduced. There are, so far as I can see, three broad rays of hope. They are, first, that either through an increase in fertility or in immigration, or through a combination of both, we can arrest the aging population; second, that we can stop borrowing so massively from the future and begin sooner rather than later the regime of thrift required to rebuild American industry and to stop the downward mobility of our children; and finally, that we can find means to prepay or otherwise compensate future taxpayers for the enormous cost of the baby boom generation's retirement. These are the challenges to which the rest of this book is dedicated.

5

Fertility and Immigration: The Politics of Population Growth

FEW AMERICANS would want to see the problems of Social Security or the terrifying medical issues discussed in the last chapter solved by dramatically increasing the population. The country is already crowded enough, most of us feel. Moreover, justice to future generations requires, somewhat paradoxically, that we not produce so many children as to reduce their quality of life. But if through increased fertility or immigration the population could be kept from falling, the baby boomers' prospects for old age could be improved without causing additional environmental strains or otherwise encumbering future generations. This chapter is dedicated to exploring these options for financing our aging society.

A Declining Population

Liberals, particularly, tend to be hostile to measures designed to bring more children into the world. But the specter of overpopulation that so alarmed liberal opinion in the late sixties and early seventies is today hardly relevant. Never before in history have Americans had to face the possibility of the nation's population actually declining. The fertility rate now averages 1.8 children per woman. Yet each woman must have an average of 2.1 children in order for the population to replace itself. This means that if the current fertility rate continues, the American population will shrink by roughly 15 percent per generation, in the absence of immigration. Geopolitical implications aside, a smaller population will all the more increase the per capita burden of servicing the national debt and of paying off all the other claims we are pushing into the future, such as the cost of promised public employee pensions and the unfunded retirement and health care benefits promised by private companies.

Bringing the fertility rate back up to replacement level is thus an option that should not be summarily dismissed. But it is by no means obvious what could be done to encourage Americans — particularly middle-class Americans — to have more children. Almost since the nation's founding, birthrates in the United States have been falling, as part of a long-term trend that has been occurring throughout the Western world (see figure 5–1). Writing in *Scientific American* during the late 1970s, the eminent demographer Charles F. Westoff once complained:

> Every time the birthrate records a new low, frequently in recent years, a demographer receives inquiries from journalists about what the trend can be attributed to: "the pill," abortion, sterilization, recession, the women's movement or some other *ad hoc* explanation. To ask what caused the latest decline, however, is to ask the wrong question. The birthrate has been coming down more or less steadily for the past two hundred years in this country — with the exception of one period. The real question, and the more perplexing one, is what caused that exception: the baby boom.[1]

Although many have tried, no demographer has ever succeeded in developing a theory that accounts both for the long-term decline of birthrates in the industrialized world and for the anomaly of the postwar baby boom in the United States. The long-term decline is frequently attributed to such disparate causes as the ebbing of religious authority, the increasing effectiveness of contraceptives, the universal education of both sexes, the declining "economic value" of children, and even the "ethos of consumerism" in industrial and postindustrial society. But none of these vague explanations stands up very well to the facts as we know them. For example, at the end of the nineteenth century, most Americans were still relying on the same methods of contraception as they had in the previous century — namely, abstinence, withdrawal, and abortion. Nevertheless, during the nineteenth century the birthrate among American women fell by half.

Moreover, all the trends thought to explain the long-term decline in birthrates seem also to have been in force during the period of the baby boom. Certainly the 1950s are not remembered as years lacking in consumerism. The movement from the

Figure 5–1. Annual Births per 1000 Women: 1810–1985

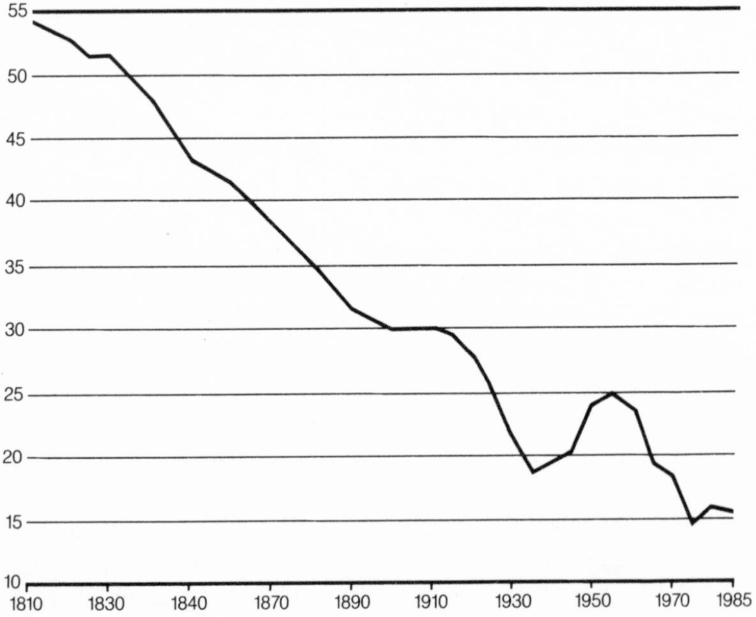

Source: *U.S. Census Bureau (1810 to 1910 data for white population only).*

farms to the cities was by then nearly complete; child labor had been abolished many decades before; the proportion of women with advanced education and paid work experience had never been higher.

One theory that attempts to reconcile all these seemingly contradictory trends has received a great deal of media attention in recent years. It is the idea, originally put forward by the economist Richard A. Easterlin, that the fertility rate is determined by how "well off" the young adults of any given period feel and that this in turn is determined by the size of their generation.[2]

The easier young adults find it to match their parents' standard of living, Easterlin claims, as part of what he calls the "relative income" thesis, the more children they will have. Easterlin then joins this "relative income" thesis with another, the "cohort size" thesis. The affluence of the young adults, he posits, depends on their numbers. Members of large generations face stiff competition for housing, jobs, and promotions; in an attempt to contain their downward mobility, they refrain from having children. Members of small birth cohorts face less competition; they therefore rapidly attain the standard of living enjoyed by their parents and feel that they can afford to raise large families.

Taken together, the relative income and the cohort size theses imply an endless series of boom and bust cycles in the fertility rate: large, poor generations will beget small, prosperous generations that will beget large, poor generations, and so on. If this theory is correct, we should expect the few children of baby boom parents to enjoy a comparatively high standard of living and to produce a baby boom of their own in the coming years.

Easterlin's theory has the virtue of at least being consistent with the trends in relative income and fertility rates during the last half-century. That it is inconsistent with the record of the nineteenth and early twentieth centuries Easterlin explains by pointing to the high rates of immigration that then prevailed. Even though the fertility rate kept falling, the numbers of immigrants kept swelling the size of each new generation. Therefore no generation enjoyed the putative advantage of being smaller than the one that came before, and so the conditions necessary for a baby boom, under this theory, were never realized.

While intuitively appealing, Easterlin's theory is beset by two overwhelming criticisms, one theoretical and the other empirical. The theoretical problem comes from supposing that the size of a cohort alone determines its economic destiny. This is the sort of claim that holds true only if all other things are equal, as they almost never are. As we saw in chapter 2, there is no reason why a large new generation must be a downwardly mobile one. The arrival of the baby boomers in the work force did cause the ratio of capital to labor to shrink, and this, most economists agree, reduced the earning power of all Americans, especially the baby boomers themselves. But it is a simple arithmetic truth that the ratio of capital to labor would not have shrunk had older Americans previously saved more and borrowed less, thereby making more capital available for productive investment. The fact that the United States has a lower savings rate than any of its major trading partners goes as far toward explaining the downward mobility of the baby boomers as does the sheer size of the generation alone. Similarly, there is no reason to believe that members of the subsequent baby bust generation will inevitably prosper because of their small numbers, so long as we are running massive deficits and otherwise borrowing against their future earnings. Indeed, their relatively small numbers may work against them throughout their lives, as politicians look to the interests of birth cohorts that command more votes.

The other problem with Easterlin's theory is that it simply fails empirical tests. The relative income thesis suggests that within any given cohort, those whose standard of living is highest compared with that of their parents' will have substantially more children than will their less fortunate contemporaries. Yet as Christopher Jencks documented in a devastating critique of Easterlin's work, all the evidence — and it is voluminous, comprising longitudinal studies going back for half a century — shows this proposition simply to be false. In the most thorough of these studies, a 25 percent increase or decrease in relative income was shown to affect the birthrate up or down by just 0.05 percent. On this evidence, Jencks concludes, "declining relative income accounts for about one percent of the decline in fertility over the past generation."[3]

Certainly, questions of "affordability" enter the minds of most young couples when they decide on the number of children they will bring into the world. In a 1983 study published by the Urban Institute, Thomas Espenshade calculated that a typical, middle-income family, with two children, a husband who works full-time, and a wife who works part-time, will spend $82,400 in 1981 dollars to rear each child to age eighteen. That figure rises to around $100,000 when such families send their children to a four-year public university or college. The proportion of family income committed to children varies little, Espenshade found, among families of different socioeconomic classes. Rather, the measure of sacrifice is determined for the most part according to the number of children in the household. Families with one child can expect to commit about 30 percent of total family expenditures to their child's consumption; in families with two children, the proportion (for both children combined) rises to between 40 and 45 percent; and in three-child families, nearly 50 percent of total family spending is for the children.[4]

Given the tremendous cost of having children, one might expect the rich to have the largest families. We are faced with the seeming paradox, however, that *within* any generation it is generally among the very poor that birthrates are highest. Further adding to the mystery, at least since the 1960s fertility rates have tended to rise temporarily during periods of recession.

One possible explanation for this puzzling situation, which would seem to apply straightforwardly to many middle-class couples within the baby boom generation, involves the enormous opportunity cost of a working wife's "taking time off" to have a baby, especially when she is in the midst of pursuing a professional career. The thesis here is that women who can earn higher wages in the labor market will have fewer children, other things being equal, because they have to sacrifice more income if they opt to become mothers. As it turns out, this thesis, which has been developed by William Butz and Michael Ward, among others, is highly consistent with the relevant trends of the post-war period and may indeed go a long way toward explaining the entire phenomenon of the baby boom and the subsequent bust.

Figure 5–2 is an updated version of a chart that originally appeared in a 1982 study published by the Rand Corporation, a highly respected public policy research institute.[5] The study's four authors offer an intriguing interpretation of the remarkable set of trends shown in the chart. During the late 1940s and during the 1950s, the percentage of working wives was extremely low. This is what explains, the authors theorize, why fertility rates in those days tended to follow the business cycle. When times were good — and they were very good throughout most of this era — couples felt that they could afford more children and still have the other luxuries they desired; since the wife typically did not work outside the home in the first place, this decision involved no loss of family income. Conversely, when times were bad, couples reacted by putting off having children. Notice that the mild recession of 1954 was accompanied by a brief slowdown in the fertility rate.

During the boom of the 1960s, however, the continuing rise in real wages at last began to attract more and more young wives into the work place, the authors posit. Another possible factor behind this phenomenon, which the authors do not discuss, was that beginning at the same time, the incomes of young men, while rising in absolute terms, had already started to slip relative to the incomes of middle-aged men, as part of a long, steep, downward trend that continues to this day. Thus, a young wife's joining the work force became more and more important to keeping her family's standard of living up to the level set by older Americans.

In any event, the crucial point is that for such young wives,

Figure 5–2. Trends in Fertility, Income, and Female Labor Force Participation Rates

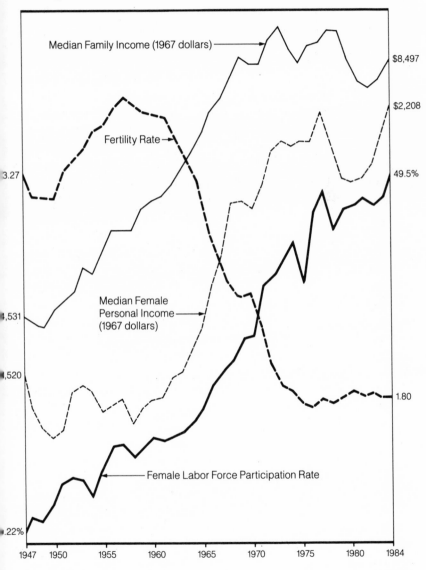

Source: *Rand Corporation; Census Bureau*

and for their husbands as well, there suddenly existed an enormous opportunity cost of having children. Notice that the fertility rate peaked at 3.8 children per woman in 1957 just as both the average working woman's hourly wage and the proportion of women employed began to turn sharply upward.

From 1958 onwards, fertility rates no longer rose with the business cycle; instead they fell. Conversely, when times were bad, as during the recessions of 1970 and 1974 and again during the prolonged recession of 1979–83, fertility rates rose, or at least stopped declining. Under their theory, the authors of the study have a ready explanation for this seeming paradox. As recession reduces the employment opportunities and real wages that women can earn in the work place, so it reduces the opportunity cost of their staying home to raise a family. Conversely, when real wages for women are rising, so too is the real cost of having children.

One may object that cultural influences, such as the force of the women's movement, the widespread fear of nuclear war, and the effects of overpopulation, may have played a greater role than shrewd financial calculation in depressing the fertility rate. Similarly, the simple availability of the pill, which first came on the market in June 1960, may have played a large role, if only in allowing women to pursue more effectively what they took to be their real emotional as well as financial self-interest. Like all theories purporting to explain human behavior on the basis of "rational expectations," this one does not prove that the skew of incentives alone produced the phenomenon. But the existence of such strong incentives not to reproduce, which are only growing stronger in our own time, should give us pause. If the relationships documented in the study hold true over the next several decades, as they appear to have since the early 1960s, they will present a no-win situation for the financing of Social Security and other old age entitlement programs. For the study presents strong evidence that the two trends upon which these systems most depend — rising wages and rising fertility — may be mutually exclusive, so long as few barriers exist to exclude women from the work place.

Implications for Family Policy

I will take it as a given that most Americans remain committed to the ideal of equal pay for equal work and opposed to all forms of discrimination against women. A just society must offer women the same chance as men to pursue careers and develop their talents. Nonetheless, providing women equal opportunity in the work place, to the extent that it actually contributes to the aging of the population, forces other sorts of equity issues that we cannot afford to ignore.

As we have seen, under Social Security, Medicare, and other programs for the elderly, each generation as a whole eventually becomes entitled to a large share of the next generation's wealth. This means that collectively each generation has a powerful interest in raising up large numbers of preferably prosperous children. But the sacrifice required to obtain that end is not equitably divided within each generation, and particularly not within the baby boom generation.

Parents in our society remain individually liable for most of the cost of raising children, with young mothers today paying an exceptionally high price in the form of interrupted careers and forgone wages. Yet the eventual economic reward that comes from this sacrifice is, by law, divided among all members of one's generation—in the form of across-the-board old age subsidies. This creates a classic free-rider problem. An individual's support in old age does not depend on his or her having made any personal sacrifice to raise up the next generation; it depends solely on others' having made the effort. The obvious incentive is to remain childless and let other people's children pay for one's old age.

This strongly implies that parents should be compensated for the sacrifice they make in the interest of their entire generation's prospects for retirement. The cost of this sacrifice has never been higher for individuals, nor the collective return greater. The higher the earning potential available to both sexes, the greater the opportunity cost endured by couples who choose to have one partner stay home to raise children. The fewer children there are, the greater the value of each one to all who will eventually rely upon them for support in old age.

Nearly every American will find something offensive in the idea of in any way paying other people to have children. To conservatives, subsidizing child care is subsidizing feminism; providing day care centers, maternity leaves, and other forms of relief to mothers, they claim, merely encourages women to abandon their traditional role in the home, while also enlarging the state and the power of professionals. Feminists, on the other hand, tend to resist any assertion of pronatalism in family policy, arguing that the state must instead seek to change the cultural expectation that women's primary role is to raise children. Racial and class antagonisms are also engaged. Through the welfare system, the state already directly subsidizes poor mothers; to liberals, this approach shores up the family as an institution, to conservatives it serves to destroy the family, leading to more unwed mothers, divorce, and an intractable "culture of poverty."

Yet wrangle as we will, the fact remains that one way or another we will all pay for the decline in the birthrate. Perhaps the government could never afford to compensate young couples enough to induce a significant number to forgo the careers now available to them and to raise children instead. For despite the yuppie stereotype, most of today's young wives, like their husbands, are not working for "pin money," or even for "self-fulfillment." They work because they must. The young middle class is beset with downward mobility. With two paychecks, the typical baby boomer couple can afford to buy a house; but if two paychecks are needed to carry the mortgage, they won't feel they can afford children, even if they wanted the house as a place in which to raise children.

Even the conservative approach of coercing women back into the home would not solve the problem. The withdrawal of women from the work force would at least temporarily raise male wages. But in the face of its low productivity growth and deficit in trade, American industry simply can no longer afford to pay the average male worker enough to support a wife and family. Aside from any nostalgia for the old sexual order one might have, the United States needs the labor women provide and will need it even more in the future, as the pool of working-aged Americans shrinks and more wealth must be sent abroad to pay back the nation's mounting foreign debts.

From these considerations I conclude that the essential challenge is to make it easier for working women also to be mothers. Dr. Benjamin Spock once observed, "It doesn't make sense to let mothers go to work making dresses in a factory or tapping typewriters in an office, and have them pay other people to do a poorer job of bringing up their children."[6] But now that most young men can no longer earn a family wage, most young wives must work. Moreover, even those who could afford not to work are not about to submit to the government's, Dr. Spock's, or any one else's telling them that they have no right to earn a living. Finally, an unprecedented number of young mothers are divorced or separated and in desperate need of child care if they are to stay off welfare. There is no point in laying blame or scoring ideological points. Instead, we should accept the reality for what it is and look to the future. The United States needs more children, and if they are to become productive citizens upon whom we can rely in old age, they cannot be allowed to grow up alone at home watching television. The debate over family policy is largely a debate over false choices. The only truly relevant question is, who is going to pay for providing working women with maternity leaves and decent child care?

Requiring employers to absorb the cost is self-defeating, because the more child care benefits they might be made to offer, the more incentive they will have not to hire women with children or even women of childbearing age. Instead, the cost should be carried by those who will depend on the next generation but who choose or are forced to remain childless. One way this might be accomplished—with particular symbolic effect—would be to require childless workers, or at least middle-class childless workers, to pay a surcharge on their Social Security taxes. The purpose would not be to condemn these workers for their infertility or choice of life style but only to make them pay their fair share of the cost of keeping old age entitlement programs solvent over their lifetimes. If and when fertility rates reached replacement levels, the surcharge could be repealed.

A universal entitlement to child care would not breed dependency among the poor. Indeed, the lack of affordable child care services is a major incentive for the working poor to go on welfare. Again and again, attempts to reform the welfare system have foundered on the problem of how to train and provide jobs for poor mothers, who cannot possibly earn enough money to have others care for their children while they are away from home.[7] Adequate provision for child care might induce more poor women to become pregnant, just as it might raise the fertility rate of middle-class women as well. We should welcome both trends. If members of the middle class expect to be subsidized in old age through Social Security and other programs, they will have to be prepared to pay much more in the meantime for educating the children of the poor and providing them with marketable job skills. This imperative will become all the greater as long as the middle class continues failing to reproduce itself.

The experience of other countries that have adopted pronatalist policies should lead us not to expect any great improvement in fertility rates even if child care subsidies are quite generous. The only measure that has proved to increase the fertility rate dramatically in developed countries is one that Americans will probably never be able to agree on, much less enforce: Rumania achieved a certain notoriety among population specialists by demonstrating the tremendous demographic impact of abortion. Rumania outlawed abortion in 1966, and within a year the birthrate more than doubled. In subsequent years, however, the fertility rate declined slowly, as illegal abortion and contraception were substituted for legal abortion.[8]

One radical measure, which has not yet been tried anywhere in the world, was proposed by the former premier of France, Michel Debré. He once drafted a bill providing for a "family vote," which would give parents an additional vote for each child under voting age.[9] This would perhaps be a more positive approach than the proposal, once floated by the *New Republic*, to disfranchise the population over age seventy.[10] In an aging population, the great danger is that the electorate will become more and more focused on the short term, for there will eventually be fewer and fewer voters who are parents of young children and more who are concerned with having the state provide either for their own aged parents or for themselves in retirement. In the absence of countervailing measures, the process of population aging may then subject democratic nations to a chain reaction ending in extinction. But before we adopt such extreme measures as rearranging voting rights, we ought at least to experiment with providing parents the same level of child care support that is offered by virtually all the developed countries of the world.

Beyond this, we must seek to change the cultural attitudes toward childbearing that grew out of the 1960s, when it seemed to many experts, as well as to ordinary Americans, that the baby boom would go on forever and that overpopulation was imminent. For the baby boomers themselves, the experience of overcrowding—first in school, later in the competition for housing and jobs—naturally has led to a constellation of values or a generational sensibility that discounts the importance of raising children. Cultural values are always playing catch-up with reality. We need to educate younger Americans on how the facts have changed. As Ben Wattenberg and Karl Zinsmeister have written, we must "call a moratorium on calling Yuppies 'selfish' [for choosing not to have children] until they understand that their private choices will have public effects which they may not like."[11]

The culture today instructs young couples that their decision to have children is no different in kind from their decision to purchase a new car, VCR, or other consumer item; to see the decision as a purely private transaction, which may or may not prove to be worth the money. Instead, the culture ought to recognize that the sacrifice that young couples, and especially young mothers, make in raising a family is vital to the nation's long-term interest, and reward them accordingly. Young parents deserve not just child care benefits but encouragement from their bosses and friends, emotional support, and a good measure of prestige.

Fertility remains the single most important determinant in the financing of Social Security and other old age benefits. Unless we are willing to take measures to increase fertility, we have no right to assume that it will automatically go up of its own accord. In 1974, after fertility rates had been falling for more than thirteen years, the Social Security system's actuaries at last dropped their assumed rate for the future to 1.9 births per woman. But three years later, when Jimmy Carter became president, they raised it again to 2.1, even though by then the actual rate had dropped to an all-time low of 1.77. At the time, Social Security was facing an acute financing crisis, which eventually resulted in Congress's passing the largest peacetime tax increase in U.S. history. By simply increasing the number of "assumed" children that would be around to support their parents in the next century, the actuaries automatically reduced the size of the pension fund's projected long-term deficit and for a long while stole the thunder from those calling for fundamental long-term reform. As one Carter administration official who was involved in the decision remembered: "We had to argue that the population would at least replace itself, that we could not stay below zero population growth for long."[12] But wishing it so won't make it so. If the government is going to stake the future of today's younger Americans on the assumption that the fertility rate will rise, then the government has an obligation to do more to help younger Americans raise families.

Immigration

After Social Security, there is no more acrimonious debate in this country than that raging over the new wave of immigration. Since the beginning of the 1970s, roughly a fifth of all population growth in the United States has been the result of legal immigration, with an average of about 400,000 foreigners lawfully taking up residence each year.[13] No one knows the precise number of illegal aliens annually entering the country, but estimates run from 500,000 to 1 million. At any one time, the total number of illegal aliens in the country may be as high as 12 million.[14]

Polls show that most native-born Americans are opposed to the new immigration and want the floodgates shut tight. Opposition is strongest among blacks and in general among those who have or who aspire to the sort of jobs most often taken by the new settlers. On the other side of the issue are large employers, especially in agriculture and the textile industry, who want the cheap labor that immigrants provide and who say that poor, native-born Americans prefer welfare to menial work. College-educated Americans, whose jobs are not usually threatened by immigrants and who often directly benefit from their services as maids, baby sitters, gardeners, and the like, also tend to support a liberal immigration policy.

But this alignment may soon change as Americans wake up to the consequences of belonging to an aging population. Currently, most Americans look forward to active, comfortable, prolonged retirement as much as they fear increased immigration. Yet, as the baby boomers pass beyond their childbearing years, more and more Americans are likely to ask how both outcomes are

interrelated. They may ask themselves whether increased immigration can save their Social Security, Medicare, and other
old age entitlements, and if so, whether they are willing to overcome their nativistic fears of becoming strangers in their own
land.

It is important to note at the outset that the issue here is not
whether immigration *at its current level* is in the long-term cultural or economic interest of the United States, or even whether
it will be sufficient to eliminate the deficits in Social Security
and other old age programs. The Social Security Administration's
"best-guess" projections for the system's future, presented in
chapter 3, already assume that today's volume of immigration
will continue indefinitely.[15] And, as we have seen, these projections show the system as a whole failing long before the passing
of the baby boom generation. Thus, we are talking about the
feasibility and the desirability of a very steep and enduring increase in immigration beyond current levels as a strategy for
funding the baby boomers' benefits.

Economists tend to divide into two camps when analyzing the
ramifications of increased immigration. One camp views immigrants and their effect on the economy in static terms: if there
are indeed jobs going unfilled, then adding new workers from
abroad with the appropriate skills will raise the level of production and with it everyone's standard of living. On the other hand,
most of these economists argue, in a slow-growing, mature economy, such as that of the United States, increased immigration
beyond current levels will inevitably aggravate the problem of
unemployment and push down wages. Provided with a swollen
labor force, employers will feel free to bash unions and cut wages.
Among workers, only those with jobs for which the new immigrants typically don't qualify, such as managers and professionals,
would benefit from increased immigration, in the form of lower
overall prices and more docile subordinates.[16]

This is the view to which most union leaders and many politicians subscribe. Colorado's Governor Richard Lamm is among

the most outspoken. "Our immigration policy is making us poorer, not richer," Lamm contends with typical bluntness. "Who needs additional people when we cannot employ our own citizens?"[17]

The other school of economists takes a more dynamic and positive view of immigration. These economists emphasize the ethos of hard work, thrift, and entrepreneurship that so many immigrants bring with them to this country. Tearing up roots and risking all in a new land is not for most of the world's citizens: wherever they come from, immigrants are likely to have been among the most resourceful and ambitious of their society. So it is, these economists argue, that the United States "skims the cream" of the Third World by pursuing a liberal immigration policy. This may be hard or even unfair to the rest of the world, but it is to the immediate benefit of the United States. When they arrive in this country, immigrants are willing to take risks, adapt, and sacrifice in ways most native-born Americans are too comfortable to try. From this point of view, new immigrants enrich the nation by increasing and improving the quality of its "human capital." Their presence may threaten the jobs of some Americans, but capitalism, after all, thrives on competition.

If both of these views seem to capture a piece of reality, that should not be surprising since both are probably true at different times and under different conditions. Talk to any California truck farmer, for example, and he will tell you he can't find native-born Americans willing to pick his crop for the wages he feels he is able to pay. Many Californians are descended from migrant workers who came from all over the country to work in the fields in the 1930s, but they won't do the work today, he will tell you, even if they are unemployed. But what if there were no army of legal and illegal immigrants to fill his fields? Would Americans stop eating fruit and vegetables before paying a higher price to cover the cost of higher wages for farm workers? Moreover, wouldn't the lack of low-cost labor provide agribusiness with a greater incentive to mechanize and to innovate with the many new biotechnologies? Obviously, any view of immigration will not hold true in all possible circumstances. Much depends on the condition of the economy, the age and educational background of the immigrants, and on just how many arrive.

But on one essential point all sides to this debate ought to be able to agree. Importing more workers requires that we form more capital, or else the ratio of labor to capital will fall and with it the average wage level. Even the most ardent supporters of further immigration must admit that all the new jobs and businesses that so many new immigrants feel driven to create require financing and that few immigrants arrive with the necessary capital. As we have already seen in analyzing the causes of the baby boomers' downward mobility, a large increase in population — whether caused by high fertility or high immigration — will eventually drive down wages unless it is matched by a commensurate increase in capital formation and productive investment.

The implications for Social Security are clear. Increased immigration might replenish the system's coffers but only if all Americans consume less, save more, and invest their assets productively. Otherwise, the growth of the labor force will increase unemployment, drive down wages, and depress the economy. The ratio of workers to retirees would improve. But with many of the workers unemployed or earning low wages, their contributions to the system would be nonexistent or small.

Thus, increased immigration hardly offers a "free-ride" solution to the problem of financing Social Security. In addition to increased capital formation, the arrival of new immigrants would require increased expenditures for education, for housing, for new water treatment facilities, for new roads and bridges, and for just about everything else, including welfare for the many who inevitably will not succeed. The same point applies if we arrest the relative aging of the population through higher fertility rates.

There is also the question of not just how many but what kind of immigrants would be required to eliminate the deficits in Social Security. As Michael Boskin has observed, because many immigrants, particularly those from South America, tend to have large families and low to moderate lifetime incomes and because Social Security promises the highest rate of return to just such households, increased immigration might actually compound Social Security's problems even in the relatively short term.[18]

Boskin also makes a moral point on this issue worth considering. It would also be unfair to the immigrants themselves, he reminds us, if they were forced to pay into a Social Security system that remains actuarially out of balance. This point applies equally to the issue, explored earlier, of whether the government ought to pursue pronatalist policies. To save Social Security for the baby boom generation solely by relying on increased fertility or immigration would be to compound the system's burden on future generations.

Finally, there is the all-important question that most thoughtful Americans prefer not to ask out loud: how might increased immigration affect America's values and political culture, which are, after all, the ultimate basis of the promises we make to one another under Social Security. In a nation in which virtually every citizen is an immigrant or descended from one, no subject is more difficult to broach.

Nevertheless, we need to bear in mind that, unless we succeed in increasing fertility among the native-born middle class at the same time, increased immigration could bring about social tensions of a kind we have never encountered before. For eventually it would leave us with a large, mostly white, native-born generation of senior citizens (the baby boomers) demanding support from a population of younger Americans composed in large measure of native-born blacks and Hispanics raised in poor families and of immigrants from the Third World. As David Hayes Bautista observes, such an outcome raises an "issue of social cohesion. Will this society of the future . . . be able to look at itself as a societal whole and be able to say, 'We are in this together: what happens to you affects me, either across ethnic boundaries or across generational boundaries'? Will there be a sense of wholeness in the society, or will the society be fragmented, divided into 'haves' and 'have-nots'? We must be concerned about the cohesiveness of society in the future."[19]

It is today's poor children who would face the greatest competition for jobs from a new wave of immigrants. Neither group would be likely to feel a great deal of sympathy for the disproportionately white older generation. It would hardly help for white senior citizens to explain to poor, younger blacks that they invited in all the foreigners with the aim of financing their own comfortable retirement on Social Security. Meanwhile, the new immigrants themselves, most of whom would hail from the Third World, would also be likely to perceive the ethnic gap between the generations. Moreover, many would have left their parents behind in the old country. Those who brought their parents along would still be likely to find them ineligible for Social Security and would for that reason resent the program. And inevitably, many of the new immigrants would have come to feel the sting of nativist slurs and prejudice, just as all previous immigrants have. The difference is that these immigrants would be expected to pay tribute, in the form of stiff Social Security taxes, to the very same class and clan with which they would most closely associate their oppression: namely, old, native-born whites.

The United States needs immigrants to keep its culture dynamic and to inject entrepreneurial energy into the economy. But there are limits to how many immigrants the nation can absorb without depressing wages or provoking social unrest. Increased immigration is thus a partial solution to the problems posed by an aging society, but it is not a panacea. Nor is increasing the fertility rate. Any increase in the fertility rate brings an attendant need to spend more on education and an attendant risk that we will succeed in convincing only the poor to have more children. If more poor children come into the world and we allow them to grow up to be poor adults, the ratio of dependents to workers will worsen in the next century and further erode the baby boomers' prospects for retirement.

Thus there are risks if we encourage population growth, and risks if we don't. Continuing with today's high rate of immigration and taking the pronatalist measures described earlier is, I believe, on balance the best course. But it requires that we also commit ourselves to spending more for education, while at the same time increasing the rate of saving and productive investment. We must find the discipline to save and invest more in raising the productivity of tomorrow's workers, whoever they turn out to be, or else increased fertility and immigration will only make things worse.

6

Consuming Visions:
Thrift and Productivity
in an Aging Society

DURING THE EARLY MONTHS of 1958, as the unemployment rate approached a new postwar high of 6.8 percent and business profits slumped, the Eisenhower administration found itself besieged from all quarters with demands that it take drastic action to avert the coming depression. President Dwight Eisenhower listened to the prophets of crisis and chose his course. He twice went before the public to urge that it was Americans' patriotic duty to save less and to Buy Now.

Advertisers across the country immediately seized upon this happy new presidential theme, launching hundreds of so-called confidence or prosperity drives to reinforce Ike's message to the consumer. An association of Cleveland auto dealers invented the clever YOUAUTOBUY slogan — later adopted by the whole industry — and were quickly rewarded by invitations to the White House and a favorable mention by Eisenhower at his weekly news conference. Businessmen in Boston offered POPS, or "Power of Positive Selling." Cleveland fathers elected a "Miss Prosperity" to reign over antirecession parades and street rallies.

In April, the *Wall Street Journal* reported that "a massive antirecession psychological offensive . . . is just getting under way in nearly every major city in the U.S. Already in existence are 'Operation Optimism,' 'Keep Detroit Dynamic,' 'Crusade for Confidence,' 'Buy and Be Happy' and 'O.K. Ike.' " Even the banks followed the siren call, abandoning their usual admonishments to thrift. "Ah gwan," the Bank of Saint Louis urged in a Sunday *Post Dispatch* ad, "buy that new car." Another bank in Saint Louis had a similar message for would-be savers: "This is the time for healthy spending." The recession, claimed the bank, was "just a state of mind. . . . In times such as these, excessive savings can be as harmful as excessive spending."[1]

Auto dealers in Essex County, New Jersey, according to the *Journal*, mounted a radio campaign to warn the public: "Buy Now. The Job You Save May Be Your Own." Elsewhere in New Jersey, a tire store, using the same "Buy, Buy, Buy" theme, added, "It's your patriotic duty."[2]

Out of such raw stuff was derived the great cultural concept of the 1950s: the idea of The Mass Consumption Society. For Eisenhower's faith in the power of positive selling was evidence of a powerful new bipartisan consensus in American economic thought—that, for better or for worse, the nation's future prosperity no longer depended much on individual savings, hard work, or entrepreneurship, but rather on the present population's propensity to consume.

In the 1870s, that most eminent Victorian and popular moralist, Samuel Smiles, became famous for his lively defense of the opposing notion—then the orthodoxy of the striving middle classes in both Europe and the United States. "It is the savings of the individual which compose the wealth—in other words, the well-being of every nation," Smiles asserted in his relentless volume, simply entitled *Thrift*. "On the other hand, it is the wastefulness of individuals which occasions the impoverishment of states. So it is that every thrifty person may be regarded as a public benefactor, and every thriftless person as a public enemy."[3] For Smiles, as for most Americans of his era, individual thrift was not only a virtue in itself; its widespread practice was considered a first requisite of civilization and nation building.

How did the ethos of thrift lose its grip on American culture and politics? Now that the United States has become an aging society, the question has a special urgency. As a larger and larger proportion of the human life span is spent in retirement, the individual need to save during one's working years has grown accordingly. Consider, for example, that in 1940 Americans at age twenty could expect to spend but 7 percent of their remaining life span in retirement; today that number has jumped to 23 percent, due primarily to increased life expectancy and the trend toward early retirement.[4]

At the same time, as the ratio of workers to retirees continues to fall, the economy as a whole requires greater amounts of savings in order to fund investments in productivity growth; if fewer workers are to provide for more retirees, their efficiency must improve proportionately. Moreover, the United States' declining balance of trade, record budget deficits, and increasing indebtedness to foreign investors issue an imperative for increased domestic savings beyond the need created by just the aging of the population. As it was in Smiles's day, but in contrast to the 1950s, the United States is once again compelled to undertake enormous investments in infrastructure, education, new factories, and research and development just because of the much greater efficiency of its principal trading partners. Because we now live in a global economy, it is not enough that today's children grow up to be much more efficient than the present work force; they must be at least as efficient at work as their counterparts abroad or the American standard of living will fall. Today's American steelworkers, for example, are the most productive in the nation's history and are also the highest paid. But because they work for the most part in obsolete mills, they are not nearly as efficient as steelworkers in Japan and Korea, and that pretty much is the whole dismal story.

But the culture has yet to adjust itself to these new realities.

As Fred Branfman has written, "Most of us cannot remember a time when America was not flush with prosperity. But only at our peril do we forget that this postwar prosperity was founded on an economic base built during a century of savings and relatively frugal investment by our grandparents and great-grandparents."5 Even as the United States has reverted to its nineteenth-century status as a net debtor nation, however, few Americans realize the role of their own personal finances in contributing to the nation's foreign indebtedness and industrial decline. Instead, we debate the size of the federal deficits, the money supply, the tilt of the tax code toward consumption or investment. But America's debt spiral is also bound up with what John Maynard Keynes liked to call "the habits of the community" — specifically, with the general demise of the thrift ethos over the generation.

Consider, for example, that between 1976 and 1986, the total amount of consumer debt more than tripled, to $664 billion. Together with the growth of mortgage indebtedness, the total amount owed by individual Americans is now over $2.8 trillion, which as of this writing is greater than the officially admitted national debt. In the first half of 1986, mortgage and consumer borrowing absorbed more than a third of all funds raised in the U.S. credit markets. The debts of the people, no less than those of the state, are depleting the supply and running up the cost of capital available for productive purposes.6

That even middle-class citizens now typically neglect to save enough to pay their own way through retirement or to be secure against a small reversal of fortune causes a clamor for "entitlements," which of course prompts in turn still more public borrowing. These trends argue for a fundamental change in our thinking about the respective roles of individual savings and consumption in our society. But these changes will not come easily.

Despite their "supply side" rhetoric, conservatives have, by and large, renounced their traditional role as defenders of the thrift ethos, celebrating instead the idea that the nation can borrow and spend its way to prosperity. But for liberals, especially, the question of how best to oppose this spendthrift policy poses tremendous difficulties. At the heart of the problem is liberalism's legacy, beginning with the New Deal, of promoting mass consumption as the principal engine of economic growth. Meanwhile, Madison Avenue and the ever expanding retail and consumer finance sectors of the economy continue to spend billions creating new appetites that tempt the average American deeper and deeper into debt.

Can an ethos of capital stewardship, of principled regard for the financial and economic interests of future generations be reconciled with the values of the prevailing culture of consumption? It is useful to recall that within the lifetime of people still alive today, the thrift ethos was a populist cause. While big government and big business may have corrupted the thrift ethos over the last generation, they have not extinguished it, nor succeeded, at least for very long, in making its values obsolete.

The Reign of the Stewards

The thrift movement, as it was called, reached its apex in this country, as well as in England, during the early 1920s. In many respects, its values and themes presaged those of the environmental movement of our own time but with a significant difference. The partisans of thrift abhorred waste and applauded conservation but extended their values to the arena of finance. It was an ethos directly inspired by the conduct of the Great War.

In 1920, the editors of the *Annals of the American Academy of Political and Social Science* devoted a special issue to the phenomenon of the thrift movement. In an introductory essay, economist Roy G. Blakey explained the essential philosophy of the cause and its origins in the home front experience of the war. "Many realized for the first time that it was a matter of life and death to thousands of soldiers and of civilians also, whether they wasted or whether they conserved food and fuel," Blakey observed. "We learned of our economic unity and interdependence as never before, we saw that the real army consisted not only of the men in uniform, but of the entire people who supported them. . . . Thrift was thus impressively shown to Americans in its true light," Blakey concluded. "Instead of suggesting stinginess, it came to connote *proper use*, the use of means in such a way as to achieve the greatest results. It was closely associated with effectiveness, loyalty, patriotism, victory. It took a new place, an exalted place, its true place in popular estimation."[7]

The thrift movement of the 1920s was an odd fusion of many diverse interests and constituencies. Andrew Mellon was an outspoken apostle of the cause; so was Stuart Chase, that perennial weathervane of fashionable, liberal opinion, who in 1928 demonstrated his late support for the movement with a popular book entitled *The Tragedy of Waste*. "We are deluged with things," Chase complained, "which we do not wear, which we lose, which go out of style, which disappear anyhow — fountain pens, jewelry, patent pencils, straw hats, mouthwashes, key rings, hair tonics, toothpastes — endless jiggers and doodads and contrivances. Here it seems, the advertiser plays on the essential monkey within us — grabbing for a rose only to pick it to pieces, petal by petal."[8]

Professional social workers of the era, as well as many partisans of the labor movement, also promoted the ideal of thrift, or its variant "wise spending," convinced that it was the surest device for enabling members of the working class to help themselves. Samuel Crowther, in his 1920 book *Why Men Strike*, argued that universal thrift would "not only destroy the budding idea of the proletariat, but also provide ever increasing facilities for higher production at higher wages." Crowther's argument was psychological, as well as economic: "The result of starting to save," he observed, "takes the feeling of property — of proprietorship — into the work, and transforms the man from a mere industrial parasite into a sturdy member of society."[9] In his popular *Book of Thrift*, T. D. MacGregor cast the movement in even more populist terms. "We the everyday men and women are the back-bone of this country," MacGregor wrote. "Let us economize! Let us save! Let us do our share in making this country the great financial power of the world! Our millions of workers can do this, not the capitalists!"[10]

Between 1912 and 1924, the amount of money deposited in savings banks increased more than two and a half times, according to a contemporary survey by the American Bankers Association; the annual per capita savings rate nearly doubled, from $89 to $186.[11] While much of this new capital formation was attributed at the time to the unprecedented publicity campaigns and aggressive marketing strategies waged by the nation's banks and insurance companies, as well as to the general rise of wages over inflation, it was also commonly accepted that the new impulse to save was inspired in large part by a genuine populist movement—a new ethos of self-help, conservation, and stewardship.

Capitalist Counterpunch

Why did the thrift movement fade? Given the threat the cause posed to the immediate interests of mass merchandisers, it is not surprising to find that the initial assaults came from capitalist quarters—principally from retailers, who found it increasingly difficult to unload their more impractical wares. In 1921, a business group calling itself the National Prosperity Bureau sprang into existence, dedicated to the promotion of easy spending. As reported by the *Nation*, the organization began "ladling cold water on the preachments of 'Thrift Week.' . . . The National Prosperity Bureau . . . is getting up at four o'clock these cold winter mornings to plaster our shop windows with posters of a figure of Uncle Sam sitting at the throttle of a locomotive. Surrounding him is the inscription: 'Full speed ahead! Clear the track for prosperity! Buy what you need now!' "[12]

The idea that informed this campaign crudely predicted the

course of mainstream economic thinking in the next decade and well into the 1970s—the idea of growth through mass consumption. In one of its leaflets, the National Prosperity Bureau argued that "the mere word 'thrift,' variously defined by thrift exponents to meet their respective objects, means in practice, if it means anything, to buy less. How can buying less open up closed mills and halt failures? We are opposed to any sort of thrift which leads to industrial stagnation."[13]

Within a few short years, writing in the *Atlantic Monthly*, William T. Foster, a former president of Reed College, and a businessman named Waddill Catchings, gave new intellectual respectability to the idea that the nation's prosperity now depended on less saving and more spending. The two men were properly impressed with the heights of production achieved during the Great War. The achievement proved, they argued, that the U.S. economy did not suffer from any lack of real industrial capacity. The implication seemed obvious:

> Since, therefore, the final end of all economic activity is consumption, and since it is always possible to produce far more than we consume, consumption regulates production. There is no use building more wooden ships, when hundreds are lying idle at the wharves; no use running all our spindles, when it is impossible to sell the cloth we have already made. Too commonplace to mention, this fact may seem; yet it is the basic fact in the whole economic problem. . . . Sustained business-depression accompanied by adequate consumer demand is no more possible than drought accompanied by heavy rains.[14]

By clear implication, the consumer was a hero, under this analysis, while the saver enriched himself at the expense of the common good.

While this formulation was widely and vigorously condemned as heresy at the time, it would soon enough become a point of liberal orthodoxy, the first premise of New Deal economics and the postwar consumer society. Anyone who has endured freshman economics during the last thirty or so years has probably encountered the identical thesis in Paul A. Samuelson's all-time best-selling college textbook, *Economics*. In the 1955 edition of his book Samuelson instructed, *"High consumption and high investment . . . go hand in hand rather than competing. This surprising result is sometimes called the 'paradox of thrift.'"* Samuelson concluded: "What once was a social virtue may then become a social vice. What is true for the individual—that extra thriftiness means increased savings and wealth—may then become completely untrue for the community as a whole."[15]

The New Deal

During the Depression years, the thrift movement's emphasis on conservation of natural resources remained an important influence on mainstream liberalism. Its legacy can be seen in the many New Deal programs that addressed environmental concerns—the Civilian Conservation Corps, for example, and the numerous bureaucracies dedicated to the problems of soil erosion and forest management. But after the shock in 1929, many liberals swiftly repudiated the ideal of thrift in economics. Because the years after World War I had been marked by a rapid increase in personal savings, it was easy to believe that the thrift movement was at least in part the cause of the downturn. At an everyday level, one could see businesses closing for lack of customers, even as Americans struggled to save more and more out of fear of the future. And as long as the Depression continued, there would be few possible ways for businessmen to invest the nation's savings profitably. The only hope for prosperity, it thus seemed, was to promote the common man's ability and proclivity to buy. Industry, liberals came to believe, was largely overbuilt; its surplus could be disposed of only by fostering mass consumption.

Stuart Chase, as usual, was quick to catch on to the shift in the liberal paradigm. Having published only three years before a spirited book in defense of thrift, in 1931 he had almost completely reversed his position. "Presumably we build up capital, equipment, the means of a more extensive life, by forgoing the full expenditure of our present resources at any given moment," Chase allowed in a pamphlet entitled *Out of the Depression.* "But since we also propose to continue indefinitely, the question ultimately arises, For what are we accumulating? At what moment in our economic history do we propose to cash in and enjoy the triumph of our thrift?"[16]

The New Deal, as is often noted, was put forth in a spirit of pragmatic experimentation. Franklin D. Roosevelt was not committed to any particular new economic theory when he came to office; his intention, as he said early on, was to try everything and see what worked. Still, by the end of his first term, the idea that brought the most consistency to his record was the thesis of prosperity through mass consumption: that by incurring large deficits, encouraging organized labor, expanding relief, and otherwise seeking to provide the common man with security from want, the New Deal was dedicated first and foremost to stimulating mass consumption as a means to recovery.

It would be many years before most ordinary Americans took the clear implication of this principle to heart. Nevertheless, the idea that personal thrift was obsolete if not socially deviant was by no means confined only to liberal intellectuals. Francis Townsend, for example, in promoting his original senior power scheme to give every citizen over age sixty-five a guaranteed monthly check of $200 — funded by a 2 percent national sales tax — was quick to reassure younger citizens that his plan would benefit them as well. "Every person accepting this monthly pension," Townsend's proposal stipulated, "shall agree under oath to spend it within the boundaries of the U.S. within 30 days." This free spending by the old, he promised, would bring swift prosperity for all generations. His movement nearly succeeded but was preempted by the passage of the Social Security Act in 1935.[17]

The Hard Sell

The period between the world wars also brought many changes outside the realm of ideas that served to erode the thrift ethos and to consolidate the modern American consumer society. It was during this period that the characteristic institutions of the consumer culture—the motion picture, the radio, the automobile, the weekly photo news magazine, installment buying, the five-day work week, and suburban living, to mention a few—assumed the central place that they still occupy in American life. As the social historian Richard Wightman Fox has written, "The Depression and the Second World War, far from undermining the consumer ethos, merely delayed for many the day of gratification."[18]

For most Americans, personal thrift remained a practical necessity during these years. Even when wages skyrocketed during World War II, there were few consumer items available, and the savings rate soared. But Americans were increasingly being exposed to the images if not the reality of high consumption. Before the 1920s, the principal mission of advertising, for example, had been to convince people to buy products they otherwise would have produced in the home. Housewives skilled in making their own soap, dressing their own meats, and baking from scratch, for instance, had to be convinced that it was more practical to pay cash to be free of such chores. The message was thus not so much to consume more, but to consume more efficiently.

By the 1920s, this situation had already begun to change dramatically. Not only had advertising become pervasive with the growth of mass circulation magazines and radio, but it increasingly sought to create new needs by appealing to the private fears and vanities of ordinary Americans. A classic example comes from Gerald Lambert, who had inherited a company that produced a lotion originally used as wound dressing. Until the early 1920s, sales were slow. But then Lambert and two copywriters hit upon the idea of promoting Listerine as "mouthwash." To do this, however, they first had to invent a disease for which Listerine became the cure. And so they created "halitosis" and set off to warn the public of its dangers. "Night after night," read a typical ad,

> she would peer questioning into her mirror, vainly seeking the reason.
> She was a beautiful girl and talented, too.
> Yet in the one pursuit that stands foremost in the mind of every girl and woman — marriage — she was a failure.
> Many men came and went in her life. She was often a bridesmaid and never a bride.[19]

In the advertising of the 1920s, the product itself came to figure less and less prominently as it was replaced by images of some ideal state of affairs, such as marital happiness or sex appeal, which its purchase was supposed to secure. In a 1928 advertisement for Drano, for example, the caption read, "Every waste-pipe faithfully flowing free . . . every day of the year." Beneath was a picture of a nude woman, towel draped over one shoulder, exposing back, shoulder, hip, and rump as she watched water swirl down the drain.[20] More important than the product's practicality was its association with a lifestyle of sensuality and leisure.

That same year, Edward Bernays, nephew of Sigmund Freud and the "father of public relations," further encouraged the advertising industry to use psychological manipulation rather than reason in persuading Americans to buy. "The group mind does not think in the strict sense of the word," Bernays wrote in his influential book, *Propaganda*. "In place of thought it has impulses, habits, emotions." To ensure that consumption kept pace with production, Bernays advised, admen would have to learn how to "make customers" through an understanding of the "structure, the personality, the prejudices, of a potentially universal public." The challenge thus became to make Americans view consumption alternatively as a form of self-expression or self-therapy.

Perhaps more than any other American businessman, Henry Ford, the father of mass production, realized that mass production's success depended on the promotion of mass consumption. A revealing anecdote has it that one year, Ford's advertising people brought him a new slogan that said: "Buy a Ford—save the difference." Although thrifty himself, Ford quickly changed that to: "Buy a Ford, SPEND the difference." The key to prosperity and to the success of his company, Ford believed, lay not in increased savings but in the working man's proclivity to turn his money over.[21]

The actual effectiveness of advertising in promoting the high-consumption ethos has been endlessly debated. Surely as important as the ads themselves was the growth of installment selling that began in this era. Although this idea had been tried occasionally before World War I, middle-class Americans had largely rejected offers to buy on time because they associated the practice with poverty. Unable to afford major purchases, the poor often paid weekly installments to a peddler, who both delivered the goods and personally collected the payments; the middle class took pride in paying cash. To break this association, merchants in the 1920s began calling consumer debt by another name, consumer credit, which connoted wealth and equity rather than misery and impoverishment. Installments were paid by mail, and the whole transaction was made to seem as businesslike as possible.[22]

The culture of consumption was also driven by the tremendous growth in forms of mediated experience apart from advertising. Radio dramas and especially movies exposed humble Americans to the proconsumption ethos of the rich and glamorous, raising expectations and inspiring imitation. The star system itself encouraged a retreat from the stolid, bourgeois commitment to work, thrift, and family. As the historian Larry May has observed, "A star—unlike the nineteenth century character actor—was a young person who experimented with a number of roles, identities and styles."[23] Personal identity thus came to be seen more

as a choice of lifestyle — of role-playing with different costumes
and trappings that could be instantly exchanged.

Finally, as more and more of what the average American knew
or thought he knew about the world came from sources outside
his own direct observation, his sense of self and of reality became
more malleable. Newsreels, as much as ads and Hollywood ex-
travaganzas, brought images of a fast-moving, dazzling sphere
where the banalities of thrift and other folk values rarely figured.
For most Americans, the "real world" thus came to seem always
to be someplace else. The desire to participate, however vicar-
iously, in this alluring world beyond direct experience led to
imitative consumption of highly symbolic commodities, such as
cigarettes, fast cars, cosmetics, fancy shoes, and jewelry. Consumption became an expression of community.

Mobilizing for Abundance

Unlike the situation in our own time, however, these trends in
the popular culture remained fully consistent with and were
reinforced by the drift of political and economic ideas among
elites. In 1936, the English economist John Maynard Keynes
published his monumental *General Theory of Employment, Money
and Interest*.[24] With its elegant algebraic equations, Keynes's
theory essentially advanced the analysis used a decade before by
the National Business Bureau and other commercial interests to
attack the short-lived thrift movement: excessive savings and
investment were causes of industrial depression, and a system
of mass production had to be matched by a system of mass consumption. Along with the New Deal liberals, Keynes went on
to argue that government must promote mass consumption by
incurring large deficits, sponsoring public works projects, and
generally redistributing income away from the rich and toward
those more likely to spend it. Keynes, of course, conceived the
need for such measures as temporary — at least in his more sober
moods. For boom periods, he prescribed that government raise

taxes and cut expenditures in order to forestall inflation. But throughout his career, he tended to de-emphasize this side of his theory, as did virtually all of his later disciples. As Robert Lekachman would write in the sixties, one of Keynes's significant "successes" was "the weakening of the identification between virtue and thrift."[25]

Keynes's period of greatest influence over American opinion makers would not come until the 1950s and 1960s. In the meantime, however, as the United States mobilized for World War II, liberal politicians and intellectuals were provided with powerful new arguments for discouraging thrift and promoting mass consumption. In a 1941 book entitled *Boom or Bust?* Blair Moody, a progressive U.S. senator from Michigan, repeated the lesson that most liberals were taking from that year's sudden recovery:

> If government spending on arms can make the factories whir, if the shortage of food abroad can reverse our whole scarcity farm plan, if the bookkeeping items that represent Uncle Sam's borrowing can increase profits and shove national income up the skylight, why cannot the factories and farms be made to whir by the spending of the people — people buying to increase their own standards of living with money they earn, in the aggregate, by producing those goods? . . . Now that we have a system of mass production, we must have mass consumption to sustain it.[26]

Starting in early 1943, a myriad of public and private study commissions as well as individual writers began issuing prescriptions along these lines, including, of course, Stuart Chase. "Building up our industrial plants over the past two hundred years, it has been inevitable that the producer should have first consideration," Chase said in an address given that May. "But now our plant is substantially built. After the war it looks as though it [will] be super-built. . . . Large sections of our magnificent new plant will just have to stand and rot, unless we develop methods to get its fabulous output into the hands of the people, unless we have mass consumption. The people as consumers, the public interest, should now come first."[27]

The home front experience of the First World War had inspired a widespread abhorrence of waste and an impulse to be thrifty in peacetime, but the country's leading liberal opinion makers drew the opposite lesson from World War II: the problem of production had been solved, and the nation's primary postwar challenge was to consume. In 1944, economist Robert Nathan, a rising star among the administration's brain trusters during the war, wrote in *Mobilizing for Abundance* that postwar prosperity would require fundamental changes not only in the role of government but also, and more profoundly, in the culture itself. "Paralleling the lesson that thrift is a virtue, we have also been taught that spending and indulgence in luxuries are undesirable and even immoral," Nathan observed. This, he allowed, presented a real problem for the new economics of mass consumption.

> In view of our long period of training in the importance of saving, it is not going to be easy to induce individuals to spend a larger share of their income without providing some other means of security to take the place of the more apparent than real security derived through individual saving. People find it hard to believe that if they spend more they will have more.[28]

For Nathan, as for many liberals of the era, this much served as an argument for expanding "social security," as the term was then used in its broadest sense. So long as the mass of Americans remained financially unprotected against the hazards of unemployment, illness or injury, and forced retirement, they would continue to put money away for a rainy day, rather than playing their prescribed role of "consumer." "Nobody is going to spend these accumulated savings if he does not know where next week's income is coming from," argued Social Security expert Eveline Burns in a 1943 address to the Institute on Post-War Reconstruction. But, said Burns, "if a man has a modest assured income, he may be inclined to spend some of these accumulated savings, as the economists hope he will spend them." So it was that the early advocates of Social Security promised that the program would decrease the savings rate and help stimulate mass consumption over investment.

The American Quarter-Century

"IT'S WONDERFUL," sang the headline in *Fortune* magazine. "When the history of the post war period was written," the magazine's editors predicted shortly after V-J Day, it would declare that "August 14, 1945, marked not only the war's end, but the beginning of the greatest peacetime industrial boom in the world's history."[29] There was nothing else, the magazine reported, of which Americans were currently more certain.

And the American people were right, in large measure because they were so certain. In 1946, successive strikes against the auto companies, Big Steel, the coal industry, and the railroads paralyzed the country, prolonging shortages of many consumer items for many months. Returning servicemen were beset by an acute housing crisis and worry over unemployment. Inflation punished everyone. But these dislocations could not hold back the mood of boundless optimism that was overtaking the country. It was a mood that produced not only the baby boom but an explosion in business investment to match the American consumer's sudden proclivity to borrow and spend without thought of a return to hard times.

Between 1946 and 1958 short-term consumer credit rose from $8.4 billion to almost $45 billion. The first credit card was issued in 1950, by Diner's Club; within fifteen years the company had more than 1 million members, as did American Express. What you thought of consumer credit and the proper way to use it depended in some degree on how old you were. Older Americans tended to uphold the old thrift ethos, but two-thirds of all younger families sprang at the opportunity to buy on time.[30] "In their desk drawer are several little books with twelve or sixteen or eighteen or more monthly payment coupons to fill out," wrote William H. Whyte, Jr., in his famous essay, "The Consumer in the New Suburbia." "But they do not worry, this is the normal estate in our economy, they know."[31]

In a very real way, Americans were indeed following Stuart Chase's advice to "cash in on the triumph of our thrift." Because of the shortages in consumer items during the war and the rise of both wages and profits, the banks were overflowing with capital and desperate to find new ways to lend it out. By the time of the Japanese surrender, individual savings had reached the enormous total of $140 billion, or more than four times the entire national income of 1932. Business liquid assets had more than tripled during the war, to an estimated $75 billion.[32]

Among other things, then, World War II had been the greatest forced savings plan ever devised. It raised enough capital not only to underwrite the postwar consumption boom with cheap loans and mortgages, but also to underwrite massive investments in new factories, schools, research and development, as well as grand-scale public works projects, such as the interstate highway system and the Saint Lawrence Seaway. While a chorus of critics condemned the United States as a consumer society in the 1950s, it was still at that time very much an investment society as well. Between 1946 and 1958, industrialists invested an average of $10 billion a year in new plant and equipment — three times the pace of the Roaring Twenties. As a result, output per man-hour soared by 35 percent, making American workers far and away the most efficient in the world. The public sector was also investing massively in the future. In 1956 alone, the federal government spent more on highways than the entire gross national product of Norway.[33]

There were many reasons to believe that the boom in both consumption and investment would continue forever. By the early fifties, the Keynesian notion that aggregate demand regulated investment was firmly in place and seemed validated by recent experience. Accordingly, many economists were convinced that the phenomenon of the baby boom by itself would provide for long-lasting prosperity. As that generation's members grew older, they would create an ever expanding consumer market, which in turn would automatically call forth new capital investment as new profit opportunities became available. The headline for a 1958 *Life* magazine cover story on the baby boom declared: "KIDS: BUILT-IN RECESSION CURE — HOW 4,000,000 A YEAR MAKE MILLIONS IN BUSINESS." In its first year, *Life* calculated, a baby is not just a child but an already prodigious consumer, "a potential market for $800 worth of products." The baby boomers, the magazine concluded, represented "a backlog of business orders that will take two decades to fill."[34]

Conversely, it occurred to many economists, Samuelson prominent among them, that because of the baby boom, the burden of the compounding national debt, as well as the eventual cost of Social Security and other old age benefits for their own generation, would be spread across a greatly expanded younger population. So there did not seem to be much need to promote increased individual saving for retirement, nor to feel inhibited, in the arena of public finance, about borrowing against future production to fund the welfare state.

"In dispassionately analyzing the growth of the [national] debt, one error we must avoid," Samuelson wrote in the 1955 edition of his textbook.

> *We must not forget that the real national product of the United States is an ever-growing thing.* Population increase has slowed down but little, and for a long time our numbers will continue to grow. . . . What seemed like a big debt in 1790 would be nothing today. What our children will come to regard as a big debt, our great-grandchildren may consider relatively unimportant.[35]

Finally, after World War II there was the obvious observation that the United States had become the most powerful nation on earth. Although there was much anxiety about the Communists, few people seriously doubted for long that the country would succeed in at least containing the threat. Accordingly, the nation's existing industrial base and technological superiority seemed secure, for just so long as it would take the rest of the world to recover from near total economic ruin. In the end, the hopes for an American Century proved exaggerated, of course. But for a long while, the country could reasonably expect to dominate its trading partners without any special effort.

Changing Values

How then did the last generation go wrong in disparaging thrift? One lesson we can take from its experience is to appreciate more fully the fragile relationship between our cultural values and the way we manage and manipulate the economy. Without consumption, production is obviously purposeless as well as unprofitable. And for a long period, roughly between the mid-1920s and the mid-1960s, consumption had to increase to keep even with the expanding productive capacity of the economy. But the systematic promotion of consumption by both business and government over the period led to an erosion of the traditional American values of work, thrift, and self-reliance that created the conditions for mass affluence in the first place. For a while, we could afford to become somewhat more self-indulgent as a people. Today, the ever increasing sense of entitlement present even in our middle class has become wholly out of balance with the actual productive potential of the economy.

This raises a hard question. We all, I'm sure, feel the tension between our roles as producers and consumers. Capitalism requires, on the one hand, that the mass of citizens be thrifty, hard working, and willing to defer immediate gratification in order to build up and finance new production. But on the other hand, the system sometimes requires—particularly during periods of recession, when profitable investment opportunities decline—

that we save less and consume more, for otherwise there will be no market for new enterprise. In pursuit of that end, both business and government can easily wind up encouraging habits of high consumption and self-indulgence that are inimical to the requirements of production and, indeed, to the long-term interests of the society itself.

As Daniel Bell has noted,

> By the 1950s, the pattern of achievement remained, but it had been redefined to emphasize status and taste. The culture was no longer concerned with how to work and achieve, but with how to spend and enjoy. Despite some continuing use of the language of the Protestant ethic, the fact was that by the 1950s American culture had become primarily hedonistic, concerned with play, fun, display, and pleasure — and, typical of things in America, in a compulsive way.[36]

After the war, just as Robert Nathan predicted, the more Americans spent, the more they had to spend, and they adjusted their values accordingly, some becoming beatniks and hippies, many becoming committed to the pursuit of leisure and early retirement. David Riesman, whose commentaries on the Zeitgeist of the 1950s were and still are widely appreciated, was among the first to proclaim that American culture had been fundamentally transformed by the perception of an imminent end to scarcity. "Whereas the explorers of the last century moved to the frontiers of production and opened fisheries, mines and mills," Riesman wrote in a 1952 essay, "the explorers of this century seem to me increasingly to be moving into the frontiers of consumption."[37]

By the mid-1960s, when the oldest members of the baby boom generation came of age, there remained few rules in the nation's mainstream culture that could serve as a check against hedonism and self-indulgence. Government policy since the end of the war had promoted a fantastic expansion in consumer installment buying and had punished savers through a variety of tax measures and banking regulations that diverted credit away from productive uses. The once thrifty and self-reliant middle class had instead become marked by an increasing collective sense of entitlement. The Wagner Act, Social Security, the GI Bill, VA and FHA mortgage guarantee programs, and other federal measures had made it possible for millions to achieve a middle-class income and lifestyle who otherwise would have remained on the farm or in the old neighborhood. But such policies did not foster — rather, they tended to erode — those familiar bourgeois values of thrift, initiative, and self-reliance that are so essential to the workings of capitalism.

Futures Trading

For students of the postwar era, one of the most perplexing riddles is how a generation of intellectuals who had experienced the shock and surprise of the Great Depression could later become so easily convinced that the nation had entered a new unbounded age of affluence. Predictably, this conviction that the economic problem had been essentially solved and that the next generation would need to be concerned only with questions of spirit eventually prompted many economists to offer new arguments directly opposed to the idea of investment and financial sacrifice on behalf of future generations, thus further eroding the thrift ethos. The debate began obscurely in the academic journals as part of a long-running technical dispute among economists over how to fix the precise "optimal" rate of savings and investment. In the 1960s a more specific question arose: By how much should social planners discount the interest of future generations in deciding whether and how much to invest in new infrastructure, such as dams and highways?

Economists argued endlessly over what they referred to as the "social discount rate," wielding against one another such arcana as alternative utility functions, mathematical axioms of cardinal welfare, and game theory matrices. But the real subject was how

to reckon the terms of the social contract between the generations. As James Tobin, in a 1966 essay, summarized the arguments of the already enormous literature, the underlying issue
was one "which has always intrigued and preoccupied economists: the present versus the future. How should society divide
its resources between current needs and pleasures, and those of
next year, next decade, next generation?"[38]

The debate was complicated by the presumption that in sacrificing for the future, no generation can expect to be repaid. As
Stephen Marglin posed the question: "Why do governments require citizens to sacrifice current consumption in order to undertake investments that will not yield their benefits until those
called upon to make the sacrifice are all dead?"[39]

The standard utilitarian reply, advanced by the so-called
growthmen, was that by forcing the present population to save
and invest at a high rate, future generations would enjoy a correspondingly higher standard of living, if only through the effect
of compounding interest. On the principle that social planners
should seek the greatest good for the greatest number over time,
it followed for the growthmen that every generation should maximize its savings for the future. Alternatively, Marglin and some
welfare economists, such as A. K. Sen, arrived at the same conclusion by arguing that long-term public investments were in the
nature of a public good—that we each desire individually to
provide prosperity for our children but that only by acting collectively can we achieve such an end.[40]

As the economy continued to grow robustly throughout the
1960s, however, the terms of the debate subtly shifted in a revealing fashion. "The next generation is going to be richer than
we are," Gordon Tulluck first interjected in 1964—regardless,
he said, of whether the rate of investment increased. Tulluck
rejected the conventional wisdom, asserting that if the present
population were forced to save more in the future, this would
in effect "clearly tax the poor to help the rich."[41] In 1968 William
Baumol, an economist at Princeton, paraphrased Tullock's de-

scription of public investments, calling them a "Robin Hood activity stood on its head." Apparently convinced that future generations would enjoy ever greater affluence, Baumol wrote, "In our economy, by and large, the future can be left to take care of itself. There is no need to lower artificially the social rate of discount in order to increase further the prospective wealth of future generations."[42]

In reexamining the course of the social discount rate debate, one is struck by a certain irony. For it was precisely during the period in which mainstream economic opinion was shifting to the view that the present population was under little or no obligation to undertake new capital projects on behalf of future generations that much of the nation's existing infrastructure was being allowed to fall into disrepair.

The cost of the Vietnam War, the War on Poverty, plus the relentless rise of social spending for the middle class and particularly for the elderly during the late 1960s and throughout the 1970s forced severe cutbacks in government spending for public works, such as new highways, mass transit, and sewer systems. Between 1965 and 1980, total public capital expenditures declined by 30 percent, from $33.7 billion to less than $24 billion. Measured as a percentage of GNP, the nation's capital budget fell by more than 50 percent, according to estimates by the Council of State Planning Agencies.

These statistics betray not only a reluctance at all levels of government to undertake new projects, but also a lack of commitment to the maintenance of existing public works. According to separate studies by the Congressional Budget Office and Congress's Joint Economic Committee, from 1983 to 2000 the country will need to spend more than a trillion dollars to repair existing public infrastructure.[43] Other estimates put the number as high as $3 trillion.[44] What economists should have been asking themselves twenty years ago, it now seems clear, was not how much people should sacrifice to build new dams, highways, bridges, and the like, but rather whether they were under any obligation to maintain the improvements that had been conveyed to them by previous generations.

From the mid-1960s onward, American society more and more rewarded consumption at the expense of future growth, as people's appetites grew beyond the actual productive capacity of the economy. While tenured educators, social critics, and presidential advisors spoke incessantly of "the challenge of abundance" and "the miseries of affluence," fiscal policy followed Keynesian prescriptions for reversing depressions, although no depression existed.

Academic economists, for example, celebrated President John Kennedy's enlightened understanding of "the thrift paradox" after he intentionally ran up the projected deficit for the upcoming fiscal year 1964 budget. The measure, later championed and imitated on a much grander scale by President Ronald Reagan, stimulated the economy to dazzling new heights. But it also marked a dramatic transformation in our political culture: never again would we find the will as a nation to avoid deficit financing of our annual wants, whether in periods of growth or of recession. The actual constituency for thrift in government receded at that moment into a permanent minority.

President Lyndon Johnson's decision in 1966 to meet the mounting cost of the Vietnam War through borrowing rather than through increased taxation established the pattern. Even in wartime, Americans learned, there was no longer any need for thrift on the home front, no reason to save up victory bonds, to endure rationing, or indeed to make any sort of economic sacrifice. Instead the war brought compounding, deficit-financed affluence to those lucky enough to stay home.

From 1970 to 1984, the accumulated debt of the U.S. government, industry, and private households more than quadrupled from $1.6 trillion to $7.1 trillion. At the same time the real value of the nation's productive facilities—its steel mills, oil wells, auto factories, and other wealth- and job-producing enterprises—increased a mere 1.6 fold.[45] This provides a rough measure of our profligacy as a nation. For every dollar of new wealth Americans created over the period, they borrowed nearly three.

Thrift and Aging

As younger Americans seek to come to terms with the legacy of a spendthrift past, they will be unable to forget that the current generation in power did indeed succeed for a long while by promoting mass consumption and the good life over savings and investment. The memory of this achievement already serves to confuse our sense of financial stewardship toward the next generation, as well as our attitude toward today's senior citizens. For it is as if the terms of the historical contract between the generations have been rendered null and void by the nation's short experience with easy affluence.

Historically, the augmentation of capital has been central to the implicit contract between the generations. In most cultures, the practice has been for people to strive during their middle years to save up or hold on to some store of value, such as land or gold, for the eventual purpose of providing their children with a legacy. Their chances of being supported and respected in old age were thus much improved. A British folktale, for example, tells of a poor old man who was mocked by his sons until a friend, hearing of his plight, lent him a bag of coins for a day. The old man allowed his sons to discover him at the kitchen table counting what they took to be his secret treasure, and thereafter they all treated him with proper veneration until he died.

In an agrarian economy, such as that which prevailed in colonial New England, the old could often retain enormous power over their middle-aged children as long as they refrained from overplanting or overgrazing their farmland and waited until the last possible moment to convey its title. "Better it is thy children should seek to thee, than that thou shouldst stand to their courtesy" went the common advice to the aged. As the social historian David Hackett Fischer has observed, in colonial New England

"land was an instrument of generational politics — a way of preserving both the power and the authority of the elderly. Sons were bound to their fathers by ties of economic dependency; youth was the hostage of age."[46]

With industrialization, however, the balance of power between the generations shifted. Factory workers could start young and achieve a tolerable standard of living without first inheriting an estate from their parents. But by the same token, having gained this freedom, most could not save enough out of their wages to provide for their own turn at being old.

In our own time, the remedy for this problem has been to allow each passing generation to tax its children through such programs as Social Security and Medicare. Because these programs are not capitalized, it may seem that the contract between the generations has been fundamentally altered: each generation appears simply to appropriate by its own laws some share of the next generation's wealth, without providing any compensation.

Yet as we have seen, the long-term solvency of these programs depends on robust economic growth. And barring extraordinary good luck, like the kind that the last generation enjoyed, the only way to bring about such compounding prosperity for our children is to build up capital and invest it wisely. In effect, then, the terms of the social contract remain the same. Each generation, in exchange for support in old age, still must provide its children with a legacy. All that has changed is that the necessary sacrifice falls not just to the individual but to the whole of his generation.

Visions of the Future

The word *thrift* connotes stinginess and hoarding; yet true thrift is the opposite of this. Its real meaning is wise spending — spending that creates greater wealth in the future.

Thus, increasing the savings rate alone would not be sufficient to prepay the costs of the baby boom generation's retirement

nor to arrest the nation's industrial decline. If the resulting pool
of capital is used for underwriting consumer credit, trading in
existing real estate, financing unproductive corporate takeovers,
and the like, rather than for investments that actually increase
the efficiency of the next generation of workers, it will bring no
real return for the next generation of senior citizens. We tend
to forget that money in the bank is not the same thing as riches.
Henry George once illustrated the difference with the example
of a "luxurious idler" who presupposed that he was living off the
legacy of his long-dead father but who in fact lived off the current
labor of those around him.

> On his table are new-laid eggs, butter churned but a few days
> before, milk which the cow gave this morning, fish which twenty-
> four hours ago were swimming in the sea, meat which the butcher
> boy has just brought in time to be cooked, vegetables fresh from
> the garden, and fruit from the orchard—in short, hardly anything
> that has not recently left the hand of the productive laborer. . . .
> What this man inherited from his father, and on which he lives,
> is not actually wealth at all, but only the power of commanding
> wealth as others produce it. And it is from this contemporaneous
> production that his subsistence is drawn.[47]

The same will be true of the baby boomers in old age; no
matter how large their individual bank accounts, their welfare
will ultimately depend on the day-to-day products and the productivity of younger workers. Thus, one obvious implication of
George's insight into the role of money is that the ethos of thrift
must extend not just to the formation of financial capital but also
to its deployment. Certainly it is preferable to approach the end
of life with large savings; there is no more certain way to secure
the support of the young than to be able to trade them dollars
for their labor. But if there are too few workers, or if those
workers are unskilled or lack the tools they need to produce
efficiently, then the savings of the elderly will buy little more
than inflation.

Another implication of George's insight is that any reduction in spending that reduces the rate of productivity in the future, or that adds to recurring expenses, is a form of false thrift. When, for example, the federal government seeks to reduce its budget deficits with cuts in spending for education, toxic waste cleanup, and research and development, the effect is to push costs on to the next generation of workers, upon whom we will ultimately depend regardless of whether we have "saved up" for the cost of our retirement. Such cuts are thus the opposite of true thrift. The next generation may gain by having to pay less interest on the national debt. But that is small compensation for being left without the skills necessary to compete in tomorrow's world economy or for being forced to live in a degraded environment. True thrift opposes borrowing that serves only to underwrite current consumption, not that which increases the general welfare in the future.

Indeed, the ideal of thrift, properly understood, suggests that we ought to be spending much more in many budget categories. More than one out of seven adult Americans, for instance, is functionally illiterate. To free these Americans from their handicap would require annual appropriations of around $10 billion. Yet in the long run, such appropriations would be a form of savings, with a return perhaps as much as twentyfold. The direct cost that illiterates impose on the economy, in the form of welfare payments, prison maintenance, and unemployment insurance, is about $20 billion annually; counting the opportunity cost in lost wages, the price of neglecting the undereducated is estimated to be as high as $200 billion a year.[48]

In saving for the future, then, human capital formation is as important as if not more important than investment in hard assets. Take wealth in some of its most useful and permanent forms — ships, dams, factories, houses. Unless constantly tended to by a skilled work force, these kinds of wealth become almost immediately useless and in any event obsolete before long. Indeed, there is virtually no form of wealth that can actually be conveyed from one generation to the next if the skills to use and maintain it are not conveyed as well.

We should also remember that, in macroeconomic terms, the nation's future would be equally well served by a drop in consumer borrowing as by a commensurate increase in personal savings. Either way, the pool of capital available for raising the productivity of the next generation expands. This means, for example, that the baby boomers might adhere to a regime of thrift in preparing for their retirement and still maintain very nearly the same rate of consumption as today; the sacrifice would come in paying for that consumption with cash rather than financing it with credit cards and other forms of unproductive borrowing. The reward would come, as George puts it, in being able to command some share of the next generation's wealth as they produce it and in having that wealth be larger than it otherwise would be.

In the end, the proper rate of savings is determined not by utility functions nor by statistical comparisons with the past, but by the real needs of the next generation, upon whom we will depend in old age. It is not necessary or even desirable that we become a nation of stern Victorians. But we do need to weigh our present appetites in the balance against predictable challenges to the American standard of living in the next century — primarily, the cost of supporting the baby boomers in retirement and of keeping up with the nation's trading partners' rapid gains in technology and efficiency. We can no longer count on mass consumption as an engine of growth, so long as what we consume is more likely to be produced abroad than at home and is more likely to be purchased on credit than with cash. Today the values of the postwar consumer society are as obsolete as its apostles once proclaimed the ethos of thrift to be.

7

Backdoor Borrowing: Generational Equity and Budgetary Reform

THUS FAR in this book, we have surveyed many reasons why Americans must direct more of their available resources away from current consumption and toward investment in the future. Already, our failure to invest adequately in education and manufacturing has brought a diminished standard of living for most of today's younger Americans. Capital that could have gone for rebuilding American industry and maintaining the U.S. lead in high technology instead went for financing the sale and resale of existing houses at ever higher prices, for credit card purchases of imported goods, for underwriting the burgeoning national debt, and for other nonproductive purposes. In the future, the aging of the population will create an even greater imperative for increased investment, as fewer workers will be available to support a growing number of elderly. Unless these workers turn out to be many times more productive than members of today's labor force, not only will Social Security become unsustainable, but the elderly baby boomers will be increasingly threatened by the horrifying prospect of health care rationing.

Far from sacrificing to meet these predictable challenges to the American standard of living in the next century, however, we continue to borrow massively against the future earnings of today's children. The recurring federal budget deficits are the most straightforward example of how we are living beyond our means. But as I will show in this chapter, the recorded deficits capture only a fraction of the actual debts the government is charging to the future. In addition to building up enormous unfunded liabilities in the Social Security and Medicare programs, the government is borrowing in many other ways that do not show up as part of the admitted national debt. The two most egregious examples are found in the financing of federal employee pensions and in the government's promise that future taxpayers will "insure" participants in private pension plans against the loss of their benefits. Both constitute forms of borrowing through the backdoor, which, unless stopped, will encumber future taxpayers with trillions of dollars in public debt.

Federal Employee Pensions

In 1818, Congress established its first federal employee pension program — a means-tested plan for Revolutionary War veterans. Today, the federal government operates thirty-eight separate retirement programs for its different types of employees and their dependents. Most of these programs are very small, ranging from the pension accounts for former presidents and their widows to the obscure National Oceanic and Atmospheric Administration Corps retirement system. The majority of federal workers, however, are covered by one of two giant programs, the Civil Service Retirement System (CSRS) or the Military Retirement System (MRS). The CSRS covers more than 2.8 million current federal employees and provides $23 billion in annual benefits to 1.4 million former workers. The MRS covers about 2.1 million active Defense Department personnel and pays $15 billion annually in benefits to another 1.3 million retirees.

A great deal of acrimonious debate has taken place in recent years over the cost of these programs. Usually the argument is about whether the benefits promised to retired federal workers are too generous in comparison with those offered by the private sector. But although the issue of whether federal employees deserve their pensions generates strong feelings, the real significance of these programs is not their generosity per se but who is expected to pay for them. As Herman Leonard has written, "These systems pay out billions of dollars each year for services received long ago. . . . Meanwhile, we continue to promise current public employees that they, too, will receive pensions — and we continue to set aside little or no money to pay for them, preferring to rely on the taxes collected from later tax payers."[1]

Because federal employee pensions are woefully underfunded, they have become one of the major means whereby we subsidize current consumption by borrowing from the future. By promising federal employees generous pensions, we persuade them to work for lower salaries than they otherwise would. By failing to prefund the cost of their future benefits, we force future taxpayers to pay for the savings we thereby realize. In effect, we commit future taxpayers to pay not only for their own federal employees but for ours as well.

The numbers are staggering. Congress has recently passed legislation that will reduce military pensions for those who have not yet joined the services. Still, because those who are currently in uniform or retired are not affected, the MRS will continue to push enormous costs on to future taxpayers. The system has no reserves. Just to pay for the pensions of those it already covers, the next generation of taxpayers will have to pay more than $444.3 billion.[2] This liability is every bit as real as any other federal obligation. Yet because of the way the government keeps its books, this liability is not counted as part of the national debt or factored into each year's recorded budget deficits.

The liabilities of the CSRS pension fund are even larger: $537 billion as of September 1985.[3] If the federal government followed the practice of private pension plans by amortizing these liabilities over a forty-year period—that is, by prepaying them in yearly installments—the cost would come to roughly 85 percent of each year's payroll.[4]

The CSRS fund does contain some reserves, but not of the kind that are of any real value to future taxpayers. As with Social Security and Medicare, its so-called assets, totaling $127 billion in 1985, are in the form of Treasury notes for which future tax-payers will be liable, both for principal and interest. The only real offset to the system's long-term liabilities are the contributions of civil servants themselves, who pay 7 percent of their salaries to the CSRS retirement trust fund. But these contributions are not even sufficient to cover more than about 12 percent of the system's *current* costs, let alone to prefund its enormous future liabilities. Taken together, the unfunded liabilities of CSRS and MRS amount to a debt of $4,130 for every man, woman, and child living in the United States.

The same pattern is evident at all levels of government. Over 5,000 separate state and local pension plans now cover a total of about 12 million public employees. Estimates of their total unfunded liabilities are difficult to come by, since different jurisdictions use different accounting methods and assumptions. But a 1983 study by Frank Arnold gives some hint of the dimensions of the looming funding crisis. Arnold studied 144 state-run pension plans, as well as some local plans, including those of the nation's twenty largest cities. Using very optimistic assumptions about the future rates of return that these plans will earn on their investments (3 percentage points above inflation), he none-theless found them to be substantially underfunded. He projected that their liabilities for future benefits totaled $295 billion in 1978, while their reserves equaled only 45 percent of this amount, or $170 billion.[5]

Other studies suggest an even deeper amount of public employee pension debt. In a more recent study for the National Economic Research Bureau, Robert Inman estimated that the unfunded liabilities of just state and local teachers' pensions amounted to more than $400 billion in 1980. Inman noted that while the officially admitted national debt rose by just 10 percent during the 1970s — adjusted for inflation — the real, unfunded liabilities of teachers' pension plans rose by 250 percent.[6] These numbers put a cloud over the movement for educational reform. Before teachers' salaries can be substantially raised and high-quality candidates recruited to the profession, today's taxpayers will first have to retire the pension debts for yesterday's teachers, which have been conveyed to them by yesterday's voters.

Of course, it is unclear to what extent the public has ever understood how unfunded pension liabilities transfer wealth and opportunity from the future to the present. The growing unfunded liabilities of public employee pension systems constitute a "quiet" crisis, which is what makes it all the more dangerous.[7] The federal government, for example, can borrow virtually unlimited resources from the future by underfunding its pension programs, without Congress's needing to raise the debt ceiling or to admit to higher deficits. Moreover, this form of government borrowing, unlike the sale of bonds by the government, does not immediately crowd out private borrowers, raise interest rates, or in any other way tax the present; instead, all the pain comes in the future. Thus, there is even less of a constituency for holding down the growth of unfunded public employee pension liabilities than there is for holding down the overt, "official" budget deficits.

At the same time, the temptation to increase this form of borrowing is overwhelming. Given the hostility most voters feel toward "pointy-headed bureaucrats" and other public employees, one might expect politicians always to be making a show of resisting any increase in public employee pensions. Yet politicians depend on public employees to deliver services to their other constituents and thus have a keen interest in seeing that they are well compensated. For a mayor, nothing loses more votes than garbage or snow piling up on the street; potholes that don't get filled; teachers, firefighters, or police officers walking out on strike. For a congressman or senator, being on the wrong side of the federal bureaucracy can make it harder to help constituents cut through red tape, win grants, recover lost Social Security checks, gain refunds from the IRS, or remedy a thousand and one other complaints and needs. A president who attacks the federal bureaucracy with more than just words must fear that his initiatives and executive orders will be quietly ignored or subverted even more than they would be normally. Meanwhile, at every level of government, public employee unions make enormous contributions to candidates who win their favor. Further, with more than a quarter of the electorate employed by the public sector, public employee unions command voting blocs that no candidate can prudently ignore.

But elected officials can't afford to be generous with public employees if this means raising taxes. The optimal short-term solution is thus for politicians to offer public employees deferred compensation in the form of generous, unfunded pension benefits. Such promises keep everyone happy, at least in the short term. Public employees receive higher lifetime compensation without today's taxpayers' having to pay the cost up-front. Politicians stay in the good graces of the public employees upon whom they depend without even having to admit any increase in public borrowing. The only losers are future taxpayers.

As Alicia Munnell, an economist with the Federal Reserve Bank of Boston, has stated, public employee pensions are inherently liable to becoming mechanisms of intergenerational transfer. "While taxpayers immediately feel the effects of increased wages [paid to public employees], they may not be aware of increases in compensation provided through liberalization of pension benefits because of the deferred nature of retirement." Thus, Munnell concludes, "unless rigorous funding practices are employed, the burden of pension costs for current employees can easily be shifted from the current to future generations of taxpayers. Because future generations are rarely the relevant constituency of current public officeholders, the discipline of public accountability is undermined."[8]

Given this skew of incentives, it is hardly surprising to find that federal workers, while generally enjoying the same overall level of compensation as their counterparts in the private sector, typically have lower salaries and higher pensions. Indeed, it is precisely the highest paid government workers who tend to receive the highest share of their total compensation in the form of pension benefits.[9] In this case, the cost of providing such workers salaries competitive with those in the private sector would be the highest in the short term. Thus they are compensated, to an even greater extent than lower-level employees, with claims against future taxpayers.

Estimating the federal government's total employee pension liabilities is nearly impossible because no uniform accounting standard exists among the many different funds it operates. The best information available comes from an obscure Treasury Department publication known in some quarters of the government as the "Saltonstall report," which is named after the late Massachusetts congressman, Leverett Saltonstall, who pressed for its creation in the mid-1960s.[10] Saltonstall brought a strong New England thrift ethos to Congress, and he was accordingly appalled to find out that the government made virtually no effort to keep track of its long-term liabilities. But while he succeeded in getting the Treasury to collect and publish what each of the government's many pension funds claimed as assets and liabilities, he did not succeed in getting the administrators of these funds to agree on the definitions of these terms. Adding up their liabilities, as reported in the Saltonstall report, is thus like adding apples and oranges.

Each program, for example, assumes different interest rates in estimating the present value of its future liabilities. Under generally accepted accounting procedures, future liabilities are reported in financial statements not at their face value but as the amount that would have to be invested today in order to be able to meet their eventual cost. This amount, in turn, depends on what discount rate is used — that is, on what one assumes the rate of return on investment will be in the future. Assume that the rate will be high, and the present value of future liabilities is correspondingly discounted, at least for accounting purposes.

It is difficult to understand why public pension systems that have no assets should be allowed to discount their future liabilities by any amount. Their costs to future taxpayers will not be offset by any return on investment, because no investments are being made. Nonetheless, all these systems do discount their future liabilities and, even more disconcertingly, do so using different assumed rates of return on their usually nonexistent reserves.

For example, using a discount rate of 6.5 percent, the comptroller general's retirement system, which pays pensions to members of Congress and their staffs, admits in the Saltonstall report to $1 million in accrued liabilities and no assets. Using a 7 percent discount rate, the pension fund for former presidents and their widows admits to $3 million in liabilities and no assets. The Coast Guard chooses to discount its considerably larger pension liabilities at 6.6 percent, arriving at a total debt of $7.1 billion, again secured by no assets.

Because of these and other accounting disparities, the Saltonstall report conspicuously lacks a bottom line. A recent estimate by the Treasury Department, however, puts the total liabilities of all federal employee pension and disability plans — discounted to "present value," as of September 30, 1985 — at $1.252 trillion. To realize the magnitude of this sum, consider that the official national debt, which does not include these liabilities, was at that time only slightly higher, at $1.499 trillion.[11]

Not all of these pension liabilities will come due in any one given year, of course. But the amount of the annual installments will inexorably grow, severely constraining the options of future Americans as they struggle to pay both for their own public servants and for those of the past. Just between 1983 and 1984, the government's liability for employee pensions and disability benefits increased by more than $62 billion; the next year they jumped by another $41 billion, according to government estimates.[12]

No previous generation has ever faced the challenge of financing such a compounding encumbrance. Because the pension benefits paid to individual federal workers are set in part according to their peak salary, any general increase in wage rates multiplies the government's pension liabilities far into the future. As people live longer and longer beyond the age of retirement, their total pensions will increase for that reason as well. The government cannot inflate out from under these liabilities, because they are all indexed for inflation.

Should federal pensions be cut? A good case can indeed be made that federal workers are promised more than their fair share in retirement benefits. Civil servants hired before 1983, for example, may retire at age fifty-five, after thirty years of service, with an annual pension equal to 56 percent of their average salary during their peak prior three years earnings. Virtually no private sector plan replaces such a high percentage of a retiree's previous salary. Of the fifty largest plans offered by *Fortune* 500 companies in 1983 none offered replacement ratios above 44 percent, and most were clustered in the 25–34 percent range, even for workers retiring a full decade later, at age sixty-five.[13]

Moreover, civil service pensions, unlike all but a handful of private sector pensions, are fully indexed to inflation. Indeed, between 1969 and 1976, retired civil servants received not only cost-of-living adjustments (COLAs), but an annual so-called 1 percent kicker, which continues to compound with all subsequent COLAs.

In addition to these benefits, fully 70 percent of all civil service retirees eventually qualify for Social Security, usually by taking on second jobs in the private sector after they retire from public service. Using conservative assumptions, the National Committee on Public Employee Pensions Systems — a public-education group committed to the reform of the CSRS and other public employee pensions — has estimated that such persons can typically expect to receive a combined lifetime annuity from CSRS and Social Security of $730,635.

Military pensions are even more generous. Full retirement becomes available at any age after only twenty years of service. Benefits are usually equal to 50 percent of a veteran's final paycheck and are also fully indexed to inflation, for life. From any point of view, this is an exceptionally good deal. A quarter of all career military personnel retire in their thirties. The average retirement age is forty-two. A thirty-nine-year-old retiree with a $25,000 annual salary will typically receive lifetime benefits in excess of $1 million. In addition, World War II veterans and all who have served in the military since 1957 are automatically covered by Social Security. In 1985 the cost of military pensions alone amounted to well over 50 percent of the Defense Department's total payroll.

Still more expensive to future taxpayers are federal employees who, by changing jobs at propitious intervals, manage to qualify for more than one federal pension. Consider the case of Hastings Keith. For many years, Keith, singularly concerned for the welfare of the next generation, has been trying to return a portion of the four federal pensions he collects. Keith began his career as a federal employee in the military, serving before, during, and after World War II. In 1958 he was elected to Congress as a Republican from a Massachusetts district that includes Cape Cod. After seven terms, Keith left Congress in 1972. For a few months he held a job in the Nixon administration and then went into business. By this time, Keith had put in twenty years on the federal payroll and at age fifty-eight was eligible for early retirement benefits.

Qualifying for a combined congressional and civil service pension, his initial benefits were $1,560 a month, or $18,720 a year. This came in addition to a military pension of $551 a month, which he began receiving in 1975, for service on active duty and in the reserves. Finally, when he turned sixty-five in 1980, Keith began collecting Social Security. All these pensions were indexed to inflation; not only that, his civil service pension offered the compounding "1 percent kicker" mentioned earlier. As a result, by the end of 1982, Keith, whose highest salary as a congressman had been $42,000 a year, found himself collecting $65,000 annually in federal pensions.

For Hastings Keith, a man who often uses the phrase "fiduciary responsibility" and who, like his mentor Saltonstall, has a New Englander's pride in thrift, accepting this windfall seemed unconscionable. In 1982 he typed out a letter to Donald Regan, then secretary of the Treasury, offering to turn over three checks totaling $3,107 if Regan would agree to participate in a public ceremony. But despite the deficits, despite the enormous unfunded liabilities in all the government's major employee pension systems, Regan refused. Since then, Keith has used his pensions to help fund a research group committed to the reform of federal pensions, stated his case on "60 Minutes," and testified repeatedly on the issue before Congress. Already Keith has received more than half a million dollars in federal pensions. Today, he estimates, assuming that inflation will never again go above 5 percent and that he has a normal life span, he will eventually collect $2,981,958 in federal pensions, plus $56,445 from a private pension, for a total of $3,038,403 in retirement pay.[14]

Keith's is an extreme case. Still, it is hard to understand why federal employee pensions, even for the average worker, should generally be set so high. Naturally if we want to attract high-quality workers to government service then we ought to be prepared to pay them well. But if the issue is discussed solely in terms of personnel management, then it is far from clear why federal employees' compensation should be so largely in the form of pensions.

The prospect of a fat pension — twenty or thirty years hence — hardly provides much incentive for talented young people to consider or remain in public service. Fewer than 13 percent of those covered by MRS, for example, will stay in the military long enough to collect a pension; nearly 80 percent of all enlisted recruits leave before serving five years.[15]

Moreover, under the current system, the government's most experienced workers are almost universally seduced into early retirement by the allure of large pensions. In 1980, over half the men covered by the CSRS retired before age sixty; only 12.5 percent worked beyond sixty-five. The trend toward early retirement is even more marked among managers, who typically receive the lowest pay compared with their counterparts in the private sector and the highest pensions. Among newly eligible top bureaucrats aged fifty-five to fifty-nine, 75 percent retired in 1980.[16] Only if one accepts the premise that older workers are invariably inefficient does this policy make sense.

But the assumption is unwarranted. Even in the military, more and more jobs require highly technical skills and experience rather than simple youthful vigor. According to a study by the comptroller general, fully 81 percent of all enlisted members of the armed services and 30 percent of the officers spend *their entire careers* in non-combat-related jobs.[17] And in any event, as the population ages, an era is beginning in which youth will be in ever shorter supply, while people in their fifties and sixties will show more vigor and have potentially more to contribute than ever before.

For reasons of personnel management, then, federal pensions ought to be cut. In compensation, salaries will probably have to be raised to avoid an increase in mediocrity and incompetence in government. But the ideal solution would address the most inequitable aspect of federal employee pensions: the fact that they are open-ended promises financed primarily by redistributing wealth and opportunity away from today's younger Americans and future generations.

Although the proposal remains politically infeasible for the moment, this hidden borrowing from the future could be corrected by a single bold reform, with no chance for accounting gimmickry or political favoritism: make all federal pensions "defined-contribution" plans. Such plans, which are increasingly common in the private sector, are analogous to a forced savings program. The amount workers must contribute each month or year is set, or "defined," in advance. Usually employers make matching contributions. All contributions are invested in assets chosen by the employee or by a portfolio manager answerable to the employee. All resulting return on investment is sheltered from taxation or receives preferable treatment.

But the benefits a worker will receive in the future are not predefined, as they are under CSRS and MRS systems, as well as under Social Security. Instead, the amount of benefits a worker will receive in the future depends on how well the plan's investment portfolio actually performs, just as the benefits of an Individual Retirement Account depend on how well the investments are managed. By definition, then, defined-contribution plans cannot have unfunded liabilities.

On the face of it, defined-contribution plans sound like a substantially worse deal for workers than do alternative "defined-benefit" plans, which promise benefits in advance on the basis of some formula, such as years of service as a function of peak earnings. But in many ways defined-contribution plans are superior, even from the worker's point of view. Like IRAs and Keogh plans, defined-contribution plans do not penalize a worker for leaving one job and taking another. The moment a contribution is placed in a worker's account, it becomes the worker's exclusive property, subject only to the condition that he or she not spend it before reaching retirement age. For this reason also public employees contributing to a defined-contribution plan would not see their benefits cut at the whim of a future Congress. Finally, because they are funded through a return on investment, defined-contribution plans offer workers the potential to realize virtually unlimited retirement income and at no expense to future generations. Indeed the capital that accumulates in these plans can be used to finance research and development, the building of new factories, and other productive projects that benefit the future.

In 1986, Congress took one step in the right direction but, unfortunately, at least one step back as well, when it created a new pension plan for recently hired civil servants. The new plan, called the Federal Employee Retirement System (FERS) arose out of the 1983 Social Security amendments discussed in chapter 3. It contains a provision that allows participants to shelter up to 10 percent of their income and to receive matching contributions from the government whenever they contribute to a special "thrift plan," which is similar to a typical, private sector, defined-contribution plan. Unfortunately, FERS also offers its participants on top of this a generous defined-benefit plan — fully indexed for inflation. In combination with Social Security, FERS was supposed to offer newly hired civil servants the same general level of retirement income as that enjoyed by CSRS beneficiaries. In reality, the total package may prove even more expensive to future taxpayers. The Congressional Budget Office estimates that 880,000 workers covered by the old CSRS plan will convert to FERS. Federal employee unions, tellingly, were nearly unanimous in their support of the new system. No reliable estimates exist yet for FERS's total liabilities, but there is no question that it too will push costs into the future.[18]

In the end, the only way to alter the skew of incentives that compels Congress to keep rewarding federal employees with unfunded pension promises is simply for Congress to declare the practice illegal, and this is not a very likely prospect. It would require Congress to dismantle all current defined-benefit programs and replace them, not supplement them, with defined-contribution plans. For now, this reform remains politically impossible. But when ordinary Americans wake up and see all the means by which the federal government is borrowing from their own and from their children's future, they will have little patience with politicians who continue to obstruct the demands of prudence.

Contingent Liabilities: Betting with Our Children's Money

As big as they are, the record budget deficits that the federal government has been admitting to in recent years also fail to include another large set of liabilities coming due in the future. The federal government is the nation's largest insurer. It insures loans to students, farmers, small businessmen, veterans, shipbuilders, home buyers, and many other favored groups. It also insures bank depositors against the loss of their savings, as well as 40 million workers and retirees against the loss of their private pensions. Through these programs, future taxpayers are exposed to a total contingent liability estimated by the president's Office of Management and Budget to well exceed $3 trillion.[19]

It is hardly likely, of course, that future taxpayers will ever have to pay that full amount. Only in the event that all the nation's banks and private pension plans collapsed at once while all beneficiaries of government-guaranteed loans also defaulted would the full liability be realized. But inevitably, with such an enormous exposure to risk, future taxpayers will be required to commit very large sums to paying off future insurance losses and loan defaults. In 1985 alone, according to estimates by the Treasury Department, the government's losses on guaranteed loans in default and other insurance claims came to $8.7 billion. And this figure, the Treasury Department acknowledges, is conservative, since "a number of agencies do not make any provision for estimated loss on loan guarantees and insurance, while others provide minimal estimates of losses."[20]

Private insurance companies build up reserves sufficient to cover the benefits they are likely to have to pay out in the future, based on actuarial assumptions rooted in past experience. Government insurance programs typically have no reserves, or reserves woefully insufficient to meet their actual accrued liabilities. This too is a form of borrowing from the future.

A good case in point is the Pension Benefit Guarantee Corporation (PBGC), a little-known government agency that stands behind the nation's private pension plans in much the same way that the Federal Deposit Insurance Corporation stands behind the country's commercial banks. Examining the PBGC's dismal financial position not only provides a major example of how the government is pushing costs into the future and understating its deficits, but it also highlights the precariousness of the nation's private pension system.

Since passage of the Employee Retirement Income Security Act (ERISA) of 1974, the government, through the PBGC, has guaranteed all Americans covered by private employer defined-benefit plans against loss of their benefits. There are over 235,000 such plans, covering over 40 million participants.

Like Social Security and other federal pension plans, private sector defined-contribution plans promise specific benefit levels to workers far in advance of their retirement, based on their eventual years of service, peak salary, and other variables. Unlike Social Security, private sector plans are required by law to set aside at least minimal reserves — invested in real, wealth-producing assets — to help defray the cost of future benefits. Nonetheless, many defined-benefit plans in the private sector remain substantially underfunded, particularly those within declining industries. According to a recent study by Richard Ippolito, director of the Office of Pension Research at the Department of Labor, the average private sector defined-benefit plan has assets equal only to about 77 percent of its actual long-term liabilities. More than a third of all plans have funding ratios below 50 percent of their actual liabilities; about 7 percent have funding ratios below 25 percent.[21]

Because these plans promise benefits without regard to the actual future performance of their investment portfolios, many disparate demographic and economic trends can unexpectedly throw them into insolvency. For instance, a decline in the ratio of workers to retirees within a company due to layoffs and to the trend toward early retirement can shrink revenues and raise costs. Similarly, when the return on the plan's investment portfolio is lower than expected or when costs rise through retirees' living longer than anticipated, the prospects for default grow inordinately. In the broadest terms, the solvency of these plans depends on the growth and competitiveness of U.S. industry, particularly heavy manufacturing—the sector in which these plans are concentrated. And because the government, through the PBGC, has guaranteed that anyone promised benefits under such plans will receive them, come what may, future taxpayers are left exposed to enormous liabilities.

Between 1942 and 1974, about thirteen thousand pension plans were terminated; about 45 percent of these plans were insufficiently funded, causing a loss of benefits to 114,000 people. The most famous case came in 1964, when the Studebaker car company declared bankruptcy. About 4,500 workers under age sixty with fully vested pension rights[22] lost all but 15 percent of the pension benefits they had been promised.[23] By the early 1970s, endless stories of workers being denied pension rights were publicized by newspapers, by a controversial NBC television documentary, and by several years of congressional hearings. Ralph Nader and Kate Blackwell published a study showing many instances in which workers who had been with the same employer for twenty years or more were denied pension benefits, due to underfunding or to ridiculous vesting requirements.[24] It was against this backdrop that Congress passed ERISA, to regulate the private pension industry, and created the PBGC, to insure benefits.

As with the government's other major insurance programs, the PBGC was not supposed to encumber either present or future taxpayers. The corporation has two major sources of revenue: the premiums it collects from the plans it insures, and claims on the net worth of any company or union that defaults on its pension plan. But as in so many other instances, Congress seriously underestimated the cost of PBGC, which, since its inception, has been racking up large unfunded liabilities of its own.

During its first few years of operation, Congress required the PBGC to charge pension plans a mere $1 in annual insurance premiums for every participating employee or pensioner. But this amount proved woefully inadequate, as ever more private pension plans failed or were terminated. In 1975, the PBGC assumed trusteeship for 3 pension plans serving 386 participants. Two years later, the PBGC had assumed trusteeship for 145 plans, covering 16,000 participants. By October 1985, the PBGC had taken over more than 1,200 pension plans covering 190,000 people and accumulated a long-term deficit of $1.325 billion.[25] In early 1986, the bankrupt Wheeling-Pittsburgh steel company alone added $476 million to this sum when it dumped its pension plan obligations on the PBGC. Later that year, the giant LTV corporation, a steel conglomerate, declared bankruptcy, leaving the PBGC to pick up unfunded liabilities from its various pension plans that, while not yet fully determined, will run somewhere between $1.5 and $2.2 billion.

Belatedly, Congress has allowed the PBGC to raise its annual premiums — to more than $8 per participant. It also has empowered the PBGC to capture up to 75 percent of a company's net worth before assuming its pension debt. (Previously, it was entitled only to 30 percent.) And still the PBGC projects that its own deficits will rise through the end of this decade. To amortize the cost of the LTV failure, while also amortizing its previously accrued liabilities, the PBGC may need to charge premiums as high as $20 per participant. If the manufacturing sector of the United States continues to decline, causing more giant corporations to default on their pension promises, eventually the PBGC's liabilities will have to be paid out of general revenues, and future taxpayers will have to pay the cost directly.[26]

Compounding this predicament, the PBGC may itself be increasing the risk of private pension plans' going into default. Especially in troubled industries, workers are more likely to accept unfunded pension promises in lieu of wage increases because they know that these promises are guaranteed by the government. At the same time, by charging the same premiums to both well-funded and underfunded plans, the PBGC in effect puts a tax on companies that manage their plans responsibly. But ending this cross subsidy, by charging weak plans higher premiums than strong plans, would put the weak plans in still greater jeopardy.[27]

A solution to these problems will not come easily. There is, however, one sweeping reform that would go a long way toward ending the crisis, although it will bring much opposition from the private pension industry. It is, essentially, the same solution suggested for public employee pension plans: let the government encourage the conversion of private sector defined-benefit plans into defined-contribution plans.

Defined-benefit plans, whether for public or private sector employees, are currently at odds with many fundamental trends that are likely to remain in effect throughout the lifetimes of today's younger Americans. These trends include the aging of the population; the rapid turnover of the labor force, especially among women as they interrupt their careers to raise children; and the pace at which whole industries now rise and fall as the United States adjusts to a global economy.

In an era when workers could reasonably look forward to remaining with the same employer throughout their careers, defined-benefit plans made sense. Even when a worker had to wait as long as ten or twenty years before earning any pension rights, he was still likely to benefit from such plans. But today this is no longer so. The 1986 tax reform bill calls for these plans to return at least partial benefits to employees who are terminated after five years of service — a significant improvement. Still, one of every twelve workers over the age of twenty-five changes jobs every year. The median job tenure for workers over twenty-five is 6.9 years for men and 4.8 years for women.[28] Moreover, even those who stay at one job for substantially longer periods are not well served by defined-benefit plans. On average, workers participating in such plans who change jobs just once, at age thirty-one, will reduce the value of their pensions by an estimated 28 percent. Workers who change jobs twice, at ages forty-one and fifty-one, will see their pensions reduced by 57 percent.[29] While roughly half of all American workers participate in defined-benefit plans, only a quarter are now entitled to a private pension upon retirement, because of vesting requirements.

Defined-benefit plans have always redistributed wealth from workers who fail to obtain seniority to those who do obtain it. But to the extent that today's younger workers are more likely to be laid off than were younger workers in the past, due to plant closings and to the general decline of U.S. industry, defined-benefit plans now disproportionately subsidize a few fortunate older workers at the expense of younger workers. Meanwhile, because these plans enjoy large tax subsidies, they contribute to the budget deficits and in that way disproportionately encumber all younger Americans. Finally, because the PBGC offers insurance worth far more than the premiums it collects, defined-benefit plans expose future taxpayers to inordinate and uncompensated risk.

By contrast, defined-contribution plans expose future taxpayers to no risks and are not at odds with prevailing economic and demographic trends. Moreover, with their immediate vesting and complete "portability" from job to job, they better serve the individual interests of today's workers—young and old alike. Under a defined-benefit system, older workers avoid changing jobs to protect their pension rights, while employers avoid hiring older workers to reduce their pension costs. As the work force ages, these perverse incentives, if allowed to persist, will affect more and more workers and will cause ever greater inefficiency in the labor markets.

As Pat Choate has written in his recent book, *The High-Flex*

Society, "What the overwhelming majority of American employees lack, but badly need, is a portable pension that is tied to the worker and not to the job—one that will allow unhampered job transfer and permit leaving and entering the work force, while pension rights continue to accrue."[30] If the United States is going to compete in world markets, it needs a highly flexible work force. Defined-contribution plans do not penalize workers for going back to school or for switching to more competitive industries; instead, they allow individuals to initiate such changes without having to compromise their security in old age.

But most important of all, moving toward a system of defined-contribution plans would eliminate the enormous liabilities that defined-benefit plans threaten to pass on to future Americans. No one can really know how long people will live in the future, how many workers any given industry will employ, where interest rates will go, and all the other imponderables that determine the long-term solvency of defined-benefit plans. In designing such plans, the best anyone can do is make educated guesses about these variables by generalizing from past experience. But what if the future does not turn out to be like the past or is otherwise inconvenient to the financing of these plans? Then a plan that was thought to be fully funded could turn out in reality to have liabilities far beyond its ability to pay. Through the PBGC, defined-benefit plans expose future Americans to a risk so large that it cannot truly be insured. The more prudent and moral course is offered by a system of defined-contribution plans, through which no generation can promise itself more money in retirement than its members have actually earned previously through savings and investment.

What's a Deficit?

Accounting is, to most of us, a sterile and bloodless subject—the province of mere "bean counters" and "number crunchers." Yet when the money involved is one's own, and the bottom line is an expression of one's future tax bills and prospects for support in old age, then the issue of how the money is counted becomes vital indeed. The federal budget deficits about which we have all been arguing throughout the 1980s are the measure simply of the difference between what cash the government takes in and what cash it pays out during the time it takes the earth to circle the sun. But while this way of defining the deficits has the virtue of being unambiguous, it at best provides only a snapshot picture of the government's true fiscal position and effect on the economy. For younger Americans especially, the government's failure to account for its long-term liabilities should be of special concern, for it is they who will pay the most in taxes and lose the most in benefits, so long as the government fails to recognize the costs it is pushing into the future.

The purpose of accounting is, or ought to be, to give as accurate and at the same time as useful a description as possible of how an institution is raising, allocating, and possibly depleting its resources over time. What defines "useful," of course, depends very much on the particular kind of questions one wants to have answered at the moment. In the day-to-day operation of a household, business, or government, cash flow is necessarily the most immediate concern. Fortunately, determining whether there will be enough cash on hand to pay the bills that have or will shortly come due is usually a comparatively simple exercise. It is performed routinely by the Congressional Budget Office and by the Office of Management and Budget when they project each year's coming federal budget deficit, which is simply a measure of the government's annual cash flow.

But suppose one is concerned with the more fundamental question of whether an institution is ultimately living beyond its means. Then a somewhat more involved approach is required. One needs to know, for example, not just about the bills coming due this month or this year but also about those coming due at some point far into the future. And this in turn depends on such factors as how fast an institution's capital assets, such as factory equipment, are likely to wear out and what it will cost to replace them. It also depends on long-term contractual obligations, such as a promise to pay employee pensions, that may eventually require large commitments of cash. While most people have little trouble keeping rough track of the expenses that they have obligated themselves to meet in the future, large institutions do have trouble in this regard, if for no other reason than the sheer size and complexity of those obligations. For this reason, the federal government requires all publicly held companies, as well as all state and some local governments, to use what is known as "accrual" accounting in presenting their finances, rather than simply counting up and displaying their annual receipts and expenses.

Under accrual accounting, revenues are put down in the books as they are accrued, or earned, rather than when they are actually received. Similarly and more importantly, liabilities are also reported as they are accrued, rather than at the time they are actually paid off, which is often in the distant future. To adjust for the time that will pass before an institution's accrued revenues and liabilities will be collected or paid out, accrual accounting calls for discounting the face value of these accrued revenues and liabilities according to prevailing interest rates. These discounted values are then amortized: liabilities are divided into yearly installments, according to the number of years before the liabilities come due. Among other things, this procedure provides a company or government with a rough measure of how much money it should be setting aside each year to cover its long-term liabilities.

Accrual accounting thus does not simply follow cash as it changes hands from day to day or from year to year, but describes how underlying economic events, such as the signing of a long-term contract, will determine an institution's future cash flow. By this method of accounting one can see, for example, whether a firm's cash reserves will be overwhelmed by enormous future expenses, such as for new inventory or equipment that the firm has ordered but for which it has not yet paid. Or conversely, one can see whether its coffers will soon be overflowing as the firm collects money for services it has previously performed. Obviously, without such information, no investor would want to invest in a company, and no company could sensibly manage itself.

For a large institution, the failure to use accrual accounting can easily lead to disastrous results. During the first half of the 1970s, for example, New York City, using a simple cash flow method to keep its books, each year reported a balanced budget. Then, in 1975, came a severe and unexpected fiscal "meltdown" that ultimately required $4.5 billion in federal loan guarantees and other aid to arrest. What caused the crisis? There were many contributing factors, but one was that for years, the city had been accruing enormous long-term liabilities, such as for employee pensions, that were not acknowledged in its annual budgets, because these budgets reflected only the difference between actual receipts and expenditures in any given year. When at last a substantial portion of these long-term liabilities began coming due, the city was overwhelmed with expenses to pay for which it had no capital reserves, and it was soon denied further credit by wary bankers.

Thus the city was forced to throw itself on the mercy of the nation's taxpayers. The federal government eventually agreed to a bailout, but only after demanding that the city thereafter use accrual accounting in order to avoid a similar crisis in the future. Nothing could have been more hypocritical. For then as now, the federal government itself insists on presenting its own finances to the public just as New York once did, on a simple cash flow basis. When it reports, for example, a $200 billion budget deficit, this figure refers only to the difference between annual receipts and expenses—in other words, to its temporary cash flow. No account is made for the enormous future liabilities it has meanwhile been accruing every day at the expense of future taxpayers.

In an era when the federal government did little more than guard the coasts and deliver the mail, cash-basis accounting could provide a fairly accurate picture of its fiscal position. In any given year, the government incurred few liabilities that were not paid the same year and thus recorded on its books. But this situation has changed dramatically over the last half-century, principally because of the growth of the welfare state. Entitlement programs, such as Social Security and Medicare, each day obligate the government to pay benefits far into the future, as workers build up future claims by paying into these systems. Indeed, since the end of World War II, nearly all the growth in federal spending as a percentage of GNP (excluding the rapid growth in the cost of financing the national debt), has been in programs that involve promises to pay future benefits. Similarly, as the government has come to own more and more capital assets, such as dams, military hardware, office buildings, and the interstate highway system, it has become liable for the enormous future cost of their maintenance, repair, and replacement. Finally, through its direct loan and loan insurance programs, the government accrues or exposes itself to still another realm of long-term liabilities. But because of the government's cash-basis accounting, none of these future liabilities shows up in its standard budget documents or is factored into its officially recorded deficits.

The government's cash-basis accounting does provide the answers to some very important questions, of course. It tells investors, for example, whether and how much the government will be borrowing from the private sector in any given year to finance the difference between its current receipts and expenses. The more capital the government borrows in any given year, the less will be available for consumer credit and investment in new industry. But this much information provides only a snapshot picture of the government's true fiscal position and effect on the economy; cash-basis accounting tells nothing about how current policies are adding or subtracting to future budget deficits because it ignores all liabilities incurred in any given year that have not yet come due.

How large, then, are the government's real budget deficits? In 1975, Arthur Anderson and Company, one of the country's "big eight" accounting firms, developed a consolidated financial statement for the U.S. government using accrual accounting and other "generally accepted accounting principles," as they are known in the industry. The study found that whereas the government's admitted, cash-basis deficit for 1974 was a mere $6.1 billion, its accrual-basis deficit was over $95 billion, taking into account not only the growth of its long-term, unfunded liabilities but also such real factors as the depreciation of its fixed assets. Ten years later, the company performed the same exercise, this time analyzing the 1984 budget. Whereas the government that year admitted to a deficit of $185.3 billion, Arthur Anderson found that the deficit was actually closer to $333.4 billion — an amount that exceeded all revenue collected from individual income taxes that year. To eliminate such a deficit would have required a 113 percent increase in individual taxes, assuming that such an increase did not itself cause a recession or depression.[31]

While these and other accrual-based estimates of the government's fiscal position remain controversial, in part because of the many uncertain assumptions about the future that necessarily underlie them, there is a strong and growing consensus among fiscal policy experts that the government's current method of keeping its books is simply inadequate to the reality it faces. Many highly technical as well as philosophical issues remain to be resolved. For example, current government accounting practices fail to provide adequate treatment of depreciation. Perversely, when a government borrows from the future by failing to maintain its assets, such as bridges, roads, and highways, this kind of borrowing is not factored straightforwardly into its deficits, even under standard accrual accounting. But when a government spends money to maintain these assets — that is, to avoid borrowing from the future — the appropriation goes down as a current expense, just like spending for a Fourth of July parade. As Herman Leonard has written,

> Using up existing capital assets — permitting a deterioration of infrastructure through deferred maintenance — is a form of public spending that operates at the lowest level of accountability. It requires no appropriation, and there is no obvious way to make it require one. It takes place by default, without explicit authorization. Not only does it *not* need an appropriated spending program to *happen*; it even takes appropriated maintenance or reinvestment expenditures to *keep* it from happening.[32]

Devising accounting standards to capture such a complex reality is a trying intellectual endeavor.

Also at issue is how to account for such hidden forms of borrowing as the sale and leasing back of public assets such as convention centers, buses, and office buildings — now increasingly common at the local level. Similarly, there is debate over the budgetary treatment of direct loans originated by government agencies, such as the Small Business Administration, which direct capital away from other, more creditworthy borrowers and which expose taxpayers to the cost of defaults but which also provide revenue so long as the loans are repaid. And there is also the eternal and politically charged issue of what forms of appropriation should be counted as capital investment: Should spending for education, for example, be treated as any less a form of investment in the future than spending for dams and highways? Should the cost of cleaning up toxic waste and other forms of pollution also be put down as investment, since it reduces costs in the future, or as a liability come due from the past? Finally, is there any way to account for the depletion of such public goods as aquifers and other natural resources?

Despite their complexity, all these issues have at their core the unifying concept of justice between generations. As the Government Accounting Standards Board wrote in a recent proposed statement of its mission,

> The Board believes that inter-generational equity . . . is fundamental to public administration and therefore needs to be considered in establishing financial reporting objectives. In short, information is needed to be able to assess whether current year revenues are sufficient to pay for the services provided and whether future taxpayers [will be] assuming burdens for services previously provided.[33]

How can accounting standards be written so as to capture the reality of resources' being transferred back and forth over time through different government policies or through the lack of any such policies at all? The political implications of such questions are so potentially volatile that the federal government will probably never agree to submit to any form of unified, accrual accounting — even if the accounting profession eventually agrees on the standards appropriate to its diverse operations. For example, in its ongoing attempt to devise a noncontroversial prototype for a consolidated financial statement of the U.S. government's assets and liabilities, the Treasury Department decided in 1986 to reclassify the Social Security system's $4.647 trillion in unfunded liabilities as merely "contingent" expenses. Thus, with the stroke of a pen, the Treasury not only appeased the partisans of Social Security — who claim, inexplicably, that the system in no way contributes to the deficits — but also inadvertently acknowledged that benefits promised to today's younger Americans are, from the government's point of view, only a matter of risk exposure: maybe the baby boomers and their children will succeed in collecting their benefits, maybe they won't.[34]

It is too much to hope that accountants can dissuade us from borrowing so heavily from the future. But we would all do well to contemplate the reality that they are seeking to describe with the concepts and standards of accrual accounting. No matter if we agree on how or whether the government's bookkeeping should be reformed, the borrowing goes on nonetheless. Better documentation will help the cause of fiscal responsibility. But ultimately, only a change in cultural values—a rediscovery of the ethos of stewardship—will save us from our greed. As I shall argue in the next chapter, we must stop acting like members of special interest groups and start deferring instead to the idea of an enduring public interest that extends equally to all generations.

8

The Broker State:
Who Speaks for the Young?

THERE IS NO RECORD that John C. Calhoun ever read or tried to write poetry. Except that once, according to a traditional gibe, he began a poem with "Whereas" and stopped.

Calhoun was bad company. "When I seek relaxation with him," complained Sen. Dixon Lewis of Alabama, his principal, although reluctant, associate in politics, "he screws me only the higher in some sort of excitement."

The senator from Alabama, weighing 430 pounds, required frequent intervals of calm. Whereas the senator from South Carolina, no matter how promising the moment, would never let up with his dialectical analysis of the evils of industrial capitalism and the coming revolution of the masses in the North—thereby attempting to demonstrate at every hour and by a thousand proofs the higher good of slavery.

"There is and always has been, in an advanced stage of wealth and civilization, a conflict between labor and capital," Calhoun would hold forth, as Dixon paled. "Under the operation of the system, wages must sink more rapidly than prices 'til the operatives [the workers] will be reduced to their lowest point — when the portion of the products of their labor left to them will be barely sufficient to preserve existence."

For his peculiarly dialectical cast of mind and for his total lack of humor Calhoun is sometimes compared to Marx, with the difference, of course, that Calhoun was seeking to justify the South's peculiar institution. "Every plantation is a community," Calhoun would say enthusiastically, "with the master at its head, who concentrates in himself the united interests of capital and labor, of which he is the common representative."

Had the Confederacy prevailed in its cause, Calhoun's exertions on behalf of the plantation state might have provided the intellectual underpinnings for American society. As things turned out, Calhoun didn't even make the Great Book series. For nearly a century after his death in 1850, the senator's place in the Great Adventure of Ideas was largely forgotten outside his home state of South Carolina.

Until, that is, America caught up with Calhoun, sometime after World War II. With the arrival of the modern welfare state, there arose in the land a new theory about how the American political process really worked and a new, quite unlikely idea of what it meant to be a liberal. The theory was pluralism, and its founding father, so said the theorists, was John C. Calhoun.

Herein lies one of the great ironies in the history of American political thought: that on his dialectical journey to the plantation state, Calhoun paused to offer, quite unwittingly, some convincing philosophical arguments in favor of the modern "pluralistic" welfare state. This is why, in some advanced circles, there was a great revival of interest in Calhoun after the war. With but a little academic revision, the theories of this splenetic, humorless racist could be made to justify new liberal agencies, such as the Social Security Administration, that brokered to Americans on the basis of their group membership, rather than according to their individual need. One did not allude, of course, to Calhoun's discussion of the virtues of slavery, but rather to his corollary proofs in support of powerful special interests, minority rule, and government by and for the organized.

Peter Drucker was the initial theoretician of the postwar Calhounical revival. In a 1948 essay for the *Review of Politics*, entitled "A Key to American Politics: Calhoun's Pluralism," Drucker sought to rehabilitate Calhoun from what he characterized as "the partisan vote of the Reconstruction Period." "There is almost no awareness," Drucker began, "of the fact that organization on the basis of sectional and interest compromise is both the distinctly American form of political organization and the cornerstone of practically all major political institutions of the modern U.S.A. . . . To find an adequate analysis of [this] principle of government . . . we have to go back almost 100 years to John C. Calhoun."

"His basic principle," Drucker continued, "that every major interest in the country, whether regional, economic, or religious, is to possess a veto power on political decisions directly affecting it . . . has become the organizing principle of American politics."

And a good thing, too, Drucker opined. For, as he concluded his essay, "the pluralism of sectional interest compromise is the warp of America's fabric — it cannot be plucked out without unraveling the whole."[1]

Within months after Drucker published his article, the neo-Calhounical revival spread beyond the province of the academy and into the mainstream of American intellectual culture. In a long and much remarked essay for *Harper's*, contributing editor John Fischer set out to popularize Drucker's thesis that Calhoun alone could explain and justify the actual practice of American politics.

"In other countries, each agency of government is at least presumed to act for the nation as a whole; here most agencies are expected to behave as servants for one interest or another," Fischer explained, with obvious approval.

The Veterans Administration, to cite the most familiar example, is frankly intended to look out for Our Boys; the Maritime Commission is the spokesman for the shipping industry; the National Labor Relations Board, as originally established under the Wagner Act, was explicitly intended to build up the bargaining power of the unions; . . . the Department of Agriculture under the old [Agricultural Adjustment Administration] became an instrument of the large-scale commercial farmers . . . while the Farm Security administration went to bat for the tenants, farm laborers, and the little subsistence farmers, as represented by the Farmers Union.[2]

Within two years, Margaret Coit produced a new, very sympathetic biography of Calhoun, following Drucker's "pluralistic" interpretation.[3] In an enthusiastic review for the *Nation*, Arthur Schlesinger, Jr., praised Calhoun's "penetrating insight in the fact that freedom derives from diversity, not from unity," and applauded his "brilliant and elaborate attempt to construct a society in which minorities would somehow be accorded, not alone the right, but the power of self-protection."

"A Calhoun revival is perhaps not inappropriate for an age like our own," Schlesinger stated. "His defense of slavery, of course, is inadmissable, but his broader philosophy has a new relevance."[4]

There is a passion in these words that seems strange today. No one gets very idealistic about pluralism anymore. The word imparts a vague legitimacy when conjoined with other phrases of state, as in democratic pluralism. It has become a notion that people are generally in favor of without knowing exactly why. But in its effect on our sense of citizenship and stewardship for future generations, pluralism remains one of the most influential and at the same time most obsolete ideas of our times. Pluralism, or what we are today more likely to call interest group liberalism, has many virtues, among them, as Schlesinger and other liberals of the last generation noted, the promotion of tolerance and the protection of minority rights. And in a country as large and diverse as the United States, some degree of deference to special interest groups is, to borrow a phrase from the historian Herbert Agar, simply "the price of union." But these points no longer outweigh the two deadly faults of a government that is dominated by special interest groups: its inability to protect the unorganized, and its inability to pursue long-term common interests. Children, the elderly poor, and future generations are the principal victims of our current pluralistic system. In an aging society, with its imperative for massive investment in raising the productivity of future workers and with its heightened need to distribute scarce resources prudently and effectively, pluralism becomes a guise for selfishness and ensures long-term national decline.

What exactly is the role of pluralism in our political culture? It is by no means unambiguous. Recall the donnybrook that followed the publication, in 1982, of William Greider's famous article "The Education of David Stockman." Stockman had set out, he confided to Greider (who then told all), to sell Reaganomics as "idea-based politics."[5] "We weren't going to get involved in tax-bill brokering of special interests," he told Greider. The idea was to avoid what Stockman called "constituency-based choice-making," which he took to be the fatal error of modern liberalism. Liberal politics, he told Greider, with but slight exaggeration, had lost the ability to judge claims and so yielded to all of them.

The new conservatism, Stockman believed at the outset, would practice a new type of politics. It would, as Greider summarized his thoughts, "honor just claims and reject spurious ones, instead of simply serving powerful clients over weak clients." The education of David Stockman consisted of his unlearning this ideal of political virtue. "The problem is, unorganized groups can't play this game," he lamented, noting that all his efforts had only changed the list of winning clients. "The hogs were really feeding. The greed level, the level of opportunism, just got out of control," he said in another remark that was widely quoted. "There were no real conservatives," went another.

Why were these statements so shocking? If, in the heat of battle, Stockman had forsaken his principles, it was nothing unusual, and it certainly was not news. What outraged the country, and especially Washington, was not that Stockman wound up playing the same old Calhounical game as everyone else. His offense was to reveal the details of the game itself.

Like the Victorians in their attitude toward sex, we do not deny that interest group politics exists. But we expect those who engage in such activities to show discretion in relating their affairs, and to use abstract terms like *pluralism* if they must refer to the subject. In his campaign debate with Ronald Reagan in 1980, Jimmy Carter is well remembered for having managed to signal every constituent group in the Democratic coalition at some point in his answers, with special phrasing meant for public school teachers. The tactic did not succeed, and indeed Carter came dangerously close to committing the same indiscretion as did Stockman. In the next presidential election, the Democrats once again learned the same lesson the hard way. Referring to the furious bidding for Jewish support during the New York primary, Murray Kempton once quipped, "Jackson may have called New York Hymietown; Hart and Mondale treated it as if it were." Throughout the campaign, Walter Mondale would lose at least as much support as he gained each time he proclaimed the endorsement of a new special interest. His careful selection of three women, two blacks, a Hispanic, and a southern white male as possible running mates reinforced Mondale's image as a broker-style politician and caused many observers to proclaim a new low point for interest group liberalism.

This is Calhoun's legacy. A candidate does well to promise a single group that he will press for their agenda. But to give the impression that he will simply broker to all groups is to fall short of the average voter's idea of leadership. We want the candidate to broker to our own group — that's leadership — not to other organized interests — that's hack politics.

The story of how pluralism, to this extent, became the accepted public philosophy, goes a long way toward explaining our current crisis of government and provides many object lessons for the future. Over the space of a generation, pluralism was transformed from a pessimistic description of how American government too often worked in practice into an intellectually respectable theory of how it should work always. For liberals, especially, stepping away from the legacy of Calhoun is extremely important, so long as liberals truly care about helping the needy and restoring growth in our aging society.

The Calhoun Legacy and the Liberal Tradition

The notion that attracted postwar liberals to Calhoun can be found deep within the midsection of his *Disquisition on Government*—copies of which can today be found in university libraries around the country thanks to the beneficence of the South Carolina legislature, which in 1851 mandated that the work be disseminated "to men of learning throughout the republic." Calhoun called his idea the "Doctrine of the Concurrent Majority," a cumbersome phrase whose essential idea is quite simple. To protect against a "tyranny of the majority," Calhoun wrote, "governments must [take] the sense of each interest or portion of the community . . . separately, through its own majority, or in some other way by which its voice may be fairly expressed."[6]

Perhaps Calhoun had in mind an organization such as the American Association of Plantation Owners, although he was not explicit about this. What he said exactly is that the "powers of government must be divided and distributed" to "give to each division or interest, through its appropriate organ, either a concurrent voice in making and executing the laws, or a veto on their execution."[7] This, sure enough, appears to be pluralism, the theory that American government is and *should* be no more than a highly organized form of collusion with and brokerage between competing special interest groups.

To the Founding Fathers, the notion that Washington should function as a sort of commodities pit for organized interests was straightforwardly subversive. James Madison, to be sure, had warned of the tendency of society to break into factions, classes and special interest groups. But in *Federalist* 10, his most famous contribution to the *Federalist Papers*, he championed the Constitution and a strong central government as means of diluting local influence and preserving the common interest of "the People."

But Calhoun saw this as nonsense. To him the People did not really exist, in any practical sense. "The first and leading error [of democratic theory] is to confound the numerical majority with the people," he asserted. Rule by numerical majority, Calhoun wrote, is never expressive of the people, since "it regards numbers only, and considers the whole community as a unit, having but one common interest throughout."[8]

So even as his contemporaries relaxed in the so-called Era of Good Feelings, Calhoun brooded. The politics of slavery at last drove him to despair of reason and of community. It was obvious that men spoke only for their own class and clan when they criticized the economic institutions of the South. Although a strong nationalist in his early life, Calhoun in the end concluded that no common good existed, save one: that each faction have the power to obstruct the designs of every other.

Given that pluralism's roots lie in the defense of slavery, it is no small irony that Calhoun's postwar resurrection was essentially a liberal movement. The vast expansion of executive power and the proliferation of clientele agencies and programs for groups as diverse as farmers, unions, and senior citizens posed a dilemma for modern liberalism. In the classical liberalism of Locke and Jefferson, and even Hoover, the atom of politics had always been the individual, not his pressure group. But Franklin Roosevelt's policies and public pronouncements had directly challenged that time-worn assumption.

In 1936, for example, during a speech to the graduating class at Rollins College, Roosevelt offered a sociological view of government that begged for Calhounical interpretation. "There are," he observed,

> groups to which almost every man and woman is tied, connected in some way. They are connected with some form of association —the church, the social circle, the club, the lodge, the labor organization, the neighboring farmers, the political party. Even business and commerce are almost wholly made up of groups. It is the problem of government to harmonize the interests of these groups which are often divergent and opposing. The science of politics, indeed, may properly be said to be in large part the science of the adjustment of conflicting group interests.[9]

Of course, amidst the misery of the Depression, relief efforts aimed at broad groups rather than at needy individuals seemed appropriate. The day Roosevelt took office, the banking system was on the verge of collapse, unemployment stood at 25 percent, and the nation's farmers were in a decade-long decline that had not yet seen the worst of the Dust Bowl. Government relief officials had no time to go door to door to ensure that only truly needy Americans received government help—particularly since so few would have been found ineligible. And while some undeserving people demanded subsidies, most Americans were instead willing to make small sacrifices and to do their part in the name of a larger good: ending the Depression. Such idealism was also strong during World War II. The nation embraced another common purpose—winning the war—and to that end Americans continued to make sacrifices, from enduring rationing of gasoline and other scarce goods, to dying for their country.

The Allies' victory brought an end to the nation's nightmare of nearly sixteen years, but in so doing it raised some disturbing questions about the kind of government Roosevelt had left behind. The challenge was to justify the continuation—in the absence of a clear national emergency—of the many clientele agencies created or expanded by the New Deal. Roosevelt had shown little inclination to dismantle these programs even as the war stimulated the economy and ended the Depression. And after the war, most people had come to feel entitled to the benefits these programs offered. But if modern-day liberalism was to continue brokering benefits to citizens on the basis of their group membership rather than according to their individual need, a new, overarching philosophy of government was needed.

John Kenneth Galbraith, most preeminently, recognized and applauded the contradiction of the old liberalism and the new. With Roosevelt, the purpose of liberalism had changed: the goal of liberalism was now to take the side of weaker special interests, he declared, to provide them "countervailing power" with which to resist the predations of the more easily organized. Indeed, Galbraith wrote, "the support of countervailing power has become in modern times perhaps the major peace-time function of the government."[10]

It followed for Galbraith, as it did for other apologists for New Deal liberalism, that government ought to embrace at least some factions, that justice was served by deferring to and even promoting certain "minority" interests. As Richard Hofstadter pointed out in a 1949 essay entitled "Calhoun and the Dixiecrats," Calhoun's only objection to modern liberalism would be that it brokered to the wrong "minority interests," for example, blacks, not that it promoted minorities per se.

There were other reasons why liberals in the late 1940s were attracted to Calhoun's ideas. Calhoun's celebration of compromise and stalemate, for example, appealed to the national yearning for normalcy after a long period of depression and world war. The impulse for security was perfectly understandable. This was a generation that had had its rendezvous with destiny and had lost many of its members in the process. It was a time to put activism and sacrifice aside, to pursue more personal goals: a college education on the GI Bill, a family, perhaps a secure corporate career as an "organization man," and a bungalow with a patio.

Though many intellectuals mocked the emerging barbecue culture of the new middle class or gravely pondered such woolly issues as Conformity and Leisure in a Mass Consumption Society, much sophisticated opinion during this era also reflected a common feeling of exhaustion. Critics such as Dwight Macdonald preoccupied themselves with making fine distinctions between the "midcult" of Hollywood and the "hi-cult" favored by true intellectuals. Daniel Bell would soon proclaim "the end of ideology." Pluralist academicians such as David Truman and Robert Dahl could find secure teaching posts that gave them plenty of time to ponder the meaning of postwar prosperity. A revival of Calhounism, according to which all viewpoints were worthy but no cause so important that it demanded personal sacrifice, seemed appropriate to the age.

Less subjectively, there was also the issue of how the good life was going to be paid for. The New Deal had been passed as a series of national emergency acts, but by the time the emergency was over, even middle-class Americans felt entitled to the beneficence of a large, central government. The GI Bill, subsidized VA and FHA mortgages, the National Labor Relations Board, Social Security, and a host of other government programs made possible the postwar idea of what it means to be middle class. Any argument that could justify more social spending for the middle class, under a more or less automatic system of brokerage and interest group politics, was thus bound to find a prominent place in the public imagination.

It was also useful, especially for liberals, to find a vessel that offered safe passage between the extremism of both the Left and the Right. In 1946, the Republicans regained control of Congress for the first time in eighteen years, and able conservatives such as Sen. Robert Taft were calling for the dismantling of much of the welfare state. Pluralism offered a ready argument in opposition, while at the same time it called for conservatives to be treated respectfully as yet another identifiable group whose ideas deserved to be heard. With the later rise of Sen. Joseph Mc-Carthy and anti-Communist sentiment, pluralism also provided a ready answer to redbaiters, for it celebrated diversity and dissent as the key to the United States' strength.

The celebration of pluralism also helped liberals deal with the peril on their left flank. Henry Wallace's Progressive party had been infiltrated by Communists and was filled with those blind to the horrors of Stalinism; Wallace's debacle in the 1948 election made many liberals seek shelter elsewhere. The group Americans for Democratic Action, for example, was formed by liberals who split off from the Progressive party because of its refusal to expel Communists. The ADA became a staunchly anti-Communist group, though it denounced McCarthy's methods in its strict adherence to more legitimate aims such as those of organized labor — a good example of pluralism at work.

Pluralism offered a third — and distinctly American — way between these ideological extremes. As Drucker observed, the great virtue of Calhoun's updated philosophy was that "it makes it almost impossible for the major parties to afford to draw strength from the kind of demagogic opposition, without governmental responsibility, which perpetually nurtures fascist and communist parties abroad."[11]

During the 1950s, pluralism quickly insinuated itself into the prevailing public philosophy. But Calhoun himself disappeared from the popular literature almost as quickly as he had appeared. Suddenly, civil rights for blacks had once again become a rancorous issue: as a result in the 1948 election the Dixiecrats bolted from the Democratic party led by another South Carolinian, Strom Thurmond, and Northern liberals were forced to recall that Calhoun truly belonged to the forces of reaction. After the *Brown v. Board of Education* decision in 1954 and the events in Little Rock three years later, how much more embarrassing the Calhounical revival of the previous decade must have seemed;

after Selma, its memory must have brought intense pangs of liberal guilt. Only gross insensitivity could have allowed liberal opinion to celebrate the theories of this unabashed slave master while dismissing his thoughts about states' rights and white supremacy with an air of intellectual amusement. Pluralism would have to do without a founding father.

So pluralists turned to the academy. Pluralist analysis became a minor cottage industry at the nation's universities; the most famous product was Robert Dahl's *Who Governs*, a book that detailed the workings of New Haven politics. The academicians didn't celebrate pluralism so much as use the notion to gain insights into politics; some, like Dahl, have expressed misgivings about its larger implications. But that did not matter as much as the fact that pluralism was subtly gaining acceptance as the American Way of Politics. Most politicians were only too happy to embrace the theory, as it sanctioned expediency, brokerage, and other behavior that tends to win votes and free politicians from hard choices. More fundamentally, pluralism encouraged ordinary Americans to think of themselves as members of special interest groups and entitled to as much subsidy as their pressure groups could wrest from the public at large. Pluralism, after all, proclaimed that whatever policies emerged from the process of collusion, competition, and compromise among special interests was, by definition, the true public interest.

A few voices of protest arose during the 1950s and 1960s, but it is a testament to pluralism's power that most such protesters were co-opted by the very theory that they had originally hoped to overcome. Some of the most prominent dissent came from the partisans of the New Left. The original manifesto of the Students for a Democratic Society, the "Port Huron Statement," written in 1962, now reads as an attack on everything Calhounical in American society. Tom Hayden and his youthful collaborators urged "the establishment of a democracy of individual participation." The specific objection was to the eclipse of the individual in a pluralistic state; the early SDS was "governed by two central aims; that society be organized to encourage independence in men and provide the media for this common participation."

Here, in its first blush, the New Left revealed its oft-remarked romanticism and celebration of the individual over the group that ultimately led many to retreat from politics into the solipsism of self-liberation. But the original intent was straightforward: the reinvention of the public man and the rediscovery of civic virtue.

The New Left attacked the pluralistic state on another valid point: its failure up to that time to offer brokerage to certain weaker special interests, specifically blacks, migrant workers, and the young. Surveying the terrain of American politics in 1968, the New Left theoretician Robert Paul Wolff likened the distribution of power to "a plateau with steep cliffs on all sides rather than a pyramid. On the plateau are all the interest groups which are recognized as legitimate; in the deep valley all around lie the outsiders, the fringe groups which are scorned as 'extremists.' The most important battle waged by any group in American politics is the struggle to climb onto the plateau."[12]

Preoccupation with the "fringe groups" was, of course, a defining feature of the New Left. It was also the source of an essential contradiction. Did the antidote to pluralism entail breaking up this system of brokerage and collusion in restoring freedom to the individual and power to the public, as the early SDS had maintained? Or was it more important to expand the pattern of interest group politics, to force the system to broker among still more categories of special interest, such as migrant workers, welfare mothers, black militants, tenants, draft evaders, women, and homosexuals?

As the sixties became more complicated and confrontational the New Left gravitated toward the second strategy. Once it was accepted that minorities required more than legal sanctions against discrimination to overcome poverty and discrimination, the path of least resistance seemed to lie in promoting affirmative action, bilingual education, special entitlement programs, the "maximum feasible participation" that Daniel Patrick Moynihan made famous in his study of the War on Poverty. The allocation of jobs, graduate school admission, and public funds was to be based not on individual circumstance but according to membership in a particular group—just as pluralism prescribed that it should be. Both the Democrats and the Republicans happily played the game. The greatest real increase in entitlement spending—particularly for senior citizens—would come during the Nixon administration.

Interest Group Liberalism in an Aging Society

Pluralism thrives on affluence and in seemingly safe times. But a government that brokers only to the organized is necessarily prone to discount the interests of future Americans and, by extension, to favor current consumption over long-term investment. This is the first reason why pluralism has become an obsolete ideal. So long as the United States required relatively little capital expenditure to remain competitive in world markets from year to year, the nation could afford—or at least many thought it could afford—the bias against investment that results from unrestrained interest group politics. But today, deferring to factions to the degree that we do comes straightforwardly at the expense of future economic growth and of justice between generations.

One way to see why pluralism is biased against the future is to consider a simple arithmetic truth. As the economist Mancur Olson has pointed out, special interest groups can always realize a greater profit by bargaining for a larger share of the existing commonweal than by joining in measures to enlarge the pie. A union, industry, or age group that wins a greater share of a society's existing wealth through such devices as trade protection, tax breaks, or entitlement programs must divide the gain only among its own members. In contrast, the return to each group and to each individual within a group that comes from growth in the overall economy is small by comparison, because the gain must be shared with everyone.

Olson has even gone so far as to argue that this logic of collective action is what explains the high growth rates of the nations that the United States defeated in World War II. The war left Germany and Japan with the opportunity to rebuild their industries virtually from scratch. But more important, Olson asserts, most organized interest groups in these two nations were dislodged during and after the war, first by repression of unions and trade groups, and then by the total political and economic transformations dictated by the triumphant occupying Allies. Italy, because it experienced less social upheaval as a result of the war, enjoyed correspondingly less economic growth in subsequent years, Olson argues.[13]

While Olson may overstate this application of his theory, his general point still has force. During the postwar period, the grand success of the U.S. economy provided a powerful argument in favor of whatever process of government we actually practiced; if it turned out that our system gave exceptional deference to special interest groups, then the implication seemed to be that we ought to promote still more pluralism. But today, the slow growth in the economy, the declining competitiveness of industry, and the mounting indebtedness of the government causes the logic of the pluralistic debate to be reversed. No longer can pluralism be championed as the driving force behind American prosperity. Far from being self-evidently "the genius of the American system," excessive pluralism seems quite likely one of its gravest flaws.

In the future, the aging of the population will force us to ask new and much graver questions about the degree to which we should allow special interest groups to dominate our politics, for several reasons. First, as the ratio of workers to retirees continues to decline, pluralism's bias against investment will increasingly be at odds with the objective need to raise productivity. As has been argued throughout this book, the American standard of living will decline as the baby boomers reach retirement age unless we invest massively to increase the output of each remaining younger worker.

At the same time, unabashed pluralism is highly likely to lead to an imprudent and unjust allocation of resources between the generations. The old will always be more likely to organize than will younger Americans. Young adults are preoccupied with establishing careers and raising families; children, to say nothing of future generations, have no ability to organize at all. At any time in history, pluralism thus has a bias against not only the long-term but also the immediate interest of the young. If we allow our politics to be dominated by special interests, this bias can only become more acute, as the population ages and the potential power of groups purporting to represent the elderly as a whole correspondingly increases.

Finally, because pluralism favors redistribution on the basis of group membership and because the ranks of one group, the elderly, will swell dramatically early in the next century, continued allegiance to interest group politics will increasingly disserve the poor of all generations. Allocating resources on the basis of seniority alone is one of the prime expressions of our current, pluralistic system. In an aging society, however, age-based entitlements are likely to be spread too thinly to rescue the elderly poor, while the overall cost of such programs increasingly strains the budgets for programs serving the poor in general.

At the heart of the pluralistic debate, then, are questions of both generational and class equity—both driven by the aging of the population. How we will resolve these questions is far from clear; we need no less than a fundamental change in our sense of citizenship and of responsibility to the common good. But the most important first step must be to re-examine the meaning of old age in our society, to ask ourselves what rights and duties we should or want to assume over our life span, and to rethink what we owe to those younger and older than ourselves. The elderly constitute the one "special interest" group that everyone hopes to join eventually. And the elderly are already the group that consumes most of our social spending. In the next chapter, we will examine the growth and contradictions of today's senior power movement and explore alternatives for how, in our aging society, the elderly of all generations can best be served.

9

Justice Between Generations: The Politics of Reform

> Elderly people, trained and experienced by life's
> activities, can be made the greatest asset humanity
> possesses if they are liberated from the slavery of
> poverty and are permitted to exercise their talents
> as circulators of money.
>
> — Francis E. Townsend, 1935

THE BIRTH of the senior power movement, according to legend, can be traced to a specific man and moment. At age sixty-six, Dr. Francis Everett Townsend, in poor health, out of a job, and with his savings running low, had come to what he thought would be his twilight years. Born shortly after the Civil War — one of seven children — to a poor but religious family, his life had never been easy. As a young man, he failed in real estate. Later, having managed to graduate from medical school, he moved to the frontier town of Bear Lodge, South Dakota, where for a while he earned a precarious living doctoring to cowhands and miners, professional gamblers and other adventurers in the still wild

229

West. For the next twenty years, he moved from one town to the next on the open range in search of paying patients. But the experience made him feel old before his time, and in 1919 he decided to move his family to what he thought would be an easier life in the sun and warmth of Long Beach, California.

There he attempted to establish a practice, but it foundered. For a while, he dabbled once again in real estate but proved to be a poor salesman. Finally, with the help of a medical school classmate, he won an appointment as assistant director of the City Health Office, but soon enough lost his job in a local political upheaval, just as the Great Depression was reaching its nadir.

Southern California had already become a haven for senior citizens. Attracted by its temperate climate, tens of thousands of pioneering older Americans from across the country had moved there in the hope of establishing a new kind of life: a comfortable, independent retirement, free from snow and family ties. But after the crash on Wall Street, most lost their meager savings, and with the unemployment rate soaring, even those fit enough to work could not find jobs. Social Security did not yet exist. It was in this setting that Townsend came to see his own misfortune as that of his generation. His moment of epiphany, he would later claim, came to him one morning when he spotted three elderly women outside his window rummaging for edibles in a trash can.

"A torrent of invectives tore out of me," Townsend recalled, "the big blast of all the bitterness that had been building in me for years. I swore and I ranted, and I let my voice bellow with the wild hatred I had for things as they were.

"My wife came a-running.

" 'Doctor! Doctor!' She always called me doctor. 'Oh you mustn't shout like that. All the neighbors will hear you.'

" 'I want all the neighbors to hear me!' I roared defiantly. 'I want God Almighty to hear me! I'm going to shout till the whole country hears.' "[1]

And before long the whole country did hear. Soon Congress and President Roosevelt himself would be struggling against the sudden potency of the Townsend movement, as local chapters sprang up in congressional districts across the nation. For in his rage, the old country doctor had hit upon a simple plan to end the Depression, a plan that, however extreme and impractical, drew legitimacy from the prevailing economic ideas of the time, while also awakening the nation's elderly to their potential power as an organized special interest group.

Townsend first formulated his plan in a letter to the editor of his local newspaper, the *Long Beach Press-Telegram*. Echoing the arguments in favor of mass consumption that Stuart Chase and others were then beginning to popularize, Townsend began by observing,

> Of late years, it has become an accepted fact that because of man's inventiveness, less and less productive effort is going to be required to supply the needs of the race. This being the case, it is just as necessary to make some disposal of our surplus workers, as it is to dispose of our surplus wheat or corn or cotton. . . . Wars have served in the past to hold down surplus population, but the last big war, in spite of the unprecedented slaughter, served only to increase production, while reducing the number of consumers.

What was to be done? Take older workers, like himself, and pay them to be full-time consumers. "It is estimated that the population of the age of 60 and above in the United States is somewhere between nine and twelve millions," Townsend reported. "I suggest that the national government retire all who reach that age on a monthly pension of $200 a month or more, on condition that they spend the money as they get it. This will insure an even distribution throughout the nation of two or three billions of fresh money each month, thereby assuring a healthy and brisk state of business, comparable to what we enjoyed during war times."

To pay for these pensions, Townsend proposed a 2 percent national sales tax. Alluding again to the proconsumption theories that would increasingly inform the New Deal, Townsend concluded, "When business begins to slow down and capital shows signs of timidity, stimulus must be provided by the National Government in the form of additional capital. . . . This function of the Government could be easily established and maintained through the pension system for the aged."[2]

The letter provoked a lively debate in the pages of the *Press-Telegram*, with Townsend taking the time to answer each of his critics, thereby provoking more letters to the editor. Soon elderly visitors began showing up at the Townsend household hoping to hear more of his "revolving pension" plan, as he began to call it. Encouraged, Townsend advertised for canvassers to obtain signatures of endorsement and within a few days had obtained two thousand names. This initial success prompted Townsend to seek out a "super salesman" who could help him build an organization and push his scheme into law. He found his man in Earl Clements, a hard-driving young businessman whose realty company had failed in the Depression. Within five weeks the two men had established an office, incorporated under the name Old Age Revolving Pensions Ltd., and were receiving an average of one hundred replies a day from the promotional material they circulated throughout the community. Soon they were publishing their own newspaper, the *Townsend National Weekly*, and excitement began to spread across California. In San Diego, a major retirement center, where 19 percent of the population was over age sixty, Townsend managed to enlist one out of six citizens into his movement. Some of these older people, convinced that Townsend would soon deliver them what was then the princely sum of $200 dollars every month, demanded that local merchants extend them credit. When the merchants refused to sell on promises, they were abused and threatened with boycotts.

At its peak, in 1935, the Townsend movement attracted an estimated 10 million members, united under the banner "Age for Leisure, Youth for Work." Ridiculed by academic economists, the business community, and New Deal brain trusters, Townsend's plan nonetheless had a popular appeal that provided a powerful impetus to the movement for Social Security. Speaking of the elderly who were attracted to Townsend's plan, David H. Bennett observed in his book *Demagogues in the Depression*, "The economy of abundance of the 1920's had provided the ideological framework for these people. . . . The Townsendites played upon these memories of prosperity and added to it their own thesis. To a generation who had largely escaped economics in school and even college, their economic arguments seemed virtually unassailable."[3]

There is an irony to the contempt that nearly all the historians of the era still show toward Townsend. He may have been a demagogue, stirring up the elderly with impossible promises without first consulting credentialed experts. But in essence, his "revolving pension plan" hardly differed from Social Security. Both were pay-as-you-go systems, designed to transfer wealth directly from taxpayers to retirees, without building up reserves. The Townsend plan was to be funded by a specially earmarked, regressive sales tax; Social Security is funded by a dedicated, regressive payroll tax. Both, by the standards applied to private pension plans, were actuarially unsound. Moreover, Townsend's rationale for the plan was completely consistent with the arguments put forward by the original architects of Social Security. Both plans were supposed to stimulate the economy by discouraging thrift and by converting workers into consumers. Both promised benefits to retirees regardless of need. And perhaps most important, both plans treated the elderly as a distinct, dependent class and thereby encouraged the elderly to view themselves as such.

As Wilbur Cohen, the "father of Medicare," would write in the early 1960s, the enduring legacy of the Townsend movement was that it "did much to make older people self-conscious and to begin to see themselves as a common interest group. It dramatized their needs and made society aware of the existence of a new group in the population."[4] By the same token, however, both the Townsend plan and Social Security stigmatized the elderly as universally needy and frail, legitimizing the view that they had no place in the mainstream of American society, except as "circulators of money."

Townsend's organization faded rapidly after passage of the Social Security Act in 1935, and until the early 1960s, despite the government's increasing deference to special interests, no comparable groups emerged. Then in 1961 came the first White House Conference on Aging. The session was itself a testament to the growing importance of the elderly vote and to the government's increasing willingness to broker to special interests. But it also brought a new dynamism to the long-dormant senior power movement by bringing many activists together for the first time and by giving them a new sense of power and political legitimacy. Within the next ten years, two major new senior power groups emerged — the National Council of Senior Citizens (NCSC) and the Gray Panthers (GP) — while two existing groups, the American Association of Retired Persons (AARP) and the National Council on Aging (NCOA), dramatically increased in membership and political influence.

Today, each of these organizations continues to lay claim to different constituencies and to emphasize subtly different goals. NCSC, for example, sprang out of the labor movement; with a largely blue-collar constituency, its primary concern is with income support for the elderly and for facilitating the trend toward early retirement. AARP draws its membership primarily from the middle- and upper-middle-class elderly. With an annual budget of over $100 million, the organization wields overwhelming force in support of Social Security, Medicare, and other age-based entitlements. But AARP also concentrates more than other groups on breaking down mandatory retirement rules, which primarily concern white-collar workers. The Gray Panthers, under the charismatic leadership of Maggie Kuhn, see themselves as a populist organization and in their rhetoric emphasize the needs of the poor — of all generations. The Panthers nonetheless display militant support for programs benefiting the elderly regardless of need and vigorously attack all proposals to means-test Social Security and Medicare.[5]

Despite these differences, two essentially contradictory ideas have come to inform the ideology of these groups and of the senior power movement generally. The first, deriving from Townsend, the social insurance movement, and the ideal of pluralism, holds that all older Americans ought to be provided benefits on the basis of their seniority alone rather than according to their individual need. This idea today continues to manifest itself in the opposition of virtually all senior power groups to any reduction in Social Security and Medicare benefits for the well-to-do, even if this would free up resources for the elderly poor. Implicit in this view is the presumption that nearly all the elderly are needy and are therefore deserving of subsidy as a class.

The other defining idea of the senior power movement, influenced by the New Left and the civil rights movement as well as by changing biological reality, stresses the diversity of the elderly. Chronological age is meaningless, goes the common assertion; many senior citizens are frail and needy, many more are active, sophisticated, and well able to contribute to society. This idea manifests itself in opposition to mandatory retirement and other forms of age discrimination. A pervasive "ageism" — or "gerontophobia," as Maggie Kuhn calls it — excludes the elderly from full participation in American life on the basis of their age alone.

Under the system of interest group politics, the gray lobby is institutionally incapable of fully supporting either view of the elderly. First and foremost, senior power groups claim to represent the elderly as a whole, or at least the current older generation. And politicians, in following the advice of these groups, presume that these organizations speak for a common interest.

For any senior power group to emphasize the diversity of the elderly would be to erode its own standing as an interest deserving of inclusion in the process of brokerage and pluralistic decision making. Thus, these groups are driven to what some have called a stance of "compassionate ageism," a willingness to reinforce prevailing stereotypes of the elderly as universally needy in the hope of winning higher benefits for all senior citizens.

As Robert Binstock has observed, senior citizens' groups

> have insisted that all programs benefitting the aged and those who make their living off of them are sacred, without regard to their distributional effects. They have fought to "Save Our Social Security" without paying much if any attention to those who are not saved by Social Security or any other program. . . . One could hardly expect otherwise. . . . The very bases, or incentive systems, on which these organizations exist dictate that they be ageist in their stance. They purport to represent or to be concerned about all older persons — the aged. To act otherwise — to emphasize differences within the constituency — would undermine their legitimacy.[6]

However, senior power groups risk offending their more affluent and alert members while also undermining arguments against age discrimination if they present the elderly as generally frail or unable to help themselves. Thus the senior power movement must live with a contradiction at its core. When it comes to the provision of benefits, partisans of the movement argue, all seniors should be treated alike and, through their representative organizations, brokered to as a distinct monolithic interest group — even if that means the elderly poor receive inadequate benefits. But when it comes to the allocation of job opportunities and social status, each senior should be judged on individual merit, with no presumption that his or her age implies any reduced capacity to be useful, creative, or independent. The elderly, they argue, have as much right and as much ability as anyone else to earn a living and pay their own way. But older Americans also have a special right, they continue, to be supported by others by virtue of their seniority and to be afforded special dignity and respect should they prefer to quit their jobs and enjoy an active prolonged retirement.

The failure of the senior power movement to resolve this conflict is tragic indeed for both young and old. No group in our society will escape resentment, much less receive veneration and respect, so long as its members are universally subsidized while at the same time many proudly proclaim their ability, if not their proclivity, to continue contributing to society. The fact that age-based entitlement programs are financed by payroll taxes that disproportionately burden the poor when they are young while promising the needy inadequate benefits when they are old compounds the tension. Finally, the fact that all of these programs are officially projected to be bankrupt or nearing insolvency during the lifetime of today's younger Americans makes a mockery of the idea that allocation on the basis of seniority alone serves all generations. We need a wholly new conception of what it means to grow old in America—one that will bring the elderly as a whole back into the mainstream of society and simultaneously afford dignity and adequate support to those in need.

Many members of the aging community have recognized the inequities and contradictions fostered by the senior power movement and have warned against their consequences. As early as 1974, for example, the prominent gerontologist Bernice Neugarten began raising the question of whether attaining age sixty-five by itself any longer served as a reliable indicator of need. In 1978, she warned that age-based entitlements were "stigmatizing rather than liberating older people from the negative effects of the label, 'old.' "[7]

The following year, Carroll Estes, in her book *The Aging Enterprise*, went further. Age-based entitlements diminish the social position of older Americans, she charged, and the fault lies with the self-styled advocates for the elderly. Conferring benefits

on the basis of seniority, she wrote, "institutionalizes and reinforces the marginality of the aged by legitimating an industry of
agencies, providers, and planners that must then continually
reaffirm the outgroup status of the aged in order to maintain and
expand their own activities."[8]

In 1981, Maggie Kuhn herself took the idea to its logical and
obvious conclusion. In an article for the *Gray Panther Network*,
she charged that "the entire aging network assumes that the
problems of the old will be solved through benefits and services
for the old. This thinking and the legislation stemming from it,
segregates the elderly from the rest of American society, thereby
enhancing hostility between generations."[9] The same concern
has been echoed by Binstock, who argues that by advocating
across-the-board subsidies for senior citizens, the gray lobby set
the elderly up to be made scapegoats for the cuts in programs
benefiting children and the truly needy.[10]

By this late date, all Americans must honestly ask themselves
what the different generations owe to one another and why.
Today, more than half of all federal social spending goes to the
population over age sixty-five, nearly all of the money distributed
without regard to need. Only about 17 percent of all families
receiving Social Security are actually poor; a mere 2 percent of
those receiving civil service and military retirement pensions fall
beneath the federal government's poverty line.[11]

The question of whether this is fair or prudent cannot be settled
by ideology. In large part, the issue involves our basic values
and ideas of community. But equally important is a firm understanding of the underlying facts and trends. Once, prevailing
stereotypes, promoted by the gray lobby, held all elderly to be
poor, frail, dependent, and, above all, deserving. Today, a new
stereotype is emerging that depicts the elderly as affluent, active,
healthy, and also selfish for refusing to relinquish any of their
benefits in the face of the compounding deficits and general
downward mobility of the young. Neither stereotype has ever
been accurate, except as applied to some varying fraction of the

elderly. Americans of all ages will eventually pay a terrible price unless we force ourselves to see past these facile generalizations and to face the complex new realities of our aging society.

Economic Status of the Elderly

On average, senior citizens enjoy higher, after-tax per capita income than do members of any age group under age fifty — a truly astounding figure when one considers that nearly all the elderly have withdrawn from the labor force.[12] Moreover, the average net worth of households headed by a person over age sixty-five is more than double that of all households headed by a younger person — and more than ten times the net worth of households headed by a person under age thirty-five.[13] But while these numbers are not meaningless — they do refute the claim that the elderly as a whole are in special need — they nonetheless mask the reality that many of the elderly are living out their final years in scandalous poverty, while many others are exceptionally well-to-do. If there is any single generalization that applies to the old, it is that no generalization holds true for all of them. As the economist Joseph Quinn has warned, "Never begin a sentence with 'The elderly are . . .' or 'The elderly do. . . .' No matter what dimension of the aged you are discussing, some are, and some are not; some do, and some do not. The central characteristic to be remembered is the diversity of the aged. The least interesting summary statistic about the elderly is their average, because it ignores the tremendous dispersion around it. Beware the mean."[14]

The percentage of elderly living in poverty has declined dramatically over the last generation. As recently as the late 1950s, more than a third of all Americans over age sixty-five were living below the government's poverty line; today about one in seven is officially poor — about the same ratio as that for the population as a whole.[15] When the market value of noncash benefits for the elderly, such as Medicare and subsidized housing, are counted, the overall poverty rate of the elderly drops to about 3 percent, according to Census Bureau estimates — the lowest rate of any age group. By way of contrast, the poverty rate among children under age six, using this same index, was 18.2 percent in 1983.[16]

Who are the elderly poor? Primarily, they are people who were poor before they became elderly — particularly members of minority groups; unmarried, widowed, or divorced women; and the very old. Those who fall into all three categories are generally poorest of all. The official poverty rate among elderly black males is 25.9 percent; for elderly black females, 35.6 percent; and for elderly black females age seventy-five or over and living alone, 56.6 percent.[17] The poverty rates among Hispanic women are comparable.

Elderly women of all races are more likely to be poor than are men of the same race, and the older they become the greater their risk of poverty. Among women of all races, aged sixty-five to seventy-one, 11.8 percent are living in poverty; but among those who live past age seventy-two, 17.4 percent fall beneath the poverty line. Divorced women are extremely likely to experience poverty in old age, and again, the older they get the greater the hazard. The poverty rate among divorced women aged sixty-five to seventy-one, is 22.5; among those aged seventy-two and over, 27.7 percent. Single and widowed women fare only slightly better. More than a fifth of all widows above age seventy-two are living in poverty.[18]

If we were really serious about eliminating poverty among the elderly, we would target old age benefits to those in the greatest need. Instead, under our current system, the highest benefits go to the richest senior citizens, while provisions for the poor remain scandalously inadequate. For the elderly who earned no more than the minimum wage during their working years, Social Security pays not even enough to bring them above the government's own poverty line. Yet such people might consider themselves lucky. *More than one out of eight families headed by a person over age sixty-five do not even qualify for Social Security.*

People who worked as maids, farm hands, day laborers, and the like frequently find themselves not covered by the system, because their employers wished to avoid paying Social Security taxes and kept their jobs off the books. As of January 1986, the maximum possible benefits such people could receive from food stamps and from the federal government's welfare program for the elderly — Supplementary Security Income — was just $4,656 a year.[19] Meanwhile, the typical, middle-class elderly couple is receiving four to five times more back from Social Security than they ever paid in, with annual, inflation-adjusted benefits running around $12,000 a year.

At a time when nearly all the elderly were poor, or close to poor, distributing social benefits on the basis of seniority alone made good liberal sense. But today, the increasing disparity of wealth among the elderly means that age-based entitlement programs wind up requiring young people to pay a significant portion of their incomes to senior citizens who are richer than they are, while at the same time too few benefits reach the elderly who are desperately in need.

Marketers, predictably, have been quicker than social scientists to catch on to the emergence of an increasingly large, prosperous class of older Americans. Until recently, the standard opinion of the industry was that companies with "upscale" products to sell should generally avoid marketing to the elderly. Indeed, consumers beyond the precise age of forty-nine, so the thinking went, were best ignored in designing advertising strategies for most luxury items; such people were perceived as more likely than younger consumers to be unhealthy, set in their ways, and reluctant to spend what little discretionary income they might possess. Now that picture of older people has changed for the most part, as the industry has become aware of the growing affluence and the new "active lifestyle" enjoyed by many older Americans, including the retired.[20]

"The glitter is off the baby boom," says Judith Langer, a marketing-research consultant who publishes a newsletter for advertisers seeking to reach the over-fifty consumer. "The baby boom was once the darling of the media, but these people, it turns out, just don't have the disposable income of older Americans."

Here are some of the statistics that are causing advertisers to turn about. Households headed by a person over fifty-five enjoy an estimated 28 percent of all the discretionary income in the United States — nearly double the amount controlled by households headed by a person thirty-four or younger. Such older households account for nearly 80 percent of all deposits in savings and loan institutions, and for 68 percent of all money market accounts. Americans aged fifty-five and over purchase 48 percent of all luxury cars, while also buying 25 percent of all cosmetics and bath products, 25 percent of all alcoholic beverages, and 21 percent of all stereos. A recent joint study by the Conference Board — a business research group — and the Census Bureau found that 26.9 percent of all households headed by a person age sixty-five or older enjoy enough income to purchase luxury items, with the average amount of discretionary income coming to an annual $5,633 per household member.[21]

The same message is echoed in the promotional material sent to advertisers by *Modern Maturity* magazine, the official membership publication of the American Association of Retired Persons, which begins recruiting members when they reach age fifty. While its legislative office has consistently lobbied on Capitol Hill against any targeting of Social Security pensions to the poor, the business staff at its magazine has been busy pointing out to potential advertisers just how rich many of today's older Americans are.

"50 & Over people . . . They've got clout," proclaims the headline in one of the magazine's media kits; "Affluent . . . Aware . . . Active buyers with over $500 billion to spend." Inside, the copy reads: "50 & Over people are putting into practice the credo of 'Living for Today.' They're spending on self-fulfillment *now* (Hedonism vs. Puritanism) rather than leaving large sums behind." AARP's advertising brochure boasts: "When viewed on a per capita income basis . . . the 50 & Over group reveals a high income profile and spending pattern that makes it one of the most affluent consumer markets in the U.S. today."

The pitch has worked spectacularly. In 1983, *Adweek* for the first time included *Modern Maturity* in its annual list of the country's ten "hottest magazines." During the previous recession year, *Modern Maturity*'s advertising revenue surged ahead by 46 percent, with a 21 percent gain in the number of ad pages.

Ironically, many firms, particularly banks, airlines, and tour-group companies, have decided that the best way to reach this new affluent class of older Americans is to offer special senior citizen discounts. Eastern Airlines, for example, has a fare policy under which a customer age sixty-five and older can buy a year's worth of travel over all its routes for $1,299 — hardly the sort of discount likely to benefit old people who are truly in need but a good marketing strategy for winning over "super citizens," as some advertisers now label the comfortably fixed elderly.

The travel industry in general has good reason for going after the senior market. In 1984, travelers over age fifty accounted for 30 percent of all domestic air trips, for 32 percent of all hotel and motel occupants, and for 72 percent of all trips in recreational vehicles, according to Robert Forbes of the AARP. In 1983, Forbes reports, nearly half of all passports issued to adult Americans went to those fifty-five and over. [22]

In the vacation travel market, the dominance of affluent senior citizens is overwhelming. According to Senior Citizens Marketing Group, a Dallas-based consulting firm, senior citizens on average spend 4 percent of their annual income on recreational travel and account for 80 percent of all commercial vacation travel trips, particularly first-class air travel and luxury cruises. Mindful of this rich and growing market, the Marriott Corporation offers room discounts of 50 percent and restaurant discounts of 25 percent to guests over age sixty-two at selected hotels. [23]

Perhaps the most egregious example of discounting to the

affluent elderly comes from Washington, D.C., where the local government has organized the "Golden Washingtonian Senior Discount Program." The City of Washington is more than 70 percent black and exceptionally poor; it is also one of the highest-priced cities in the nation. Nonetheless, Mayor Marion Barry has acted to make the cost of living still higher for everyone below age sixty-five by persuading local merchants to offer 10–25 percent discounts to anyone above that age — both D.C. residents and tourists. In a letter to local merchants, Barry explains his program and its rationale:

> The Golden Washingtonian Club senior discount program is a tested tool you can use to attract a *truly golden market*, and boost your bottom line. . . . *It's a matter of numbers.* More than four million seniors visit the District each year — and 103,000 live here. . . . *It is also a matter of money.* Seniors have more after-tax disposable income than members of any other age group. Combining this $175 million local total with the $250 million or more senior visitors spend here each year spells big business.[24]

Merchants who agree to participate in the program are listed in a handy "Gold Mine" directory, which the city mails to local seniors and to all local hotels and tourist offices.

Banks, having become aware of the tremendous pool of savings controlled by older Americans, now routinely offer such incentives as free checking, reduced fees for safe-deposit boxes, as well as special credit lines to any customer over sixty-five, or in some cases, fifty-five. At least indirectly, such discounts must, of course, come at the expense of younger customers.

The very existence of this large new prosperous class of older Americans undermines one of our most central ideas about the nature of old age in America. The thesis goes back to the Progressive era: when reform-minded Americans first "discovered" the elderly, early in this century, it seemed inevitable to many observers that the rise of industrialism entailed a common misery for the old — that the rapid pace of technology and the new stress on efficiency would necessarily lead to the impoverishment of each succeeding older generation.

As Edward T. Devine, an early advocate of old age compensation, wrote in 1909: "It is notorious that the insatiable factory wears out its workers with great rapidity. As it scraps its machinery, so it scraps human beings. . . . Middle age is old age, and the worn-out worker, if he has no children and if he has no savings, becomes an item in the aggregate of the unemployed."[25]

But it has turned out otherwise. We should not be surprised that many of today's senior citizens are doing well. After a rough start during the Depression, the current older generation, it should be recalled, went on to experience the greatest, most prolonged period of mass affluence the world has ever known. The nature of work changed drastically over this period. An ever smaller percentage of Americans worked in factories, and those who did worked shorter hours and usually enjoyed the protection of a strong labor movement. At the same time, most Americans came to be employed in the service sector of the economy, where jobs are less physically demanding. Home ownership also became the norm during this period, not only insulating the majority of Americans from inflation, but also providing many with large windfalls. Moreover, by the 1970s, for the first time a third of the elderly would be receiving private pensions in addition to Social Security and Medicare. Meanwhile, medical technology continued to advance, allowing more and more Americans to escape or delay the disabilities that once made old age almost universally an unpleasant and impoverished time of life.

All these changes are to be applauded. But to pretend that they have no implications for a Social Security system invented more than half a century ago, or for our welfare state more generally, is simply to be obtuse.

Today, both the public and private pension systems are seducing millions of Americans into early retirement long before their productive years are over. Even those who want to remain at work frequently find this ambition too costly, because the longer they delay retirement, the lower the lifetime value of their Social Security and other pensions. Using data from a survey by the Social Security administration, for example, Joseph F. Quinn and fellow economist Richard V. Burkhauser have shown that among men who were sixty-five in 1974 and who qualified for Social Security only, the median loss of benefits for remaining another year in the work force came to $3,000. For those who qualified for both Social Security and a private pension, the median loss of benefits came to over $5,000—an amount that equaled 48 percent of the annual median earnings of such senior workers.[26]

In 1977, amendments to the Age Discrimination in Employment Act banned mandatory retirement before age seventy; in 1986, mandatory retirement rules at any age became illegal—except in colleges and universities. Yet as important as this civil rights legislation may be in principle, it has so far proved practically irrelevant in practice, largely because of the incentives that Quinn and Burkhauser have documented. Using the same longitudinal data that they studied, Herbert S. Parnes has found that only 3 percent of senior workers were actually "forced out" by mandatory rules; the others all opted for the increasingly generous (and coercive) benefits available to them before they reached the age at which they would have been forced to retire.[27]

Meanwhile, as we have seen, the system has caused many other pernicious effects. The cost of these pensions reduces the ability of younger Americans to save for their own retirement and also to afford children, thereby undermining the long-term solvency of these systems. At the same time, the provision of benefits on the basis of seniority carries with it an implicit, demeaning assumption that the elderly as a whole are unfit to contribute to society. As partisans of the senior power movement alternately promote and debunk this stereotype, they first unwittingly provide a rationale for age discrimination and then provide powerful arguments for why the young should resent being forced to support the old. The able elderly lose respect and their rightful place in the mainstream of American society, while those in need suffer from neglect and inadequate benefits. It is surely time we redrafted the so-called contract between the generations.

Beyond Entitlements

Three arguments have traditionally been used to defend age-based entitlements. The first we have already heard from Townsend. Paying the elderly to consume, he promised, would stimulate the economy and provide more jobs for younger workers. In an era of massive unemployment and surplus capacity, the notion could not be summarily dismissed. But in an aging society that is at the same time beset with a declining industrial base and flooded with imports, it makes no sense to promote consumption or to encourage idleness. Whether it was true or not in the past, today the United States needs the talent and experience of its older citizens.

As the baby boom generation ages and the pool of younger workers shrinks, we will need the contributions of the elderly still more. In the meantime, if we are to afford the cost of rebuilding U.S. industry, of repairing our dilapidated infrastructure, and of providing today's children with the skills and knowledge that they will need to compete in a global economy, we cannot afford to promise today's elderly, or our future selves, that for the last 20–25 percent of adult life we will all be automatically entitled to subsidized consumption and be free from labor.

As Jarold A. Kieffer, former staff director of the 1981 White House Conference on Aging has written,

> The pro-retirement philosophy may have made sense to policy makers and employers in the 1950s and 1960s, when high U.S. productivity and low inflation made it seem possible to support a large retired population. . . . Younger workers needed jobs. Most older workers had been engaged in farming or other work requiring

heavy manual labor. Many were physically spent or in poor health. . . . But policies that encourage premature retirement are no longer appropriate in a time when the solvency of our retirement systems is a growing problem, older people are healthier and longer-lived, and most jobs do not require heavy labor.[28]

The second argument in favor of age-based entitlements is that because they promise benefits to rich and poor alike, they enjoy broad-based political support and are therefore immune to budget cuts. "A means test makes for a mean program," goes the common saying. Put another way, the affluent must be bribed to support the needy. As the political writer Bob Kuttner has written in defense of the status quo in Social Security, the current system "is able to redistribute so much income to the poor precisely because it distributes within a context of a universal program that provides benefits to the middle class. Isolating those portions of Social Security that function as an anti-poverty program might make fiscal sense, but this would quickly erode the system's political logic."[29]

But programs that ignore fiscal sense tend toward insolvency, regardless of what the polls show. As we have already seen, Social Security, Medicare, and the other age-based entitlement programs are all likely to strand the baby boomers in old age, or else to present an impossible encumbrance on the next generation. In either event, these programs will create generational conflict, thereby creating an entirely new and vicious political logic.

Moreover, in thinking concretely about this issue, it is important to remember who the elderly poor are. At any given moment, most younger and middle-aged Americans are sure that they won't soon find themselves in need, and consequently they do indeed tend to resent programs that deliver only to the non-elderly poor. But it is much more difficult for any of us to know what hazards we may face in old age, or even what our parents may face. Middle-class women are especially vulnerable to poverty as they grow older, particularly if they are single or outlive their husbands, as most do. Men and women alike know that as they age, they will be increasingly susceptible to catastrophic illnesses for which they could never pay without public support. The high cost of nursing home care can wipe out the savings of any middle-class couple within a few months, whether they are paying for their own care or for an elderly, destitute parent. In short, because old age is such a vulnerable time of life, even for the well-to-do, there is no reason to suppose that younger Americans, rich and poor alike, won't support programs that insure their parents and themselves against becoming both old *and* in need.

Indeed, in the future such programs would be far more likely to attract the support of the young than our current age-based entitlement system. They would cost less and would relieve the young of having to pay benefits to the affluent. Moreover, it will eventually become clear to more and more of the young that while they can reasonably expect their children to insure them against becoming needy in old age, they cannot expect their children to pay for programs that insure against the extreme and increasing probability that they will simply succeed in living past age sixty-five.

The third argument used to justify age-based entitlements is that they do not expose the elderly to the "humiliation" of having to prove their need. Submitting to a means test is indeed humiliating to most people. But it is not nearly as humiliating, let it first be said, as enduring grinding poverty, becoming dependent on one's children, or being denied access to adequate medical care. Under our current system, the elderly poor are denied the benefits they need to live in dignity, while the young must face the prospect of not receiving any benefits at all. We cannot do more for the elderly poor of any generation as long as we all promise ourselves subsidies in old age without regard to need.

Furthermore, the principal reason we find means-testing humiliating is that we associate the practice with welfare programs. But there is no reason why a means-tested program for the elderly cannot be provided as social insurance to which everyone has an "earned right." This would be no more or less accurate than our current practice of describing Social Security as a form of insurance. Let there be a specially earmarked tax to pay for the program. By paying this tax, younger Americans will in fact insure themselves against the very real possibility that through bad luck, bad planning, or poor health they will find themselves needy in old age. In that eventuality, filing for a claim would be no more humiliating than filing for fire insurance after one's house has burned down. And those who never needed to file a claim would have no more reason to feel resentful than the happy home owner who pays for fire insurance all his life but who never sees his house actually consumed by flames.

From Here to There

The case for reforming Social Security and changing it from a program that insures one against becoming a senior citizen into a program that insures one against becoming dependent in old age is, I think, logical and fully consistent with both the needs of the economy and with the true interests of the elderly of all generations. Unfortunately, we are not, however, starting from scratch. Today's affluent elderly have been promised their benefits and have laid their retirement plans accordingly. Certainly there is a moral problem with changing the rules of the game on those already collecting, or soon to collect benefits, to say nothing of the political problem.

The insistence of the affluent elderly that they receive their benefits, come what may, creates endless dilemmas. Every day that younger Americans continue subsidizing the affluent elderly, they build up in themselves the rightful expectation to be subsidized in turn when they retire, regardless of their means. Gradual reform means reform principally at the expense of younger Americans. No reform means that, at the very least, younger

Americans will be exposed to the risk of a poor and shameful old age while their children are unjustly encumbered with unpaid bills.

There is no easy answer for this predicament. Today's older generation, in devising Social Security, Medicare, and other age-based entitlement programs, bet that today's younger Americans would be much richer than they have turned out to be and also less healthy and more inclined to raise large families. Those errors probably will not wind up costing today's affluent senior citizens their entitlements. But they do point up the need for young Americans to be more prudent in devising their own institutions of retirement. For the baby boomers, especially, the margin for error is small.

One incremental reform that is frequently suggested is simply to roll back the retirement age farther and faster than Congress has already done. Under the 1983 amendments to the Social Security Act, the retirement age for full benefits will begin increasing by two months per year starting at the turn of the century and ending in 2022. Thus, under current law, sixty-seven will become the standard retirement age for people born after 1960.

At first glance, this approach seems fair, since the baby boom generation will probably be longer-lived than any that has gone before. But raising the retirement age will only compound the class inequities perpetuated by the current system. The poor do not live as long as middle- and upper-class people do. Black males born in 1982, for example, had a life expectancy that year of 64.9 years. In contrast, white males born the same year could expect to live past 71. Moreover, morbidity varies greatly among the elderly. Some citizens are simply worn out even before they reach age sixty-five, especially if they have worked as manual laborers or endured the tedium of assembly line work. Others, especially white-collar workers, are physically able to continue at their jobs into their eighties and nineties. Distributing benefits on the basis of age alone thus tends to work to the advantage of those least in need. In the absence of other reforms, raising the retirement age will only compound the inequity between rich and poor within each generation.

What we need instead is a way to convince today's affluent elderly that they can preserve their interests and at the same time be part of the solution to the problems faced by younger Americans. To do this, we must remember that the elderly — even those who are quite well-to-do — are exposed to exceptional risks. Why are the affluent elderly so often militant in their demands for subsidy? One important reason is that they fear just one catastrophic illness will wipe out their savings. Similarly, they know they are vulnerable to enormous nursing home care expenses and to other quick reversals of fortune caused by deteriorating health. If the government were to offer the elderly true protection against such calamities, senior citizens would be provided with social security in the true meaning of the term; in return, the affluent elderly might agree to forgo some of their public pensions and subsidies for routine medical treatment.

Three factors must come together in order for social insurance to be practical. First, the problem insured against must occur comparatively rarely. Second, it must be extremely harmful to its victims. Finally, there must be a problem of adverse selection that prevents private insurers from offering adequate protection. Private insurance against long-term and catastrophic health problems is available, but it is extremely expensive, primarily because Americans are loath to buy such insurance until they are old or otherwise likely to qualify for benefits. Social insurance against these needs, because it would be mandatory, would solve this problem of adverse selection. At the same time it would satisfy the other two conditions of practicality. Reaching age sixty-five or living much beyond that age was once the exception rather than the rule; it also brought near universal hardship. But this is no longer the case, which is the fundamental reason why our system of age-based entitlements must be reformed. But social insurance against catastrophic illness, nursing home care, and even poverty itself can be offered on an actuarially sound basis while also relieving the elderly of tremendous anxiety. Most of us will die without needing or qualifying for such benefits, but all of us will enjoy a much greater sense of security in old age if we do not have to worry about paying for such misfortunes.

It might well be asked, why not abandon the mask of social insurance altogether, and pay each according to his need rather than to his age or previous work experience? Why should poor, younger Americans be asked under any circumstances to pay for the rich—even those who are residing in nursing homes or suffering from catastrophic illnesses? The answer is practical politics. Today's affluent elderly will not accede to any reduction in their Social Security and Medicare benefits unless given something of real value in return. In some cases, the opposition of the affluent elderly to the reform of these systems is motivated by selfishness, in some cases by misunderstanding of what is being proposed, but most often by justified fears that the hazards of old age will not leave them affluent for long. They do not want to see themselves pauperized by illness or frailty. Only by offering them insurance against these real risks can younger Americans hope for anything more than gradual reform of Social Security and Medicare, which amounts to reform principally at their own expense. The proposal is by no means a perfect solution—by itself, it is probably not a solution at all. But it may be the best deal that younger Americans can expect.

The great danger with this approach is, of course, that it will lead to the affluent elderly's being granted new benefits at the same time that the gray lobby succeeds in blocking any cuts in existing old age entitlement programs. Younger Americans have no lobbies. As was discussed in the last chapter, under our pluralistic system of politics, a built-in bias exists in favor of expanded benefits for older citizens. Moreover, as the baby boomers move through midlife, an increasing number will look to the government to support their own aged parents—regardless of need—in hopes of preserving their inheritances. Finally,

another factor may come to play. As we have already seen, the
Social Security pension fund is projected, under relatively optimistic economic assumptions, to begin building up large surpluses in the next two decades. If these surpluses materialize,
they will provide Congress with a powerful temptation to accede
to the demands of the gray lobby and increase old age benefits
across the board. Unfortunately for the baby boomers and their
children, the fiscal position of at least the pension trust fund, if
not the Medicare fund, may actually improve before deteriorating during their own retirement years. Only if younger Americans succeed in holding politicians accountable for the long term
will the momentum for reform be preserved — a less than encouraging thought.

Fallback Positions

If Americans are unable or unwilling to stop promising themselves universal subsidies in retirement, then at least we must
look for ways to finance old age entitlements that promote rather
than erode the long-term solvency of these programs. The current payroll tax puts the greatest burden on the working poor,
thereby increasing their dependency and reducing their ability
to save for retirement. At the same time, as a tax on paid labor,
it discourages employment while also making American-built
products more expensive and American business less competitive
in world markets. In all these ways, the payroll tax is inconsistent
both with the liberal purpose of the programs it finances and
with the rapid rates of economic growth these programs require
in order to remain solvent over the long term.

To remedy this inconsistency, programs that pay benefits on
the basis of seniority alone, if we must have them, ought to be
financed with a tax on consumption rather than on labor. The
more people consume, at any time of life, the less they save.
And the lower the savings rate, the less capital is available for
economic growth. At the same time, the less thrifty people are

in their younger years, the less the likelihood that they will be able to support themselves in old age without public assistance. Thus, today's payroll tax, by discouraging savings, not only serves to increase the dependency of the future elderly, but makes it less likely that programs such as Social Security and Medicare will be able to pay them adequate benefits.

There are many ways to tax consumption. The most progressive would be simply to require Americans to pay taxes on the difference between what they earn in a given year and what they save, with tax rates set higher according to income. Revenues accrued through this tax could be earmarked for the Social Security trust funds, just as today's payroll taxes are. To the extent required by political expediency and the demands of the gray lobby, benefits could be related to a worker's "contributions" to the system, just as they now are. The advantage would come in providing younger Americans with increased incentives to save. If the tax were extended to those already receiving old age benefits, it would provide the additional advantage of forcing the rich elderly to assume some of the burden for supporting the poor of their own generation.

The best argument against this reform is that younger Americans, within each economic class, tend to consume a higher proportion of their income than do older Americans of the same class. The young must pay the high cost of setting up a household — buying furniture, appliances, and if they're lucky, an actual home of their own — whereas older Americans usually have most of these expenses behind them. But only if one takes a short-term view are the young particularly encumbered by a tax on consumption. In the long run, the incentives to save created by such a tax not only will provide the young with more assets of their own when they retire, but will also encourage economic growth, create more jobs, and thereby eventually improve the chances of today's younger people for receiving public support in old age.

In keeping with the second condition upon which the long-term solvency of the Social Security System depends—population growth—Social Security taxes should be reduced for those Americans who make the sacrifice of raising children. The consumption tax just described should allow large deductions or credits for each dependent child. Childless Americans would of course be forced thereby to pay higher taxes than they otherwise would, but this would only be fair since their support in old age depends in large measure on the expenditures other people make to raise and educate the next generation.

There are, however, no purely technical solutions to the crisis in Social Security, Medicare, and other age-based entitlement systems. The crisis results ultimately from the way we live. Some improvements could be realized by changes in other government policy areas. Many needed reforms are simply beyond the scope of even the most intrusive government.

The single most important reform that can be legislated is that of ending the recurring budget deficits. I have argued earlier that the surpluses projected to build up the Social Security pension fund are illusary, because they are not invested in real wealth-producing assets and because future taxpayers will ultimately become liable for any funds Social Security lends to other government agencies. Although this analysis is controversial in some quarters, virtually all economists agree that as long as the surpluses in the Social Security trust funds are used to help finance each year's overall budget deficit, they will do nothing to help defray the cost of the baby boom generation's retirement, and many would agree that the net effect will be to drain resources from the future.

Moreover, the budget deficits themselves, to the extent that they are used to subsidize current consumption rather than to invest in the future, straightforwardly encumber the young by crowding out private investment and by causing more and more resources to be committed to servicing the mounting national debt. Finally, remember that under current law, nearly all baby boomers will wind up paying income taxes on their Social Security pensions. If the current deficits continue, tax rates will eventually have to be set much higher than they are today, and the baby boomers will accordingly see their real Social Security pensions reduced still more.

By increasing support for education, the government can also do a great deal in easing the pressures on the various old age entitlement programs. Similarly, by investing more in the repair and maintenance of the nation's public works and by paying the cost of cleaning up toxic wastes and other forms of pollution sooner rather than later, the government can help ease the burden on future taxpayers of supporting the ever growing number of elderly. Strict enforcement of laws against age discrimination would also help achieve this end, while at the same time providing more of the elderly with the chance they deserve to remain productive and independent.

But ultimately, cultural values must change before we can achieve real reform. Liberals and conservatives may differ on which social problems are best alleviated by government and which by market forces. But we live in an era in which both the public and private sectors are marked by exceptional devotion to short-term gain at the expense of the future. Corporate America is increasingly preoccupied with rearranging existing assets rather than in creating new ones, as can be seen in the merger mania that has swept over Wall Street in recent years. The best and the brightest of the business world now concentrate not on restoring productivity growth and rebuilding U.S. industry, but on inventing new forms of "junk bonds," "greenmail," and computer-driven arbitrage techniques. As many commentators have noted, American business generally has come to use investment criteria that systematically discount future earnings, while also creating a bias against productive investment.[30] Meanwhile, ever more individual Americans are managing their own finances as if tomorrow doesn't matter, racking up unprecedented levels of consumer debt while saving next to nothing.

These trends are symptomatic of a culture that no longer believes in or cares about its future. We worry constantly about the threat of nuclear war but very little about how we will live during the next century in the likely event that the world does not end. Members of the baby boom generation are showing exceptional devotion to exercise, proper diet, and other means of prolonging life, but few have given any hard thought to how they will pay their bills if indeed they succeed in living to a ripe old age. Older Americans tend to be awed by the technological marvels that have come into the world since they were children and by the unprecedented increase in living standards. But they tend to forget that these achievements did not come automatically and that there is no particular reason to assume that today's younger Americans won't also experience depression and hard times. The future cannot necessarily be left to take care of itself.

Our culture no longer builds large monuments; skyscrapers are constructed to last no more than a few decades, roads and bridges for even less time. Rather than building for the future and seeking to impress future generations, we instead devise ever more numerous and sophisticated means of borrowing from posterity. Children are the first victims of a culture that begins to discount its future; those who will eventually depend on today's children, the baby boomers, will be next, unless we change our ways.

Generational Equity

Every generation requires a strategy for its old age. An odd folk tale that has been told throughout Europe since the thirteenth century shows how far-reaching the repercussions of such strategies can be. "The Tale of the Ungrateful Son" begins with a description of an old merchant, who day by day grows more infirm. The old man's wife has long since passed away, and he is miserably lonely. Fearing that he will soon lose his powers of mind, the old man finally decides to ask his middle-aged son and daughter-in-law if he may move in with their family in the country.

At first the couple is overjoyed, for by way of compensation the merchant promises to bequeath his small fortune to them before he dies. But the old man, in his dotage, becomes increasingly troublesome to clean and feed. Eventually, his daughter-in-law grows resentful of his constant demands and senile chatter. Indeed, she nags her husband night and day, until at last he reluctantly agrees that the time has come to retire the old man to the barn.

The ungrateful son is too embarrassed, however, to confront his father directly with his shameful decision. He gives that chore to his own youngest child.

"Take your grandfather to the barn, and wrap him in the best horse blanket we have on the farm," he tells the boy. "That way, the old man will be as comfortable as possible until he dies."

With tears in his eyes, the child does as he is told. Except that, having selected the farm's best horse blanket, he tears it in half. He uses one part to swaddle his beloved grandfather but sets the other part aside. The merchant's son is furious when he learns what his child has done. "What sort of boy are you," he shouts, "who would put his own grandfather out in the barn to freeze with only half a horse blanket?"

"But father," the child replies, "I am saving the other half for you."

Any generation that neglects its elders must be prepared to suffer in kind. But by the same token, any generation that neglects its children must also be prepared for a miserable old age. The challenge of each generation, as it passes through its middle, productive years, is thus to strike a prudent balance between the needs of the young and the old. If, for example, the middle generation spends so much on the elderly that it must skimp on the education of the young or on investments in economic growth, then when the time comes for the young to govern, they may be unable to provide their elders with enough support. Alternatively, if the middle generation is stingy with the elderly, the young may come to feel like the child in "The Tale of the Ungrateful Son"—free to shirk their responsibilities to the old.

For many years, we could afford, or at least we thought we could afford, a political system that ignored this reality of the human condition. So long as the American standard of living continued to rise throughout the postwar period, there seemed to be little harm and much virtue in a system of government that brokered to the elderly as a whole, even while the young and future generations remained unorganized. But today we can't afford to avoid the hard choices that the partisans of interest group liberalism pretend don't exist. Either we must have senior power *and* junior power, or we must have neither.

Liberals, if they will be liberals in more than name only, must recognize this unavoidable truth. As programs for the poor have been cut while entitlements for the affluent elderly have been preserved, our welfare state acts more and more like an airdrop program. Flying over a certain neighborhood in an airplane, we know that somewhere below are citizens of all ages living in scandalous poverty. But rather than go door to door and seek out those who need help, we cast bushels of dollars over the entire area, hoping that some of the money will flutter down to the truly deserving.

Politically, of course, such methods of redistribution have been very popular. The middle and upper classes receive all sorts of benefits intended for the poor, bureaucracy is kept to a minimum, and everyone avoids the "humiliation" of a means test. But ultimately, the money runs out, the poor are still poor— and everyone feels overtaxed.

Is there any realistic chance that we will overcome interest group politics and reform the welfare state to meet true liberal ends? Though there are many reasons for doubt, there are also some for hope. Consider that in an aging society, the political party that promotes age-based entitlements for the rich and for the middle class will be the party of ever higher taxes and/or deficits. As long as the population was growing rapidly, it was possible to promise every American much more in old age benefits than he or she ever contributed to the cost of retiring the preceding generation, because the cost of old age benefits could be spread across an ever increasing number of younger taxpayers. Today it is just the opposite. Middle-class members of the baby boom generation will be lucky to receive back from Social Security and Medicare as much as they paid into these systems, even while younger Americans are forced to pay in much more of their income with still less prospect of return.

This circumstance presents the opportunity for a wholly new coalition in American politics: the truly needy allied with the truly overtaxed. The idea may seem paradoxical, but it is firmly validated by the arithmetic of an aging society. Why should middle-class Americans pay a dollar in taxes one year just on the promise that they might receive it back some years later? Since the relative number of younger Americans is shrinking, this is the question that must repeatedly be asked. For an ever increasing majority of Americans, Social Security promises a lower return on their contributions than they could realize by investing their tax dollars even in federally insured savings accounts. Can any party hold on to power for long by offering that sort of a deal?

But social insurance can provide all Americans with something the private sector can't: blanket protection against poverty — in old age, or, if we have the will, at any age. And it can do so at a much lower cost than our current system of universal age-based entitlements. The conjunction of interest, brought on by the aging of the population, between the poor and the young middle class — and the whole middle class of the future — can form the political basis for a liberal agenda that combines compassion with thrift, fairness with equity, individual interests with family values.

But to get there, we need our parties and our politicians to lead and educate the American people, not simply to broker to the loudest, most organized interests. We can never do away with faction. But we can have a political culture that holds factions accountable for their greed and that forces all special pleaders to show how their agendas just might serve the long-term public interest. Above all, because of where the money is spent, we need to penalize politicians and groups who plead for "our senior citizens" as if no distinction existed between the rich and the poor, the present or the future elderly.

The aging of the population need not force the American dream to end in this century. But it does require that we invest far more of our available resources in educating the young and more generally in raising the productivity of the next generation of workers. And it requires that we be far more prudent in the claims we make against the young, whether in the form of budget deficits, unfunded pension and health care promises, deferred maintenance of public infrastructure, or delayed cleanup of toxic wastes. At no time in history has mankind possessed so many different means and cumulatively wielded so much power to improve or diminish the near and distant future. With that power must come a new ethos of stewardship, a willingness to conserve and husband resources, not just in the interest of future generations but of our future selves as well.

Notes

Index

Notes

Chapter 1. The Challenge of an Aging Society

1. U.S. Bureau of Labor Statistics, *Recent Trends in Labor Force Participation Rates: A Chartbook* (Washington, D.C.: U.S. Government Printing Office, 1980).

2. In a 1950 study of steelworkers age fifty-five and over, for example, the majority felt that retirement was only for the physically impaired; by 1960, less than 25 percent of older workers in the same company agreed with that assessment. Philip Ash, "Pre-Retirement Counseling," *The Gerontologist* (June 1967): 97–99. Quoted by Anne Foner and Karen Schwab, "Work and Retirement in a Changing Society," in *Aging in Society*, ed. Matilda White Riley et al. (Hillsdale, N.J.: Lawrence Erlbaum Associates, 1983), 71.

3. Thomas Griffith, "Generations Are a Passing Thing," *Atlantic* 246:5 (November 1980): 24.

4. U.S. Bureau of the Census, *Historical Statistics of the United States, Colonial Times to 1970*, bicentennial edition, part 2 (Washington, D.C.: U.S. Government Printing Office, series B1–4, 1976), 49; U.S. Bureau of the Census, *Statistical Abstract of the United States: 1986*, 106th edition, (Washington, D.C.: U.S. Government Printing Office, 1985), table 81, 56.

5. U.S. Bureau of the Census, *Historical Statistics of the United States, Colonial Times to 1970*, (series A119–134), 15.

6. U.S. Bureau of the Census, Current Population Reports, *Projections of the Population of the United States, 1982 to 2080* (Washington, D.C.: U.S. Government Printing Office, series P-25, no. 952, 1984). The accompanying charts are based on the bureau's "middle series" projections, which

assume 1.9 lifetime births per woman, life expectancy at birth in 2080 to be eighty-one, and yearly net immigration of 450,000 persons.

7. Official estimates of the fertility rate are published by the National Center for Health Statistics' *Monthly Vital Statistics Report* (Washington, D.C.: U.S. Government Printing Office).

8. Selected Gallup poll opinion surveys, collected in *Public Opinion* (December–January 1986): 28.

9. Further arguments against the likelihood of any future increase in fertility rates are presented in chapter 5.

10. U.S. Bureau of the Census, Current Population Reports, *Projections of the Population of the United States, 1982 to 2080.*

11. Robert L. Clark and J. J. Spengler, "Changing Demography and Dependency Costs: The Implications of Future Dependency Ratios," in *Aging and Income: Essays on Policy Prospects*, ed. Barbara R. Herzog (New York: Human Sciences Press, 1977), 55–89.

12. Samuel H. Preston, " Children and the Elderly in the U.S.," *Scientific American* 251: 6 (December 1984): 45.

13. This figure includes the portion of a worker's wages that is forwarded to Social Security directly by his or her employer. Although advocates of Social Security sometimes argue that this tax is actually borne by the employer, economists are nearly in unanimous agreement that the funds actually come out of the worker's salary, as common sense would also confirm. For further discussion of this issue, see chapter 3.

14. D. P. Rice et al., "Changing Mortality Patterns, Health Services Utilization, and Health Care Expenditures, United States, 1978–2003," *Vital and Health Statistics* (Washington, D.C.: Public Health Service, U.S. Government Printing Office, series 3, no. 23, DHHS pub. no. (PHS) 83-14-7, September 1983), table 4.

15. U.S. General Accounting Office, *Social Security: Past Projections and Future Financing Concerns* (Washington, D.C.: U.S. Government Printing Office, GAO/HRD-86-22, March 1986), appendix 2, p. 80.

16. U.S. Bureau of the Census, Current Population Reports, *Money Income of Households, Families, and Persons in the United States: 1984* (Washington, D.C.: U.S. Government Printing Office, series P-60, no. 151, 1986), 121.

17. Frank S. Levy and Richard C. Michel, "The Economic Future of the Baby Boom" (Paper presented at the first annual conference of Americans for Generational Equity, Washington, D.C., 10 April 1986. Research originally prepared in December 1985 under contract with the Joint Economic Committee of the U.S. Congress and authorized by Chairman David Obey and Vice Chairman James Abnor).

18. Louise B. Russell, *The Baby Boom Generation and the Economy* (Washington, D.C., Brookings Institution, 1982), table 4–6, and U.S. Bureau of the Census, Current Population Reports, *Money Income of Households, Families, and Persons in the United States*, selected years.

19. Bryant Robey and Cheryl Russell, "The Year of the Baby Boom," *American Demographics* 6:5 (May 1984): 21.

20. Janet Bamford, "Degrees of Debt," *Forbes*, 7 April 1986, 122.

21. Levy and Michel, "The Economic Future," 8.

22. Jane Seaberry, "Two-Tiered Wages, More Jobs versus More Worker Alienation," *Washington Post*, 7 April 1985, p. Gl. "Two-Tier Plans Grow Like Topsey" (Labor Letter), *Wall Street Journal*, July 9, 1985, 1.

23. U.S. Bureau of the Census, Current Population Reports, *Money Income of Households, Families, and Persons in the United States*, 1975, 1985.

24. John Weicher and Susan Wachter, "The Distribution of Wealth Among Families: Increasing Inequality?" Paper presented to

the Working Seminar on the Family and American Welfare Policy, American Enterprise Institute, 10 November 1986.

25. Robert B. Avery, Gregory E. Elliehausen, and Glenn B. Canner, "Survey of Consumer Finances, 1983: A Second Report," *Federal Reserve Bulletin* (December 1984); Levy and Michel, "The Economic Future," 17.

26. U.S. Bureau of the Census, Current Population Reports, *Household Wealth and Asset Ownership: 1984*, series P-70, no. 7, 8.

27. Levy and Michel, "The Economic Future," 13. For Levittown prices, see Kenneth T. Jackson, *Crabgrass Frontier: The Suburbanization of the United States* (New York: Oxford University Press, 1985), 236.

28. U.S. Bureau of the Census, Current Population Reports, *Household Wealth and Asset Ownership: 1984*, series P-70, no. 7, 14.

29. Avery, Elliehausen, and Canner, "Survey of Consumer Finances, 1983," *Federal Reserve Bulletin* (September 1984).

30. See, for example, Yankelovich, Skelly, and White, Inc., *A Fifty Year Report on Social Security*, 1985 (survey sponsored by the American Association of Retired Persons, Washington, D.C.). Nearly two-thirds of the respondents aged twenty-five to forty-four stated that they were "not too confident" or "not at all confident" about the future of Social Security. For a comprehensive study of public attitudes toward Social Security, see Robert Y. Shapiro and Tom W. Smith, "The Polls: Social Security," *Public Opinion Quarterly* 49 (Winter 1985): 561–72.

31. Office of Management and Budget, *Special Analyses of the Budget of the United States Government, Fiscal Year 1987* (Washington, D.C.: U.S. Government Printing Office, 1986).

32. E. S. Andrews, *The Changing Profile of Pensions in America* (Washington, D.C.: Employee Benefits Research Institute, 1984).

33. Frances FitzGerald, *Cities on a Hill: A Journey Through*

Contemporary American Cultures (New York: Simon and Schuster, 1986), 209.

34. Social Security Administration, *The 1986 Annual Report of the Board of Trustees of the Federal Old-Age and Survivors Insurance and Disability Insurance Trust Funds* (Washington, D.C.: U.S. Government Printing Office, 1986), table 10, p. 32. The number is arrived at by compounding the annual growth in real wages assumed by the system's actuaries under "Alternative I," the only model that shows both the disability and pension trust funds remaining solvent past 2030. See, for example, table 31, p. 75. Note as well that these estimates do not take into consideration the cost of financing the Hospital Insurance or Medicare trust funds. A full discussion of the actuarial issues surrounding the Social Security system's trust funds is presented in chapters 3 and 4 of this book.

35. Daniel Patrick Moynihan, *Family and Nation* (San Diego: Harcourt Brace Jovanovich, 1986), 112.

36. U.S. Bureau of the Census, Current Population Reports, *Characteristics of the Population Below the Poverty Level: 1984* (Washington, D.C.: U.S. Government Printing Office, series P-60, no. 152, 1986).

37. Mary Bordette (Director, Government Affairs, Children's Defense Fund), "Investing in the American Family: The Common Bond of Generations" (testimony before the Select Committee on Aging, U.S. House of Representatives, 8 April 1986).

38. Sheldon Danziger and Peter Gottschalk, "Families with Children Have Fared Worst," *Challenge* (March–April 1986): 40–47.

39. Bordette, "The American Family."

40. Arthur J. Norton and Jeanne E. Moorman, "Marriage and Divorce Patterns of U.S. Women" (Revised version of paper given at the 1986 Population Association of America meetings, 11 June 1986), quoted by Peter A. Morrison, "Changing

Family Structure: Who Cares for America's Dependents" (testimony before the Subcommittee on Economic Resources, Competitiveness, and Security Economics of the Joint Economic Committee of Congress, 31 July 1986).

41. Among women aged thirty-five in 1985, for example, a quarter of those who were ever married experienced divorce before reaching age twenty-nine. Robert Shoen et al., "Marriage and Divorce in Twentieth Century American Cohorts," *Demography* 22 (February 1985): 101–14.

42. Preston, "Children and the Elderly," 46.

43. National Center for Health Statistics, *Advance Report on Final Natality Statistics, 1984*, supplement 35: 4 (18 July 1986).

44. National Commission on Excellence in Education, *A Nation at Risk: The Imperative for Educational Reform* (Washington, D.C.: U.S. Government Printing Office, 1985), 5.

45. Education Commission of the States, *Action for Excellence: A Comprehensive Plan to Improve Our Nation's Schools*, a report by the National Task Force on Education for Economic Growth (Washington, D.C.: U.S. Government Printing Office, 1983).

46. National Science Board Commission on Precollege Education in Mathematics, Science, and Technology, *Educating Americans for the 21st Century* (Washington, D.C.: U.S. Government Printing Office, 1983), p. v.

47. Survey results reported by the National Science Board, *Science Indicators: The 1985 Report* (Washington, D.C.: U.S. Government Printing Office, 1985), and by Wayne Riddle, *Comparison of the Achievement of American Elementary and Secondary Pupils with Those Abroad — The Examinations Sponsored by the International Association for the Evaluation of Educational Achievement*, Congressional Research Service, Library of Congress (Washington, D.C.: U.S. Government Printing Office, 2 May 1986). See also "U.S. Pupils

Lag from Grade 1, Study Finds," *New York Times*, 17 June
1984.

48. International Association for the Evaluation of Educational
Achievement, *Second International Mathematics Study: U.S.
Summary Report* (Urbana: University of Illinois at Urbana/
Champaign, U.S. National Coordinating Center, January
1985). And Riddle, *Comparison of Achievement*, 30–33.

49. National Science Board, *Undergraduate Science and Engineering Education* (Washington, D.C.: U.S. Government
Printing Office, March 1986), 2.

50. Ibid., 30.

51. National Science Board, *Science Indicators: The 1985 Report*, 92.

52. Simon Ramo, *What's Wrong with Our Technological Society
and How to Fix It* (New York: McGraw-Hill, 1983), 182.

53. National Science Board, *Science Indicators: The 1985 Report*, 92.

54. Congressional Budget Office, *1986 Annual Report* (Washington, D.C.: U.S. Government Printing Office, February
1986), table D-2.

55. Office of Management and Budget, *Special Analyses*, p. E-
12, table E-5.

56. Abba Lerner, "The Burden of the National Debt," 1948, in
Ralph Cecil Epstein and Arthur D. Butler, eds., *Selections
in Economics* (New York: Smith, Keynes and Marshall, 1958),
168–89.

57. Office of Management and Budget, *Special Analyses*, table
E-6.

58. Barry P. Bosworth, "Fiscal Fitness: Deficit Reduction and the
Economy," *Brookings Review* 4:2 (Winter–Spring 1986): 3.

59. Henry Kaufman, *Interest Rates, The Markets and the New
Financial World* (New York: Times Books, 1986), 31.

60. Although the hazards of protectionism are clear, it remains
true that in the long run, a large imbalance in the trade

budget subtracts from the wealth and opportunity of future Americans as much as if not more than a large deficit in the federal budget. For an informed analysis of the intergenerational transfer latent in our free trade policies, see John M. Culbertson, "The Folly of Free Trade," *Harvard Business Review* (September–October 1986): 122–28.

61. Bosworth, "Fiscal Fitness," 3.

62. Lester Thurow, *Zero Sum Solution* (New York: Simon and Schuster, 1985), 36.

63. Friedrich Her, *The Challenge of Youth* (University of Alabama Press, 1974).

64. Daniel Yankelovich, *New Rules: Searching for Self-Fulfillment in a World Turned Upside Down* (New York: Random House, 1981), 104.

65. Kingsley Davis and Pietronella van den Oever, "Age Relations and Public Policy in Advanced Industrial Societies," *Population and Development Review* 7:1 (March 1981): 3.

66. Reported by Alan L. Otten, "Deceptive Picture," *Wall Street Journal*, 25 September 1986, p. 1.

67. See Preston, "Children and the Elderly," for a fuller discussion of these trends.

68. David Hayes Bautista, "Hispanics in an Aging Society," in *Hispanics in an Aging Society*, ed. Fernando Torres-Gil (New York: Aging Society Project, Carnegie Corporation, 1986), 24–25.

69. Davis and van den Oever, "Age Relations and Public Policy," 9.

70. Frank G. Dickenson, "Economic Aspects of Our Population," in *Problems of America's Aging Population: A Report of the First Annual Southern Conference of Gerontology* (Gainesville: University of Florida Press, 1951); excerpted as "The Coming Class War—Old vs. Young," *Harper's*, July 1952, 81.

71. Eric R. Kingson et al., *The Common Stake: The Interdepen-*

dence of Generations (Washington, D.C.: The Gerontological Society of America, 1986).

72. Bernice L. Neugarten, "Age Groups in American Society and the Rise of the Young-Old," *Annals of the Academy of Political and Social Sciences* 415 (1974): 189.

73. Robert N. Butler, *Why Survive? Being Old in America* (New York: Harper & Row, 1975), 323. For other early warnings of generational conflict over equity, see Pauline K. Ragan, "Another Look at the Politicizing of Old Age: Can We Expect a Backlash Effect?" *Urban and Social Change Review* (Summer 1977): 6–12.

74. Preston, "Children and the Elderly," 48.

Chapter 2. The Mortgaging of America: Real Estate and the Future of Retirement

1. Henry George, *Progress and Poverty*, 15th ed. (New York: Robert Schalkenbach Foundation, 1966), 40.

2. H. James Brown and John Yinger, "Home Ownership and Housing Affordability in the United States: 1963–1985," Joint Center for Housing Studies, Harvard University and the Massachusetts Institute for Technology (Paper prepared for the National Gypsum Co., Dallas, Tex., 1986).

3. U.S. Bureau of the Census, *Historical Statistics of the United States, Colonial Times to 1970*, bicentennial edition part 1, (Washington, D.C.: U.S. Government Printing Office, series N259–269, 1975), 647.

4. Lewis H. Brown, "Durable Goods Industry Committee to Study the Housing Act," *New York Times*, 27 May 1934, sec. II, p. 2.

5. For a fuller discussion of the federal government's housing policies during this era, see Martin Mayer, *The Builders* (New York: W. W. Norton, 1978), and Kenneth T. Jackson,

Crabgrass Frontier: The Suburbanization of the United States (New York: Oxford University Press, 1985).

6. John P. Dean, "Don't Get Stuck with a House," *Harper's*, July 1945, 92.

7. Marriner S. Eccles, "Inflationary Aspects of Housing Finance," *Federal Reserve Bulletin* (December 1947): 1463.

8. Eric Larrabee, "The Six Thousand Homes That Levitt Built," *Harper's*, September 1948, 85.

9. U.S. Census Bureau, *Historical Statistics*.

10. Kenneth T. Jackson, *Crabgrass Frontier*, 234.

11. U.S. Census Bureau, *Historical Statistics*, 647.

12. A Decent Home: The Report of the President's Committee on Urban Housing (Washington, D.C.: U.S. Government Printing Office, 1969), 119, quoted by Mayer, *The Builders*, 16.

13. U.S. Census Bureau, *Historical Statistics*.

14. Anthony Downs, "Are We Using Too Much Capital for Financing Housing?" in *Housing Finance in the Eighties: Issues and Options* (Papers presented at the Federal National Mortgage Association symposium, Washington, D.C., 10–11 February 1981), 75.

15. Economics Department, U.S. League of Savings Associations, *Homeownership: Coping with Inflation* (Chicago: 1980), 20.

16. Carl F. Horowitz, "Downsizing the Single-Family Home: Prospects for the Current Cycle," *Real Estate Issues* 9 (Spring–Summer 1984), 9.

17. U.S. Census Bureau, Current Population Reports, *Household and Family Characteristics: March 1978* (Washington, D.C.: U.S. Government Printing Office, series P-20, no. 340, 1979). Cited by Landon Jones, *Great Expectations: America and the Baby Boom Generation* (New York: Coward, McCann & Geoghegan, 1980), 231.

18. National Commission on Urban Problems, *Building the American City* (Washington, D.C.: U.S. Government Printing Office, 1968), part 3.

19. William F. McKenna and Carla A. Hills, *The Report of the President's Commission on Housing* (Washington, D.C.: U.S. Government Printing Office, 1982).

20. William J. White, *Final Report of the Task Force on Housing, U.S. Department of Housing and Urban Development* (Washington, D.C.: U.S. Government Printing Office, 1978), 180.

21. Mayer, *The Builders*, 246.

22. Bernard J. Frieden, "The Exclusionary Effects of Growth Controls," in *Housing: Supply and Affordability*, ed. Frank Schnidman and Jane A. Silverman (Washington, D.C.: Urban Land Institute, 1983), 110.

23. Adam Smith, *Paper Money* (New York: Dell, 1981), 86.

24. Scott E. Hein and James C. Lamb, Jr., "Why the Median-Priced Home Costs So Much," *Federal Reserve Bank of St. Louis Review* 63 (June–July 1981), 13.

25. For a full discussion see J. Fred Giertz and A. James Heins, "Real Estate: The Legacy of Tax Advantage," *Illinois Business Review* (June 1984); also, Henry J. Aaron, *Shelter and Subsidies* (Washington, D.C.: Brookings Institution, 1972).

26. Anthony Downs, *The Revolution in Real Estate Finance* (Washington, D.C.: Brookings Institution, 1985), 326.

27. Louis Harris & Associates, *Buying a Home in the 80's: A Poll of American Attitudes* (Washington, D.C.: Federal National Mortgage Association, 1982), table 11, p. 17.

28. This number is derived by comparing the book value of mortgages held by thrifts against the market value. See Andrew S. Carron, *The Plight of the Thrift Institutions* (Washington, D.C.: Brookings Institution, 1982), 18.

29. *Federal Home Loan Bank Board Journal* 17 (February 1984): 36, quoted by Downs, *The Revolution in Real Estate Finance*, 208.

30. Quoted by Dale Russakoff, "Tax Breaks' Fertile Ground," *Washington Post*, 4 November 1985, p. A1.

31. Brown and Yinger, "Home Ownership."

32. Bureau of Economic Analysis and Federal Reserve Board data, cited by Giertz and Heins, "Real Estate," 7.

33. George Sternlieb and James W. Hughes, "Housing: Past and Futures," in *Housing Finance in the Eighties*, 34.

34. Lester Thurow, *Zero Sum Solution* (New York: Simon and Schuster, 1985), 84.

35. Jackson, *Crabgrass Frontier*, 295.

36. Office of Management and Budget, *Special Analyses, Budget of the United States Government, Fiscal Year 1987* (Washington, D.C.: U.S. Government Printing Office, 1986) table G-1, p. G-38.

37. "The Decaying of America," *Newsweek*, 2 August 1982, 13.

38. Federal Highway Administration, *Status of the Nation's Highways: Conditions and Performance* (Washington, D.C.: U.S. Government Printing Office, 1983), iv–7, quoted by Pat Choate, *Bad Roads: The Hidden Cost of Neglect* (Riverdale, Md.: National Asphalt Pavement Association, 1983).

Chapter 3. Social Security and the Baby Boom Generation

1. Geoffrey Kollmann and David Koitz, "How Long Does It Take for New Retirees to Recover the Value of the Social Security Taxes?" Congressional Research Service, 21 January 1986, report no. 86-10 EPW, table 1, p. 11.

2. *Congressional Record*, 97th Congress, 1st session, 1983, 129, S4098.

3. "Ponzi Dies in Brazil," *Life*, 31 January 1949, 63.

4. U.S. Department of the Treasury, *Statement of Liabilities and Other Financial Commitments of the United States Government as of September 30, 1985*, 31 U.S.C. 331(b) (Washington, D.C.: U.S. Government Printing Office, 1985).

5. "Paul A. Samuelson on Social Security," *Newsweek*, 13 February 1967, 88.

6. *1986 Annual Report of the Board of Trustees of the Federal Old-Age and Survivors Insurance and Disability Trust Funds* (Washington, D.C.: Social Security Administration, 1986).

7. The SSA defines growth in real wages as the difference between the percentage increases in average annual wages in covered employment, and the average annual consumer price index.

8. The economic and demographic factors underlying these forecasts are contained in tables 10 and 11 of the system's *1986 Annual Report.* Table 31 presents the expected outcome for the system's various trust funds. Table E3 contains the estimates of the increase in payroll taxes needed to keep the system solvent.

9. For a full discussion of the behind-the-scenes politicking leading up to the passage of the 1983 amendments, see Paul Light, *Artful Work: The Politics of Social Security Reform* (New York: Random House, 1985).

10. *Developments in Aging*, Senate Special Committee on Aging, vol 1., Rept. 98–360, p. 139. Also, *Background Material and Data on Programs within the Jurisdiction of the Committee on Ways and Means*, 1986 ed., Ways and Means Committee Print: 99:14, p. 281; and the *1986 Annual Report of the Board of Trustees of the Federal Old-Age Survivors Insurance and Disability Insurance Trust Funds*, table 29, p. 71.

11. Anthony Pellechio and Gordon Goodfellow, "Individual Gains and Losses from Social Security Before and After the 1983 Amendments," *Cato Journal* 3: 2 (Fall 1983): 417–42.

12. Michael J. Boskin, "Government Policy Instruments and Inter-generational Transfers" (Paper presented to the first annual national conference of Americans for Generational Equity, 11 April 1986, Washington, D.C.). For a fuller discussion, see Boskin, *Too Many Promises: The Uncertain Future of Social Security* (Homewood, Ill.: Dow Jones–Irwin, 1986).

13. In essence, the reason for discounting is to adjust for the return that the average taxpayer would have earned had he or she been free to invest contributions to Social Security in the private economy. The 2 percent discount rate used in accord with historical experience is consistent with the SSA's II-B, or "best-guess" forecast for the system's future. The SSA also calculated rates of return using a 3 percent discount rate, which may well reflect the real opportunity cost of future contributions to Social Security. This calculation showed younger Americans receiving back only 72 cents on the dollar for their payroll taxes to OASI and DI.

14. Harry C. Ballantyne (Chief Actuary, Social Security Administration), "Long-Range Estimates of Social Security Trust Fund Operations in Dollars," Actuarial Note 125, Social Security Administration, U.S. Department of Health and Human Services (April 1985). My thanks to Peter Ferrara for bringing this document to my attention.

15. Eveline M. Burns, *The American Social Security System* (Boston: Houghton Mifflin, 1948), 115–16.

16. Alva Myrdal, *Nation and Family: The Swedish Experiment in Democratic Family and Population Policy* (Cambridge, Mass.: MIT Press, 1968), 87. For the analysis in this section, I am heavily indebted to the work of Allan Carlson of the Rockford Institute. See, for example, his stunning critique, "The Time Bomb within Social Security," *Persuasion at Work* 8:9 (September 1985): 1–8. See also his fine essay, "Depopulation Bomb: The Withering of the Western World," *Washington Post*, 13 April 1986, Outlook section.

Chapter 4. Death and Taxes: Confronting America's Health Care Crisis

1. Victor R. Fuchs, " 'Though Much is Taken': Reflections on Aging, Health and Medical Care," *Milbank Memorial Quarterly/Health and Society* 62:4 (Spring 1984): 164–65.

2. Joseph A. Califano, Jr., *America's Health Care Revolution* (New York: Random House, 1986), 176.

3. House Committee on Ways and Means, *Background Information on Programs Under the Jurisdiction of the Committee on Ways and Means*, 99th Congress, 1st session, 1985, WMCP, 99–2.

4. Bureau of the Census, Current Population Reports, *Projections of the Population of the United States, by Age, Sex, and Race, 1983 to 2080* (Washington, D.C.: U.S. Government Printing Office, series P-25, no. 952, 1984).

5. Edward L. Schneider and Jacob A. Brody, "Aging, Natural Death and the Compression of Morbidity: Another View," *New England Journal of Medicine* (6 October 1983): 855.

6. *Trends and Strategies in Long-Term Care* (Washington, D.C.: American Health Care Association, 1985).

7. House Select Committee on Aging, *The Twentieth Anniversary of Medicare and Medicaid: Americans Still at Risk*, press release, 30 July 1985.

8. Estimated by the Department of Health and Human Services, as reported in the *Washington Post*, 30 July 1986, p. A6.

9. Congressional Office of Technology Assessment, *Medical Technology and the Costs of the Medicare Program* (Washington, D.C.: U.S. Government Printing Office, 1984), 15.

10. Department of Health and Human Services.

11. Barbara Boyle Torrey and Douglas Norwood, "Death & Taxes: The Fiscal Implications of Future Reductions in Mortality," Paper presented at the annual meetings of the American Association for the Advancement of Science, Detroit, 26–31 May 1983.

12. Demographers employ statistical standards called "model life tables" to compare the death rates in different age groups with trends that would be expected from international and historical experience. Such tables show that the greatest improvements in death rates over the last twenty years have

occurred in older age groups. See, for example, Samuel H. Preston, "Children and the Elderly in the U.S.," *Scientific American* 251:6 (December 1984): 46.

13. Eileen M. Crimmins, "Recent and Prospective Trends in Old Age Mortality" (Paper presented at the annual meetings of the American Association for the Advancement of Science, Detroit, Mich., May 26–31, 1983).

14. Torrey and Norwood, "Death & Taxes."

15. Reuel A. Stallones, "The Rise and Fall of Ischemic Heart Disease," *Scientific American* (November 1980): 53.

16. James F. Fries, "Aging, Natural Death, and the Compression of Morbidity," *New England Journal of Medicine* (17 July 1980): 130.

17. Francisco R. Bayo and Robert J. Myers, *United States Life Tables for 1979–81* (Itasca, Ill.: Society of Actuaries, 1985), tables 33, 34.

18. Jacob A. Brody, "Limited Importance of Cancer and of Competing Risk Theories in Aging," *Journal of Clinical Experimental Gerontology* 5:2 (1983): 141–54. For a rebuttal of Fries's work, see Schneider and Brody, "Aging, Natural Death and the Compression of Morbidity: Another View," *New England Journal of Medicine* (6 October 1983): 854.

19. Rosalie S. Abrams, "Hunger among the Elderly" (testimony before the House Select Committee on Hunger, 22 April 1986).

20. Quoted by Andrew Achenbaum, *Old Age in the New Land: The American Experience Since 1790* (Baltimore: Johns Hopkins University Press, 1978), 12.

21. Lynn Etheredge, "An Aging Society and the Federal Deficit," *Milbank Memorial Quarterly/Health and Society* 62:4 (Spring 1984): 531.

22. Statement of Carolyn K. Davis, Ph.D, Administrator, Health Care Financing Administration, before the House Select Committee on Aging, 30 July 1985.

23. Quoted by Phil Keisling, "Protection from Catastrophe: The

Medicare Reform We Really Need," *The Washington Monthly* (November 1983): 39.

24. Quoted by A. Haeworth Robertson, *The Coming Revolution in Social Security* (McLean, Va.: Security Press, 1981), 124.

25. Linda E. Demkovich, "When a Booming Population of Old Vets Checks in for VA Health Care, Look Out," *National Journal* (2 June 1984): 1091.

26. Califano, *Health Care Revolution*, 178.

27. Senate Special Committee on Aging, "Retiree Health Benefits: The Fair-Weather Promise?" Staff report (7 August 1986), 4–5.

28. Califano, *Health Care Revolution*, 14, 30.

29. Marilyn Much, "Retiree Benefits out of Control," *Industry Week*, 17 February 1986, 33.

30. Glenn Pascall, *The Trillion Dollar Budget* (Seattle: University of Washington Press, 1985), 187.

31. T. Timothy Ryan, Jr., "Overview of an Employer's Right to Modify Health and Welfare Benefits for Active and Retired Employees," Testimony presented to the Special Committee on Aging, U.S. Senate, 7 August 1986, 1.

32. M. Chassin et al., "Variations in Medical Health Services," *New England Journal of Medicine* 314:5 (30 January 1986): 285.

33. *United Nations Demographic Yearbook*, 35th ed. 1983 (New York: United Nations, 1985), table 22.

34. Elizabeth Ann Kutza, *The Benefits of Old Age* (Chicago: University of Chicago Press, 1981), 72.

35. See, for example, Douglas W. Nelson, "Alternative Images of Old Age as the Bases for Policy," in *Age or Need: Policies for Older People*, ed. Bernice L. Neugarten (Beverly Hills, Calif.: Sage Publications, 1982).

36. Daniel Callahan, "Adequate Health Care and an Aging Society: A Moral Dilemma," in *Our Aging Society: Paradox and Promise*, ed. Alan Pifer and Lydia Bronte (New York: W. W. Norton, 1986), 328–29.

37. John Rawls, *A Theory of Justice*, (Cambridge: Harvard University Press, 1971).

38. Lester Thurow, *Zero Sum Solutions* (New York: Simon and Schuster, 1985), 254.

39. Norman Daniels, *Just Health Care* (New York: Cambridge University Press, 1985), 86–113. I am heavily indebted to Daniels for this whole line of argument and for much that follows. While wishing to acknowledge this debt, I hasten to add that Daniels's conclusions are highly qualified and that he is entitled to be dissociated from my own views to whatever extent he desires.

40. Henry J. Aaron and William B. Schwartz, *The Painful Prescription* (Washington, D.C.: Brookings Institution, 1984), 34.

41. Message to Congress on 7 January 1965, in *Public Papers of the Presidents of the United States, 1965* (Washington, D.C: U.S. Government Printing Office, 1966). Quoted in W. Andrew Achenbaum, *Social Security: Visions and Revisions* (New York: Cambridge University Press, 1986), 169.

42. I am indebted for this analysis to Prof. Norm Daniel of Tufts University. See his essay "Why Saying No to Patients in the United States Is So Hard: Cost Containment, Justice and Provider Autonomy," *New England Journal of Medicine* (22 May 1986).

43. Califano, *Health Care Revolution*, 78.

44. Robert Kuttner, *The Economic Illusion* (Boston: Houghton Mifflin, 1984), 251.

45. David Durenberger, *Prescription for Change: Health Care Reform Through Consumer Choice* (Minneapolis: Piranha Press, 1986), xxix.

46. William B. Schwartz, "The Inevitable Failure of Current Cost-Containment Strategies," *Journal of the American Medical Association* 257:2 (9 January 1987): 220–21.

47. Marc S. Tucker, testimony before the Joint Economic Committee of the United States Congress, Subcommittee on Eco-

nomic Resources, Competitiveness, and Security Economics, 29 July 1986.

Chapter 5. Fertility and Immigration: The Politics of Population Growth

1. Charles F. Westoff, "Marriage and Fertility in Developed Countries," *Scientific American* 239:6 (December 1978): 53.
2. Richard A. Easterlin, *Population, Labor Force, and Long Swings in Economic Growth: The American Experience* (Palo Alto, Calif.: National Bureau of Economic Research, no. 86, 1968). For a more recent and popular exposition, see Easterlin, *Birth and Fortune: The Impact of Numbers on Personal Welfare* (New York: Basic Books, 1981).
3. Christopher Jencks, "Destiny's Tots," *New York Review of Books*, 8 October 1981, 30–32.
4. Thomas J. Espenshade, *New Estimates of Parental Expenditures on Children* (Washington, D.C.: Urban Institute, February 1983). See also Carolyn Summers Edwards and Linda J. Beckham, "Child Cost User Data Updated to 1983," *Family Economics Review* no. 3 (1984): 13. This study places the cost of raising a child born in 1984 at $140,927 in constant dollars, under a "moderate cost level in the urban North Central region."
5. William P. Butz et al., *Demographic Challenges in America's Future* (Santa Monica, Calif.: Rand Corporation, 1982), 4–11.
6. Benjamin Spock, *Baby and Child*, 1947 ed., *Broken Promises: How Americans Fail Their Children*, quoted in W. Norton Grubb and Marvin Lazerson (New York: Basic Books, 1982), 34.
7. See, for example, Mickey Kaus, "The Work-Ethic State," *New Republic*, 7 July 1986.
8. Charles F. Westoff, "Marriage and Fertility," 56.
9. Ibid.

10. Douglas J. Stewart, "Disfranchise the Old," *New Republic*, 22–29 August 1970, 20. Stewart remains notorious among aging advocates for writing: "The vote should not be a privilege in perpetuity, guaranteed by minimal physical survival, but a share in the continuing fate of the political community, both in its benefits and risks. The old, having no future, are dangerously free from the consequences of their own political acts, and it makes no sense to allow the vote to someone who is actuarially unlikely to survive, and pay the bills for, the politician or party he may help elect." Stewart must himself by now be getting on in years.

11. Ben J. Wattenberg and Karl Zinsmeister, "The Birth Dearth: The Geopolitical Consequences," *Public Opinion* 8:6 (December–January 1986): 13.

12. Quoted in Paul C. Light, "Social Security and the Politics of Assumptions," *Public Administration Review* 45:3 (May–June 1985): 369.

13. One frequently hears asserted that as much as half the population growth in the United States is the result of immigration, but this fraction is probably exaggerated. For an excellent discussion of the new immigration wave, see James Fallows, "The New Immigrants: How They're Affecting Us," *Atlantic* 252:5 (November 1983), 45.

14. See, for example, Leon F. Bouvier, *The Impact of Immigration on U.S. Population Size* (Washington, D.C.: Population Reference Bureau, January 1981).

15. The actual net immigration number assumed by the SSA under its II-B scenario is 500,000 per year. See the *1986 Annual Report of the Board of Trustees of the Federal Old-Age and Survivors Insurance and Disability Trust Funds* (Washington, D.C.: Social Security Administration, 1986), 34.

16. For a popular expression of this economic school's ideas, see Gail Garfield Schwartz and William Neikirk, *The Work Rev-*

olution: The Future of Work in the Post-Industrial Society (New York: Rawson Associates, 1983), 116–21.

17. Quoted by Fallows, "The New Immigrants," 48.

18. Michael Boskin, *Too Many Promises: The Uncertain Future of Social Security* (Homewood, Ill.: Dow Jones–Irwin, 1986), 99.

19. David Hayes Bautista, "Hispanics in an Aging Society," in *Hispanics in an Aging Society*, ed. Fernando Torres-Gil (New York: Carnegie Corporation, 1986), 25.

Chapter 6. Consuming Visions: Thrift and Productivity in an Aging Society

1. "Buy and Be Happy," *Wall Street Journal*, 14 April 1958, p. 1.

2. For a fuller account of the "Buy Now" campaign, see Paul A. Carter, *Another Part of the Fifties* (New York: Columbia University Press, 1983).

3. Samuel Smiles, *Thrift* (New York: Harper & Row, 1876), 14.

4. Barbara Boyle Torrey, "The Lengthening of Retirement," in *Aging from Birth to Death*, vol. 2, ed. Matilda White Riley et al. American Association for the Advancement of Science, Selected Symposium no. 79.

5. Fred Branfman, "Unexplored America: Economic Rebirth in a Post-Industrial World," *World Policy Journal* (Fall 1984): 35.

6. *Federal Reserve Bulletin* 72:7 (July 1986), selected tables.

7. Roy G. Blakey, "America's New Conception of Thrift: Forward," *Annals of the American Academy of Political and Social Science* 87 (1920), 1.

8. Stuart Chase, *The Tragedy of Waste* (New York: Macmillan, 1926), 120.

9. Samuel Crowther, *Why Men Strike* (New York: Doubleday, Page & Co., 1920), viii, 213.

10. T. D. MacGregor, *The Book of Thrift* (New York: Funk & Wagnalls, 1915), 15.

11. "We Become a Nation of Savers," *Literary Digest*, 3 January 1925, 68.

12. "The Menace of Thrift," *Nation* 12:2902 (16 February 1921), 256.

13. Ibid.

14. William T. Foster and Waddill Catchings, "The Dilemma of Thrift," *Atlantic Monthly* 137 (April 1926): 533–43.

15. Paul A. Samuelson, *Economics: An Introductory Analysis*, 3d ed. (New York: McGraw-Hill, 1955), 236–37.

16. Stuart Chase, *Out of the Depression* (New York: John Day, 1931).

17. Russell Porter, "Looking for Utopia Along the Townsend Trail," *New York Times Magazine*, 5 February 1939.

18. Richard Wightman Fox, "Epitaph for Middletown," in *The Culture of Consumption: Critical Essays in American History, 1880–1980*, ed. Richard Wightman Fox and T. J. Jackson Lears (New York: Pantheon Books, 1983), 103.

19. Quoted in Roger Draper, "The Faithless Shepherd," *New York Review of Books*, 26 June 1986, 15.

20. Quoted in T. J. Jackson Lears, "From Salvation to Self-Realization," in Fox and Lears, eds., *The Culture of Consumption*.

21. David Halberstam, "Citizen Ford," *American Heritage* 37 (October–November 1986): 50.

22. Daniel Bell, *The Cultural Contradictions of Capitalism* (New York: Basic Books, 1976), 69.

23. Larry May, *Screening Out the Past*, quoted in Fox and Lears, eds., *The Culture of Consumption*.

24. John Maynard Keynes, *General Theory of Employment, Money and Interest* (New York: Macmillan, 1936).

25. Robert Lekachman, *The Age of Keynes* (New York: Random House, 1966), 111.

26. Blair Moody, *Boom or Bust* (New York: Duell, Sloan and Pearce, 1941), 7.

27. Stuart Chase, "Goals for America" (Paper presented to the Institute for Post War Reconstruction, New York University, 19 May 1943, p. 14).

28. Robert Nathan, *Mobilizing for Abundance* (New York: McGraw-Hill, Whittlesey House, 1944), 149.

29. "It's Wonderful," *Fortune* (October 1945): 125.

30. Quoted in C. Hartley Grattan, "Buying on Time: Where Do You Stop?" *Harper's* (April 1956), 75.

31. Quoted in Grattan, "Buying on Time," 76.

32. "It's Wonderful," *Fortune* (October 1945): 125.

33. William E. Leuchtenburg, *A Troubled Feast: American Society Since 1945* (Boston: Little, Brown, 1979), 37ff.

34. *Life*, 16 June 1958, quoted in Landon Y. Jones, *Great Expectations: America and the Baby Boom Generation* (New York: Coward, McCann & Geoghegan, 1980), 37.

35. Samuelson, *Economics*, 356.

36. Bell, *Cultural Contradictions*, 70.

37. David Riesman, "Some Observations on Changes in Leisure Attitudes," reprinted in Riesman, *Individualism and Other Essays* (Glencoe, Ill.: The Free Press, 1954), 211.

38. James Tobin, *National Economic Policy: Essays* (New Haven: Yale University Press, 1966), 89.

39. Stephen A. Marglin, "The Social Rate of Discount and the Optimal Rate of Investment," *Quarterly Journal of Economics* 77 (1963): 95.

40. A. K. Sen, "On Optimizing the Rate of Savings," *Economic Journal* (September 1961): 11–23.

41. Gordon Tullock, "The Social Rate of Discount and the Optimal Rate of Investment: Comment," *Quarterly Journal of Economics* (May 1964): 334.

42. William J. Baumol, "On the Social Rate of Discount," *American Economic Review* 58:4 (September 1968): 801.

43. Congressional Budget Office, *Public Works Infrastructure: Policy Considerations for the 1980s* (Washington, D.C.: U.S. Government Printing Office, April 1983); Joint Economic Committee, U.S. Congress, *Hard Choices: A Summary Report of the National Infrastructure Study* (Washington, D.C.: U.S. Government Printing Office, February 1984).

44. Mark Starr, "The Decaying of America," *Newsweek*, 2 August 1982, 12.

45. U.S. Bureau of the Census, *Statistical Abstract of the United States: 1986* (Washington, D.C.: U.S. Government Printing Office, 1985), tables 817, 897.

46. David Hackett Fischer, *Growing Old in America* (New York: Oxford University Press, 1978), 52.

47. Henry George, *Progress and Poverty*, 15th ed. (New York: Robert Schalkenbach Foundation, 1966), 75.

48. Jonathan Kozol, *Illiterate America* (New York: New American Library, 1985), cited in the *Economist*, 27 September 1986, 26.

Chapter 7. Backdoor Borrowing: Generational Equity and Budgetary Reform

1. Herman B. Leonard, *Checks Unbalanced: The Quiet Side of Public Spending* (New York: Basic Books, 1986), 7.

2. Treasury Department, "Statement of Liabilities and Other Financial Commitments of the United States Government as of September 30, 1985," *Treasury Bulletin* (Winter 1986), 204.

3. Ibid.

4. President's Private Sector Survey on Cost Control, *Report on Personnel Management* (Washington, D.C.: U.S. Government Printing Office, 1983), 12.

5. Frank S. Arnold, "State and Local Public Employee Pension Funding: Theory, Evidence and Implications" (Ph.D. diss.,

Harvard University, 1983), cited in Leonard, *Checks Unbalanced*, 34

6. Robert P. Inman, "The Funding Status of Teachers' Pensions: An Econometric Approach," working paper no. 1727, National Bureau of Economic Research, Cambridge, Mass., October 1985, cited in Leonard, *Checks Unbalanced*, 35.

7. For a useful but by now somewhat outdated discussion of the public employee pension issues, see *The Quiet Crisis of Public Pensions* (New York: Aspen Institute for Humanistic Studies, 1980).

8. Alicia H. Munnell, *Pensions for Public Employees* (Washington, D.C.: National Planning Association, 1979), 1.

9. Robert W. Hartman, *Pay and Pensions for Federal Workers* (Washington, D.C.: Brookings Institution, 1983).

10. The Saltonstall report is published every year as an appendix in the winter issue of the *Treasury Bulletin* under the title "Statement of Liabilities and Other Financial Commitments of the United States Government."

11. Treasury Department, Financial Management Service, *Consolidated Financial Statements of the United States Government: Fiscal Year 1985, Prototype* (Washington, D.C.: U.S. Government Printing Office, 1986), 27, n. 8.

12. For the 1984–1985 change, Ibid., 11; for previous change, see *Federal Government Reporting Study: Illustrative Annual Financial Report, 1984* (Gaithersburg, Md.: U.S. General Accounting Office, 1986), 30. Both studies are designed as prototypes for a possible consolidated statement of assets and liabilities for the U.S. government, which budget reformers want to see published every year.

13. The Wyatt Company, "The Top 50," *Management Overview and Survey Report*, 1984.

14. Among the many political writers to whom Keith has told his story is James Fallows. See his excellent account in "Entitlements," *Atlantic* (November 1982):51, from which I have borrowed. Keith's research group, headquartered in Wash-

ington, is called the National Committee on Public Employee Pensions, and he cochairs it with John W. Macy, Jr., former chairman of the Civil Service Commission.

15. General Accounting Office, *The 20 Year Military Retirement System Needs Reform: Report to the Congress by the Comptroller General of the United States* (Washington, D.C.: U.S. Government Printing Office, 13 March 1978).

16. Hartman, *Pay and Pensions*, 38, 74.

17. General Accounting Office, *The 20 Year Military Retirement System Needs Reform.*

18. During the debate over FERS, the Congressional Budget Office estimated that it would save $7 billion over the next five years compared with the cost of including new hires in CSRS. But this purported savings was arrived at by counting the contributions made by federal workers to the thrift plans as part of the system's assets. In reality, these contributions must be returned and are thus liabilities to the government and to its future taxpayers.

19. Office of Management and Budget, *Special Analyses: Budget of the United States Government, Fiscal Year 1987* (Washington, D.C.: U.S. Government Printing Office, 1986), table F-16, p. F-45. The precise estimate is $3.060603 trillion. This number, OMB comments, represents "the overall contingent liability or exposure of the Government resulting from all potential insurance claims and guaranteed loan defaults."

20. Treasury Department, Financial Management Service, *Consolidated Financial Statements of the United States Government: Fiscal Year 1985, Prototype*, table, p. 11, and n. 10, p. 22. This estimate does not include contingent liabilities for private pension insurance offered through the Pension Benefit Guarantee Corporation, which exposes future taxpayers to tremendous risks, as is discussed later.

21. Richard A. Ippolito, "The Economic Burden of Corporate Pension Liabilities," *Financial Analysts Journal* (January–

February 1986), 611–51. The definition of pension fund liabilities used by Ippolito is the amount that will be due workers in the future assuming the plan is not terminated. By contrast, the unfunded pension liabilities reported by companies in their annual reports usually express only the amount that the company would be legally bound to pay vested workers if its pension plan were terminated at any given time. Ippolito argues persuasively that this latter definition understates the true economic burden of pension liabilities, because it fails to account for the reality that workers expect the company not to terminate their pension plans and most companies have no plans to do so.

22. Under a defined benefit plan, a worker's benefits are said to be "fully vested" when he or she has satisfied all the requirements, such as age and length of service, set out in advance by the plan as a precondition for receiving benefits.

23. Edward J. Harpham, "Private Pensions in Crisis: The Case for Radical Reform," study by the National Center for Policy Analysis, Dallas, Tex., p. 6.

24. Ralph Nader and Kate Blackwell, *You and Your Pension* (New York: Grossman Publishers, 1973), quoted in Alicia Munnell, *The Economics of Private Pensions* (Washington, D.C.: Brookings Institution, 1982), 131.

25. Pension Benefit Guarantee Corporation, *Annual Report to Congress, Fiscal Year 1985* (Washington, D.C.: U.S. Government Printing Office, 1985).

26. The Economic Report of the President (Washington, D.C.: U.S. Government Printing Office, 1986), 206.

27. Vincent Amoroso, "Termination Insurance for Single-Employer Pension Plans: Cost and Benefits," *Transactions* 35 (1983), 93–110.

28. Ellen Sehgal, "Occupational Mobility and Job Tenure in 1983," *Monthly Labor Review* (October 1984): 24.

29. David A. Wise, "Labor Aspects of Pension Plans," *NBER Reporter* (Winter 1984–85): 24.

30. Pat Choate and J. K. Linger, *The High-Flex Society* (New York: Alfred A. Knopf, 1986), 246–47.
31. *Sound Financial Reporting in the U.S. Government: A Prerequisite to Fiscal Responsibility*, Arthur Anderson and Company, February 1986.
32. Leonard, *Checks Unbalanced*, 177.
33. Government Accounting Standards Board, "Exposure Draft: Proposed Statement of Governmental Accounting Concepts," project no. 3–2, 24 July 1986, 44.
34. Treasury Department, Financial Management Service, *Consolidated Financial Statements of the United States Government: Fiscal Year 1985, Prototype*, p. 22, n. 9.

Chapter 8. The Broker State: Who Speaks for the Young?

1. Peter F. Drucker, "A Key to American Politics: Calhoun's Pluralism," *The Review of Politics* (October 1948):412–26.
2. John Fischer, "Unwritten Rules of American Politics," *Harper's* (November 1948):27–36.
3. Margaret L. Coit, *John C. Calhoun, American Portrait* (Boston: Houghton Mifflin, 1950).
4. Arthur Schlesinger, Jr., review of Margaret L. Coit's *John C. Calhoun*. The *Nation* (1 April 1950): 302.
5. William Greider, "The Education of David Stockman," *Atlantic* 248:6 (December 1981): 27–54.
6. John C. Calhoun, *Disquisition on Government* (New York: D. Appleton, 1851), 1:25.
7. Ibid., 25.
8. Ibid., 28.
9. *The Public Papers and Addresses of FDR 1936: The People Approve* (New York: Random House, 1938), 5:148.
10. John Kenneth Galbraith, *American Capitalism: The Concept of Countervailing Power* (White Plains, N.Y.: M. E. Sharpe, 1980), 136.

11. Drucker, "A Key to American Politics."
12. Robert Paul Wolff, *The Poverty of Liberalism* (Boston: Beacon Press, 1968), 155–56.
13. Mancur Olson, *The Rise and Decline of Nations* (New Haven: Yale University Press, 1982), 18.

Chapter 9. Justice Between Generations: The Politics of Reform

1. Richard Milne, *That Man Townsend* (Los Angeles: Prosperity Publishing Co., 1935), 5.
2. Francis E. Townsend, *New Horizons* (Chicago: J. L. Stewart, 1943), 137–40.
3. David H. Bennett, *Demagogues in the Depression* (New Brunswick, N. J.: Rutgers University Press, 1969), 157.
4. Wilbur Cohen, introduction to *The Townsend Movement: A Political Study*, by Abraham Holtzman (New York: Bookman Associates, 1963), 13–14.
5. Henry J. Pratt, *The Gray Lobby* (Chicago: University of Chicago Press, 1967), and "The 'Gray Lobby' Revisited," *Phi Kappa Phi Journal* (Fall 1982).
6. Robert H. Binstock, "The Aged as Scapegoat," *The Gerontologist* 23:2 (1983):142.
7. Bernice Neugarten, "Policy for the 1980s: Age or Need Entitlement," in *National Journal Issues Book, Aging: Agenda for the Eighties* (November 1979):48–52.
8. Carroll Estes, *The Aging Enterprise* (San Francisco: Jossey-Bass, 1979), 17.
9. *Gray Panther Network* (January–February 1982):20–22.
10. Binstock, "The Aged as Scapegoat," 142.
11. Estimates are for 1983. Congressional Budget Office, "An Analysis of Selected Deficit Reduction Options Affecting the Elderly and Disabled," (Washington, D.C.: U.S. Government Printing Office, March 1985).
12. U.S. Bureau of the Census, *Current Population Reports,*

series P-23, no. 147, "After Tax Money Income Estimates of Households: 1984" (Washington, D.C.: U.S. Government Printing Office, 1986), table 1.

13. U.S. Bureau of the Census, *Current Population Reports*, series P-70, no. 7, "Household Wealth and Asset Ownership: 1984" (Washington, D.C.: U.S. Government Printing Office, 1986), table 3.

14. Joseph F. Quinn, "The Economic Status of the Elderly: Beware of the Mean" (Keynote address for the 1983 Family Economics–Home Management Workshop, Madison, Wis., 24–25 June 1983, p. 2).

15. U.S. Bureau of the Census, *Current Population Reports*, series P-23, no. 138, "Demographic and Socioeconomic Aspects of Aging in the United States" (Washington, D.C.: U.S. Government Printing Office, 1984), table 8–7; U.S. Bureau of the Census, *Current Population Reports*, series P-60, no. 152, "Characteristics of the Population Below the Poverty Level, 1984" (Washington, D.C.: U.S. Government Printing Office, 1986), table 8.

16. U.S. Bureau of the Census, Technical Paper 52, *Estimates of Poverty Including the Value of Noncash Benefits: 1983* (Washington, D.C.: U.S. Government Printing Office, 1984), table E, p. xiv.

17. U.S. Bureau of the Census, Current Population Reports, *Characteristics of the Population Below the Poverty Line, 1984*, series P-60, no. 152, table 11. Last statistic estimated by the House Select Committee on Hunger.

18. U.S. Bureau of the Census, Current Population Reports, *Characteristics of the Population Below the Poverty Line, 1984*, series P-60, no. 152, table 11.

19. House Select Committee on Hunger, press release for hearings entitled "Hunger and the Elderly," 22 April 1986.

20. Carole B. Allan, "The Older Consumer: The Time Is Now," *National Journal* (24 November 1979):1998–2003; "Over 55: Growth Market of the '80s," *Nation's Business* (April 1981);

Betsy D. Gelb, "Discovering the 65+ Consumer," *Business Horizons* (May–June 1982):42–46.

21. U.S. Bureau of the Census and the Conference Board, *A Marketer's Guide to Discretionary Income* (Washington, D.C.: U.S. Government Printing Office, 1985).

22. Robert Forbes (Special Services Department, Membership Division, American Association of Retired Persons), "The 50+ Traveler: The Market, the Myths, and the Realities" (Paper presented to the Travel Industry Association of America, National Conference and Marketing Showcase, New Orleans, La., September 1985).

23. "There's Gold in Seniors," *Target Marketing* (October 1986):19–21.

24. Marion Barry, Jr., letter addressed "Washington Business and Service Providers," dated 29 May 1986.

25. Edward T. Devine, *Misery and Its Causes* (New York: Arno Press, 1971), 125.

26. Joseph F. Quinn and Richard V. Burkhauser, "Influencing Retirement Behavior," *Journal of Policy Analysis and Management* 3:1 (Fall 1983). See also their article, "The Effect of Pension Plans on the Pattern of Life Cycle Compensation," in *The Measurement of Labor Cost*, ed. Jack E. Triplett, National Bureau of Economic Research: Studies in Income and Wealth, vol. 48 (Chicago: University of Chicago Press, 1983).

27. Parnes's findings were reported by *Society* (November–December 1982):5.

28. Jarold A. Kieffer, "The Coming Opportunity to Work Until You're 75," *Washington Post*, 9 September 1984, p. Dl.

29. Robert Kuttner, "The Social Security Hysteria," *New Republic*, 27 December 1982, 20.

30. See, for example, Robert H. Hayes's and William J. Abernathy's seminal essay, "Managing Our Way to Economic Decline," *Harvard Business Review* (July–August 1980): 67–77.

Index

abortion, 143
accelerated cost recovery system (ACRS), 57
accounting systems, 204–10
accrual accounting, 204–5, 207–9
advertising: consumerism and, 152–53, 162–65
Adweek, 243
Agar, Herbert, 215
age-based entitlement, 108–12; arguments for, 247–50; and generational conflict, 237–38; promoting solvency in, 254–58; reforming, 247–54; *see also* Medicare; Social Security
age composition of the population, 3–6
age discrimination, 235, 236, 257
Age Discrimination in Employment Act: 1977 amendments, 246
"ageism," 33, 235, 236
Aging Enterprise, The (Estes), 237
aging of the population, 6–8, 129; and decrease in population growth, 130; and future of America, 262; and generational conflict, 29–30; and health care crisis, 88–90; and interest group liberalism, 225–28; and pronatalist measures, 143; and prophets of crisis, 32–33
Aging Population Growth (APG), 66
agrarian economy: generational contract in, 177
Aid to Families with Dependent Children, 17–18
Alzheimer's disease, 96
American Airlines, 13
American Association of Retired Persons (AARP), 234, 242, 243
American Bankers Association, 158

American Express, 168
Americans for Democratic Action (ADA), 222
American Social Security System, The (Burns), 80–81
Annals of the American Academy of Political and Social Science, 156
Armco, Inc., 105
Arnold, Frank, 185
Arthur Anderson and Company, 207

baby boom generation: aging of, 2, 6, 7–8; and consumer ethic, 170, 172–73; and crisis in education, 19–23; decline in home ownership, 38, 47; development of (1950s–1980s), 1–2; downward mobility among, 11–13, 14, 18, 134; educational level of, 12; family income with children, 18–19; family size of, 7; fertility rate among, 6–7, 8; and financing of Medicare, 98–100; financing their retirement, 10–16; generational conflict vs. generational equity, 27–32; life expectancy of, 6, 8; lifestyle of, 47; median family income of, 14; and national debt, 23–27, 34; net wealth of, 14–15; numbers of, 1, 3; rate of return from Social Security, 74–76; and Social Security, 62–85; standard of living among, 11–12, 18; tax incentives to save, 16
balance of trade, 25, 34
banks: and consumerism, 153; and FHA, 41–42; and real estate mortgages, 39–40, 55–56; and senior citizen discounts, 244; and thrift ethic, 158